Chaucer to Shakespeare, 1337–1580

transitions

General Editor: Julian Wolfreys

---

transitions Series
Series Standing Order ISBN 0–333–73634–6
(*outside North America only*)

You can receive future titles in this series as they are published by
placing a standing order. Please contact your bookseller or, in case of
difficulty, write to us at the address below with your name and address,
the title of the series and the ISBN quoted above.

Customer Services Department, Macmillan Distribution Ltd
Houndmills, Basingstoke, Hampshire RG21 6XS, England

---

transitions

Chaucer to Shakespeare, 1337–1580

SunHee Kim Gertz

palgrave

First published 2001 by
PALGRAVE
Houndmills, Basingstoke, Hampshire RG21 6XS and
175 Fifth Avenue, New York, N.Y. 10010
Companies and representatives throughout the world

PALGRAVE is the new global academic imprint of
St. Martin's Press LLC Scholarly and Reference Division and
Palgrave Publishers Ltd (formerly Macmillan Press Ltd).

ISBN 0–333–72198–5 hardback
ISBN 0–333–72199–3 paperback

This book is printed on paper suitable for recycling and made from fully managed and sustained forest sources.

A catalogue record for this book is available from the British Library.

Library of Congress Cataloging-in-Publication Data

Gertz, Sunhee Kim, 1951–
    Chaucer to Shakespeare, 1337–1580 / SunHee Kim Gertz.
    p.cm – (Transitions)
    Includes bibliographical references and index.
    ISBN 0–333–72198–5 — ISBN 0–333–72199–3 (pbk.)
    1. English literature—Middle English, 1100–1500—History and criticism. 2. English literature—Early modern, 1500–1700—History and criticism. 3. Shakespeare, William, 1564–1616—Criticism and interpretation. 4. Chaucer, Geoffrey, d. 1400—Criticism and interpretation. 5. Authors and readers—Great Britain—History—To 1500. 6. Authors and readers—Great Britain—History—16th century. 7. Narration (Rhetoric) I. Title. II. Transitions (St. Martin's Press)

PR251 G47 2000
820.9—dc21   00–042067

10 9 8 7 6 5 4 3 2 1
10 09 08 07 06 05 04 03 02 01

Printed in China

To my nieces and nephews
present and future college students
Andrew, Elizabeth, Sarah, and Brendan

Contents

General Editor's Preface

Transitions: *transition-*, n. of action. 1. A passing or passage from one condition, action or (rarely) place, to another. 2. Passage in thought, speech, or writing, from one subject to another. 3. **a.** The passing from one note to another **b.** The passing from one key to another, modulation. 4. The passage from an earlier to a later stage of development or formation ... change from an earlier style to a later; a style of intermediate or mixed character ... the historical passage of language from one well-defined stage to another.

The aim of *Transitions* is to explore passages and movements in language, literature and culture from Chaucer to the present day. The series also seeks to examine the ways in which the very idea of transition affects the reader's sense of period so as to address anew questions of literary history and periodization. The writers in this series unfold the cultural and historical mediations of literature during what are commonly recognised as crucial moments in the development of English literature, addressing, as the OED puts it, the 'historical passage of language from one well-defined stage to another'.

Recognising the need to contextualise literary study, the authors offer close readings of canonical and now marginalised or overlooked literary texts from all genres, bringing to this study the rigour of historical knowledge and the sophistication of theoretically informed evaluations of writers and movements from the last 700 years. At the same time as each writer, whether Chaucer or Shakespeare, Milton or Pope, Byron, Dickens, George Eliot, Virginia Woolf or Salman Rushdie, is shown to produce his or her texts within a discernible historical, cultural, ideological and philosophical milieu, the text is read from the vantage point of recent theoretical interests and concerns. The purpose in bringing theoretical knowledge to the reading of a wide range of works is to demonstrate how the literature is always open to transition, whether in the instance of its production or in succeeding moments of its critical reception.

The series desires to enable the reader to transform her/his own reading and writing transactions by comprehending past developments. Each book in the second tranche of the series offers a pedagogical guide to the poetics and politics of particular eras, as well as to the subsequent critical comprehension of periods and periodisation. As well as transforming the cultural and literary past by interpreting its transition from the perspective of the critical and theoretical present, each study enacts transitional readings of a number of literary texts, all of which are themselves conceivable as having effected transition at the moments of their first appearance. The readings offered in these books seek, through close critical reading, historical contextualisation and theoretical engagement, to demonstrate certain possibilities in reading to the student reader.

It is hoped that the student will find this series liberating because the series seeks to move beyond rigid definitions of period. What is important is the sense of passage, of motion. Rather than providing a definitive model of literature's past, *Transitions* aims to place you in an active dialogue with the writing and culture of other eras, so at to comprehend not only how the present reads the past, but how the past can read the present.

Julian Wolfreys

Acknowledgements

I've enjoyed writing this book. It's allowed me the 'space in my head' to mull over and write about subjects I've wanted to approach for years. For the opportunity, I thank the Transitions Series Editor, Julian Wolfreys, who also read and commented on the manuscript. The Reference and Interlibrary Loan Librarians at Clark University made my various research tasks exponentially easier, and I am deeply grateful to them. Finally, I wish to thank my students, whose questions and conversations sustain and inspire me.

SUNHEE KIM GERTZ

The author and publishers wish to thank the following for permission to use copyright material:

AKG London/Erich Lessing for Paolo Uccello (*c.* 1397–1475) 'The Battle of San Romano'. Right panel of a three part series. On wood, 180 × 316 cm, Paris, Musée du Louvre.

The Bridgeman Art Library/National Gallery, London for Paolo Uccello (*c.* 1397–1475) 'St George and the Dragon' *c.* 1460, oil on canvas, National Gallery, London.

The Bridgeman Art Library/Musée Jacquemart-Andre, Paris for Paolo Uccello (*c.* 1397–1475) 'St George and the Dragon', panel.

Research by ISI.

Introduction

While walking through the Louvre, you may happen upon a rather large painting by Paolo di Dono Uccello (1397–1475) called the *Battle of San Romano* – a mural 1.8 meters high and 3.16 meters long. Glancing at the painting, you're likely to be most struck by the central figure gallantly straddling a spirited black horse. The elegant knight wears an elaborate hat, and his right arm grasps a raised sword as if to inspire his men to glory. Banners and lances punctuate the darkened background, and everything about the scene seems to elicit the sense that you're witnessing a patriotic call to arms. Looking to the left of the central horseman, you see support for your surmise, as a bugler sounds his trumpet, and, to his left, knights, complete with plumed helmets, are poised to charge (see page 2).

Uccello's painting serves as the introduction to this study for a number of reasons. For one, a viewer's initial encounter with it seems to emblematize what many of us think we know of the periods traditionally called the Middle Ages and the Early Modern or Renaissance era: in *those* days, some might say, noble knights fighting for a worthy cause would, in the thick of excruciating battle, somehow find the energy and courage to launch heroic charges against the enemies of virtue and nation.

But upon looking more closely, Uccello's mural also reveals less-obvious detail, the kind of detail that will occupy a good part of our time here. If you look to the right of the central horseman, for example, the knights on this side seem unprepared, their lances criss-crossing or at angles with one another. Likewise their plumed helmets are sunk, facing downward; even their horses seem to be at rest. And although many of the painting's cues seem to point you to looking upward, you might nonetheless glance between the horses, to see the legs, now and again the faces, of foot soldiers. Further below, patches of grass and mud.

Such detail necessarily conflicts with our first impressions and

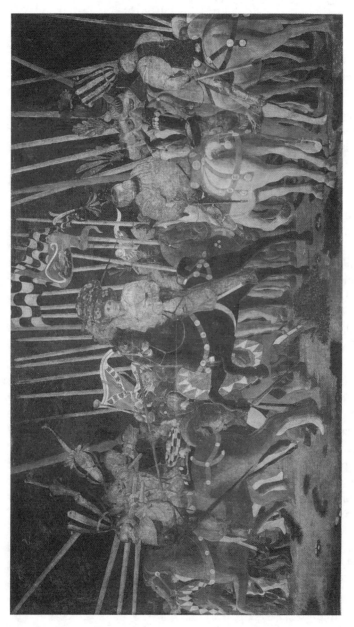

'The Battle of San Romano' by Paolo Uccello (c. 1397–1475). Right panel of a three part series on wood, 180 × 316 cm, in the Musée du Louvre, Paris.

encourages a dialogue with the mural, an attempt to understand how the apparent oppositions can form one narrative. It is such detail we'll be reading in juxtaposition to the obvious, sometimes grand, images greeting us, since this kind of detail will help us understand, and texture, written materials from the years 1337–1580.[1] In other words, in our readings of these narratives from the past, we'll look at the *relations* between images or ideas as well as at modifying details. For, if anything, *Chaucer to Shakespeare* is about the love of reading, the kind of reading that tries to imagine as full a picture as possible, not the kind that speeds us breathlessly along to see how the story will end (as if we couldn't guess).

Thus, to return to our introductory image, in contrast to what may have been our initial expectations, Uccello's mural mingles glory and misery, rather than separating these experiences into a black-and-white dichotomy. In this sense, the painter creates a 'full moment', one complete with the oppositions, anomalies and emotions that fuel life's experiences. Uccello achieves this effect in part by playing with the conventions audiences understand to belong to the genre of military glory. For example, the central figure, Micheletto da Cotignola, proudly raises his sword arm to attack, and, a little to his left, slightly above his head, the unicorn flies as his standard. By such means, Uccello relies on the viewer to infer that this is the leader and that his call to glory will inspire a fierce attack.

What our sense of *the presentation* of military glory 'in those days' doesn't prepare us for is that rather than a uniformly brave attack, Uccello also depicts confusion. 'Nowadays,' we may very well be inured to the conventions of the anti-hero through novels and films that portray the ugly aspects of military encounters, but 'in those days'? And how are we to interpret Cotignola's single-mindedness of purpose in view of the lack of unity? At least in our literature and films, heroes know what they're up against and express some dissatisfaction with the sordidness of war. Here, whatever coherence exists in the melée – the glory and all the painful, bloody losses – all this is brought together and evoked in the figure of Cotignola, who is calling his men to arms under a banner depicting a unicorn, a sign depicting a mythical creature.

Rhetoric, semiotics and arcs

This kind of broad look at structural components that refuses to erase away apparent contradictions constitutes the first step in the type of analyses we'll be undertaking here. It presumes that an author, or artist, *presents* messages in various kinds of material *for an audience* by means of *shared conventions* – in this case, the emblems, themes, and dynamics of warfare. Without such value-imbued conventions, this mural might seem an exercise in idiocy: what individual in his or her right mind goes into battle without a helmet? Conventions, whether literary or from the domain of visual arts, provide a meeting ground for *literati* – writers and readers of any kind of narrative or text – and, as in this mural, allow messages to be communicated telegraphically.

The attempt to reach an audience is, in and of itself, *the* hallmark of *rhetorical theory*, which we tend to think of today as that which is used by advertising agencies, politicians and outdated English teachers. In this volume, however, we will be analyzing, rather than using, implied author–audience interaction (rhetorical interaction) through instances that are intended for audiences smaller than those aimed for by ad companies or spin-doctors, instances that furthermore have multiple, more complex messages than 'Buy into the Cosmo image' or 'Vote for me'. Indeed, rarely do ads and campaigns present contradictions of the kind Uccello conveys – they opt for streamlining all complexity out of their messages, since all they need from their audiences is a clear, unambiguous purchase or vote.

In addition to assessing rhetorical structures and frameworks, it will be necessary to address their *contexts* to some extent. As is clear – especially to the ad agency or spin-doctor – targeting audiences means considering aspects of their lives that may affect their purchase or vote. Returning to the Louvre, we could, in this particular case, try to understand more of the context of Uccello's painting by surfing the web to land at the address, www.uq.net.au/iacobus/uccello/san_romano.html. We would then not only be able to view Cotignola leading his forces, we would learn that this complex painting is actually part of a larger project. At the Uffizi in Florence, you may view his depiction of the opposing leader, Bernadino della Ciarda of the Sienese forces, while in London's National Gallery you would be able to study Uccello's portrayal of Cotignola's ally, Niccolò da Tolentino.

You might then surmise that the three murals were intended to be read one against another, in juxtaposition, and with the supplementary information provided by the web page construct a narrative whereby the Sienese suffered defeat at the hands of the Florentines. You might go on to extend the domain of context through another text-specific evaluation. The lavishness of the paintings might make you wonder about the financial support that allowed their creation and that consequently implies that the battle being depicted, although not known to you, was of some importance to whoever commissioned the paintings. In other words, you might correctly guess that the three murals demonstrate the importance of patronage. Cotignola and Tolentino, not coincidentally, are depicted in their glory, while the Sienese Ciarda is depicted in the moment of his being unhorsed. It will come as no surprise to you, then, to learn that Uccello was commissioned to paint these murals for Florence's ruling family, the Medici.

Of course, you should always check your surmises and web information against standard sources, since often enough, incorrect information floats all too freely in the ether. But once you've corroborated your information against standard sources (for example, Borsi 1993), you'll probably have acquired a broader context for your analysis. In this case, as a result of our hunt to flesh out contexts, we need to adjust our perspective on the mural in Paris and accommodate a larger vision. I won't explore the other two murals here, but I do want to note this: the patriotically stirring call to glory conveyed by Uccello's three murals is sounded by leaders who were all *condottiere*, mercenary leaders of mercenary armies. Such knowledge creates dissonance – can patriotic causes be executed through mercenaries? – and leads us necessarily to try to learn more about warfare in this period as well as to examine our own reactions to such information. With such contextual information, we probably can then come to a better understanding of what informed the artist's vision while attempting to transform the ordinary into the extra-ordinary.

Such attention to dissonant detail – in contexts as well as in a text (verbal or visual) – marks the use of our second main theoretical tool: *semiotic theory*. Semiotics concerns, essentially, the analysis of signs. It presumes the existence of relations that express meaning by means of some vehicle, whether these vehicles are letters, geometric figures or images. For example, gravity *per se* is a relation to the earth that obtains for every object on the earth. Hence, the force itself is not a sign, since the force doesn't *stand for* anything. In contrast, you, as an individual, may also have a relation to the earth beyond that of gravity, one that is expressed, say, in pounds or in the image of Gaia. Pounds and Gaia become signs when they *stand for* something – time to diet or the wholeness of nature, for example.

Since semiotics is concerned with the representation of meaning, you can imagine how the language of semiotic theory can very rapidly fly off into obscure abstraction. I'll do my best to minimize the degree of abstraction in this study, but consider what a difficult enterprise semioticians have: not only are *all words* signs, but *everything* can be made into a sign. Part of the problem is that, traditionally, semiotic theory is articulated in the language and conceptual framework of formal logic, a language that causes many of us story-lovers to glaze over, doomed to reading the same page over and over again. Regardless of how it is expressed, semiotic theory is nevertheless primarily a reader's tool and, as such, complements and often over-laps with rhetorical theory, which is primarily an author's tool. I have used the term *primarily* in both cases, because as I hope we'll see, effective writers need to be effective readers, and effective readers need to be effective writers.

Like rhetorical theory, semiotics has been studied and developed since the classical Greek era, and quite a few approaches have been developed since then. Here, we'll look at a few of them, but we'll be grounded in the perspective articulated in the work of Maria Corti, who sees semiotics as a way to understand literary communication. In other words, we'll use a semiotic approach that – although expressed in the framework and language of logic – is focused on rhetorical dynamics. After all, *communication* is concerned with messages sent between authors and audiences, and, as stated above, the hallmark of rhetorical theory is the author's attempt to reach an audience. Thus, it will be useful to keep the following model in mind, which combines semiotic and rhetorical concerns, and which was articulated by Roman Jakobson, who, however, is mostly concerned with linguistic properties (Innis 1985, 150):

Context
Message
Addresser..Addressee
Contact
Code

In his words:

> The ADDRESSER sends a MESSAGE to the ADDRESSEE. To be opera-
> tive the message requires a CONTEXT referred to ... seizable by the
> addressee, and either verbal or capable of being verbalized; a CODE
> fully, or at least partially, common to the addresser and addressee ...
> and finally, a CONTACT, a physical channel and psychological
> connection between the addresser and the addressee, enabling both
> of them to enter and stay in communication.

Thus, I, as writer, am sending a multiply stranded message about
theory and literature to you, the reader. Our context is multifarious,
but perhaps the most relevant aspect of it here is the university. Our
code involves the complex conventions that have evolved around
learning. Last but not least, our contact is this book, which is not only
a physical channel, but also one which conveys a certain set of connotations, which you were able to grasp as soon as you saw what
Macmillan did with it graphically to make it look like a volume in a
series concerned with literary theory rather than, say, a lurid detective
novel.

Keeping the Addresser–Addressee axis in mind allows us to remember that the *literary system*, to use Corti's term, serves as the framework, the primary context for any literature we read. For the literary
system includes not only those texts which we tend to call 'canonical'
or 'authoritative', like Shakespeare's plays, but also every poem, short
story, novel, image and convention that will allow us to read materials
in a given period and in a given culture with understanding. Here,
we'll broaden this framework now and again to include other artifacts
we commonly associate with a society, like paintings, since they too
share common ground with literature.

For example, as suggested above, Cotignola's leadership at San
Romano on Sunday 1 June 1432 is somehow more striking by his not
donning a helmet. Nonetheless, we don't understand Cotignola to be
hopelessly stupid or even careless; the thought might not even occur
to us, for we do understand this pose to be a *presentation*, whose relation is not to data-specific reality, but to the reality of fiction which
telegraphically communicates *ideas* by such signs. Thus, when we
read this dissonant marker against our knowledge of literary conventions – against the literary system – what is communicated by the sign
is the extraordinary courage and special dispensation of our hero. In

other words, Uccello – who painted the three panels some time after the battle, the first two around 1435-36, and the one we're viewing in about 1440, about mid-way through the period we're studying – fictionalized the historical battle by playing against the images and patterns of narratives that depict war as a glorious undertaking, while at the same time undercutting them.

Actually, this particular battle was fought in the war between Florence and Milan; the Sienese were allies of the latter. Tolentino and a small band of his men accidentally came upon Siena's main forces. He nonetheless attacked and was about to be soundly defeated by Bernardino and his troops, when the forces of Cotignola (our man, who, by the way, less than a decade earlier was still fighting for the Milanese) arrived and engaged in a short battle before the Sienese retreated. Contemporary chroniclers of both sides claimed victory, while later sources barely treat the battle, and Machiavelli doesn't even mention it. But Cosimo de' Medici, who essentially funded the war, needed a victory to return from exile and establish a power base in Florence. This was the only 'victory' the Florentines could claim. When Tolentino, who was also a good friend of his, died (or was killed, the circumstances aren't clear), Medici commissioned the paintings to depict the battle in all its Florentine glory. As we know from presentations of Marilyn, the Kennedys, or Princess Di: once a story has ended (the battle is over, the star has died), known human foibles (mercenary armies, numerous affairs) may surface, but tend to be marginalized, and what remains most prominent is the framework that emphasizes the story of greatness.

In our study of English literature from 1337 to 1580, I will use one more tool, although less prominently, which I call an *arc*. What I mean by the term is something like a path. We tend to think of the past as directly and causally related to us in the present, and hence we select events or literature of the past that help us see these relations. Although past is certainly prologue to the present, in thinking in this manner, we tend to forget that in any single moment of time there are multiple possibilities – there are multiple ways for 'our story to end'. It's only when we perceive an ending that we select the events leading to it. To remind us, now and again, of the myriad events that are part of any moment, I plan to isolate *arcs*. I use this term heuristically, just as a helpful tool, to remind us that a straight line is not the only way to connect two points, that multiple arcs can *also* exist between points. Thus, arcs will complement our use of rhetorical and semiotic theory when they reveal strands of the context that illuminate aspects of a literary text which we might not otherwise have considered … since we know the ending.

Back again to Uccello. It certainly wasn't a necessary consequence that the paintings created for Cosimo de' Medici are housed where they currently are – they left Florence some time between 1787 and 1844; in 1857 the National Gallery purchased the Tolentino mural, and in 1863 the Louvre acquired the Cotignola. But the fact that they are in these three different cities functions as a useful, serendipitous, arc insofar as they represent the relations among England, France and Italy that are also vibrant during the 250 years under study here. For example, the English literary system of the period includes narratives and conventions in Latin, French and Italian, as well as in English, and is influenced by and often meant to be read against Latin writers like Vergil, Ovid and Boethius; French poets like Guillaume Machaut, Guillaume de Lorris and Jean de Meun, and Italian authors like Dante Alighieri, Francesca Petrarca and Giovanni Boccaccio.

Less serendipitously, and more in accordance with the meaning of arc I intend here, it is useful to arc back in time to gather, for example, details on the longstanding rivalry between Siena and Florence, information that will enhance an arc forward that notes differences in the cultural fabrics of these two Tuscan cities that exist to this day in painting styles, economic prosperity and architecture. It is this kind of arc that will enable us to examine the English literary system at a time when English evolves into the language of literary art as well as of state and religious policy; authoritative literary genres are making space for additional forms such as drama; the reading public is growing; and writers produce England's first, most widely spread, national narratives in English.

1337–1580

Thus, rather than just strolling by Cotignola to witness what at first seems 'simply' a glorious moment, we should pause before this magnificent mural. Doing so will, hopefully, prove invigorating, as we examine it from rhetorical and semiotic standpoints, while arcs back and forth between various points will emerge that can shade the painting with yet more vibrant detail. This is, in essence, the model we will be using for reading the literature in this volume.

To start us off, however, let me note here that the years focused upon, 1337–1580, do not represent a conventional historical or literary period. Ordinarily, the Middle Ages are said to cover from *c.* 450–1450, and the Early Modern era, from *c.* 1485–1700. Likewise, conventional literary history records Geoffrey Chaucer (*c.* 1343–1400) as the last great English poet of the medieval period, after which there is no literary artist his equal until William Shakespeare (1564–1616) illuminates the Renaissance. Here, we'll look at some of the obvious central figures (like Cotignola), but also pay attention to lesser figures (like the knights to the leader's right), to dissonant figures (like the other warriors to Cotignola's left), to transcendent signs (like the helmetless pose of military glory), and to a bit of the contexts (those foot soldiers mulling around in the lower half).

These 250 years may be perceived as forming the transition between the Middle Ages and the Early Modern era. A transition, however, is something *perceived*; it is a *sign* that stands for an ending giving way to a beginning. Yet, we can be pretty certain that no person living during these years stopped on the way to a play and smacked herself on the forehead, crying out, 'Well, there we are, I forgot to set my watch for Early Modern time'. Although I think we all know what is meant when we say these 250 years form the transition between the Middle Ages and the Early Modern era, we should remember we're talking about a transition between heuristic constructs, between academic fictions, between presentations, between signs. For our purposes, the transition is not a space where an ending meets a beginning. It's a place where multiple arcs criss-cross, creating multiple strands that raise multiple possibilities. It's only from our endpoint that we perceive this space as finite.

Indeed, periodization works something like Uccello's banner of the unicorn – it rallies forces and efforts under one *sign*, even though it is, actually, a presentation of a fictional construct. Looking at the past through such traditional signs resembles how Francesco Petrarca (1304–74) looked at the years between his fourteenth-century Florence and the Roman empire that was dissolved in the fifth century. For, it was Petrarca who called this intervening period the *Medium Aevum*, which in Latin means 'Middle Ages'. He did so to signal a *Renaissance*, a 'rebirth' of past values that he perceived as belonging to the Roman empire, and, in the process, to suggest that the intervening years were not worth exploring.[2] (By the way, scholars used to follow his cue, but now the period is called Early Modern.)

So, the title of this volume signals this space of about 250 years by using the names of England's preeminent poets prior to 1600 – authoritative today as well as in their own times. If we were to separate them from each other into two separate periods, we would miss out on the multiple strands that link the two poets. For example, both Chaucer and Shakespeare write in a literary system that emphasizes the importance of rhetorical training and the highly crafted use of images (and yet another reason why we'll be using rhetorical and semiotic theories). Moreover, these two poets are not only recognized in their own times as exceptional writers. Among other things, Chaucer was a diplomat and bureaucrat as well as a controller of customs, and Shakespeare was also probably an actor as well as an entrepreneur.

Likewise, the dates chosen to cordon off this period are associated with traditionally important historical events, but they also serve to signal less obvious social, economic and aesthetic markers. Thus, 1337 marks the beginning of the Hundred Years War as traditionally designated by historians, but it is also the year in which William Merlee of Oxford recorded the first scientifically conducted weather forecasts (whose methodology has become more sophisticated, while its results still remain inaccurate). The second date is notable not only because it is the year in which Sir Francis Drake returned from his circumnavigation of the world. It is also the year during which an earthquake disrupted London and the last performance of a miracle play in Coventry took place.

Dynastic ambition, science, exploration, disasters – these also texture England's cultural fabric of the time and provide contexts as well as stimuli for its literature. And this principle necessitating the relation of literature to its cultural contexts is a constant. Could 1997 ever have produced *Gattaca* had technology not made computers and genetics a dominant part of our daily encounters with science? It won't be difficult to isolate arcs in this 250-year period; radical and far-reaching events punctuate these years. To illustrate with perhaps the most obvious, early example: the English monarchy not only engages in the Hundred Years War (1337–1453), it is also straddled by the War of the Roses (1455–85) and wages ongoing, nation-defining battles against the Irish and Scottish as well. These military efforts not only fuel the diminishing of the island population, but also alter British economy, military organization, class structure, religious self-definition, consumer behavior and, certainly not least, the arts.

The Order of the Garter

By isolating an obviously influential set of events such as nation-defining warfare, it's possible to identify less visible but clearly inter-related arcs as well. One such arc is established at the beginning of our 250-year period. That is, some time between 1344 and 1351, Edward III (1327–77) created the Order of the Garter to honor 26 knights (including himself and the Prince of Wales) on St George's Day. Probably inspired by the Arthurian literature composed in the prior two centuries and certainly part of *his* literary system, Edward created – he authored – an elite institution. This sign is enhanced over the years by the creation of other signs of its importance: Windsor becomes the Order's home, and the Chapel of St George its collegiate church.

In effect celebrating his victories at Crécy (1346) and Calais (1347), Edward III signals with the Order a new kind of alliance between regent and nobility, which simultaneously seems to set this chosen circle apart from the rest of English society. Its effect, however, extends beyond a celebratory marker of class distinction. Drawing upon the literary system and articulating symbols in architectural edifices as well as in other emblems, Edward III is able to disseminate a call to glory not unlike that represented by Cotignola and the unicorn banner in Uccello's mural, whose message is indeed heard. For example, lay as well as national orders are subsequently established in western Europe, with France founding its own, the Order of the Star. Another interesting marker of response, around the time of the Order's inception, St George is the patron saint of all knights, thereby marrying medieval feudal and religious ideologies in a seemingly universal sign. By the end of the century, however, St George becomes the patron saint of England. If we arc forward to our own times, Edward's creation still resonates today beyond the Order's continuing significance for English nobility. After all, scholars still cling to tradition when they celebrate Shakespeare's birthday (which is not actually known) on 23 April, St George's Feast Day.

One of the fascinating aspects of this particular arc is its popularity. It seems that at least in part its attraction stems from the fact that traditional, medieval formulations of knighthood are treated in a sign communicating not only Arthur-like glory, but also that all is well in the realm. In this sense, the Order functions very much like Uccello's murals. After all, although Edward does win critical military victories, they are costly, and, moreover, England is severely affected by them as well as by internal disruption. Thus, in the midst of warfare against France and Scotland, the Black Death, first appearing in Dorset in 1348, ravages England in 1349, decimating the population by at least a third and maybe by a half, with outbreaks of the dread disease continuing well into the seventeenth century – throughout the period explored here. As one of many results, the virulent illness forces a shift of perspectives, transitions: new, economically defined classes evolve; new demands are made of the Church; and new economic pressures are experienced by the nobility. In this context, the Order of the Garter serves not only as a marker of elitism and national identification, it also functions as a dissonant sign. Indeed, through its very 'necessity', it quietly comments on less than satisfactory public policy, while it nonetheless encourages an odd sense of belonging – not unlike the tensions created by Henry's St Crispin's Day speech in Shakespeare's *Henry V*, 'Be he ne'er so vile,/ This day shall gentle his condition' (IV, iii, 62–3).

At least by the end of this 250-year period, the allure of the Order of the Garter should have been tarnished. Certainly, a more objective assessment of the kingdom might have stimulated the Order's demise, since, among other things, England had by then lost all right to the French throne as well as to English dominions in France. In spite of all the problems, the glorification of the elite does not subside. On the contrary, along with other European powers, England transformed battles over imperial identity into efforts to define colonialism in the Americas. And alongside such investments in national identity, contradictory or anomalous strands texture English life. It is during these years, for example, that England experiences the Peasants' Revolt; the royally supported usurpation of religious authority; the creation of a poorer North and a trade-rich London; the emergence of economically redefined social classes; and radical shifts in education, as manifest in the increasing number of universities, specialized schools and grammar schools.

With fewer people, incessant wars and taxation, devastating outbreaks of the plague, and the redefinition of political boundaries, economic opportunities in the British Isles are also necessarily wrested from the knightly class. Not surprisingly, then, as much as the Order of the Garter celebrates itself with pomp and ritual, opposing modes of *authorized* participation in elite activities concurrently multiply. I italicize 'authorized' because much of the access to such participation is effected through literary vehicles. For example, drama, which had begun in close connection with the Church, emerges in this period as a secular and viable economic institution that gains support from the nobility.

As the following chapters attempt to illustrate, looking closely at the literature from the years between 1337 and 1580 reveals tensions and details that when analyzed rhetorically and semiotically allow for a more textured understanding of these times as well as of our own.

Here's the plan

I've found it more difficult than I anticipated to present literature of this period through the auspices of semiotic and rhetorical theory, so, I decided it would make more sense to cover less material than throw a series of titles at you. Consequently, I've found it necessary to eliminate many really wonderful narratives. In recompense, at the end of the volume the annotated bibliography contains a few suggestions for further reading.

But I also found myself going back and forth over details. For example, should I include quotations from texts I refer to in their original languages or not? This is a more difficult question than it may at first seem, since English literature *is* influenced by other national literatures. In addition, during this period, there is no standardized spelling. Furthermore, modern-day editors (which means scholars from the Victorian era to ours) have different methods for presenting this irregular spelling to their audiences.

Somewhat reluctantly, I decided to present materials as found in the various editions used, without trying to normalize them. This way, I think, the layering of decades devoted to recovering these texts might in some way be experienced, along with a sense of how varied spelling slows down the reading process (as you may also gather from my American orthography). What I have changed in very few of the older edited texts is this: I've omitted the italics or brackets which indicate an editor's judgment call, and I've provided full words instead of unusual contractions. I've also tried to use editions that are relatively easy to access, sometimes finding inexpensive volumes, but also sometimes using very old editions even though they may no longer be in print, either because they are the only ones available or because university libraries are likely to have them.

Finally, when deemed necessary, I've included loose translations along with the originals, or the translations of others, although I recommend that you take the time to peruse the original texts. Some of the usages may surprise you. If they do, rest assured, some earlier readers join you, as Chaucer's words in the prologue to Book II of his late fourteenth-century *Troilus and Criseyde* suggest:

> Ye knowe ek that in forme of speche is chaunge
> Withinne a thousand yeer, and wordes tho
> That hadden pris, now wonder nyce and straunge
> Us thinketh hem, and yet thei spake hem so ...
>
> [II. 22–5: You know also that there is change in the form of speech within a thousand years, and words that then were valued, now we think of them as silly and strange, and yet they spoke them in that manner ...]

Notes

1. I will try to give dates for the births and deaths of those we study from this period, although for regents the dates refer to their reigns. Frequently, however, dates aren't known, which is more often the case for the earlier part of the period.
2. Two major scholars writing on the relation of Latin antiquity to western European culture are Ernst Robert Curtius, who argues for a continuous relation (Curtius 1973), and Erich Auerbach, who essentially argues for discontinuity by taking into account the modifications introduced by Christian discourse (Auerbach 1965). Both scholars bring excellent materials, arguments and perspectives to the problem.

1   Authors and Audiences in Transition

In an indirect way, the battle depicted in Uccello's murals suggests how many of us orient ourselves to the new. In a single defining moment, it seems, everything can be resolved, and new projects can be launched, new adventures at once different and exciting. In contrast, we often associate the old, the past, with much that weighs us down – conventions; rules; listening to parents and others with more experience; learning dates, authors and quotations. The idea that all past conflicts can be completely eradicated is embodied in Cotignola's portrait – confronting the enemy with one glorious sweep of his arm in a defining gesture that promises a new order, the brave and elegant warrior of San Romano conveys a quintessentially romantic vision.

But actually, what we call the past – or the future, for that matter – does not exist separately at any given moment. There are traces of the past weaving through our lives, just as intimations of the future shape our consciousness. From our names to our use of language to the churches and banks we glimpse as we drive through town, traces of the past help construct the frameworks in which we can know anything. Likewise, we make calls to meet friends, desperately access the www to research essays that are due the next day, plan dates along with our careers, and otherwise project a framework into what we call the future. Yet, neither the past nor the future can exist as a separate continuum at any given moment, because what *exists* is a past-modified and future-expectant present.

What we call the past and the future are essentially heuristic constructs we use to order our lives and to help make sense of what would otherwise be a never-ending confrontation and negotiation with a continual flux of data. With the help of these temporal constructs we can perceive trends, progress, failures and causalities. Moreover, the ability to perceive temporally is fundamental to how we acquire knowledge. Not only does one bit of information depend on other *already* acquired bits of information, but also what we know depends on what we've received as knowledge while part of a larger set of audiences, and, of course, what we've received depends on the heuristic constructs that frame our knowledge, temporality among them. So, when we receive information about our past in school or are told what our destiny is by politicians, we are part of a larger set of audiences who receive this information in heuristic frameworks, in narratives, that have already been formed. How we individually assess this information depends on frameworks we've adapted along the way.

One of the many consequences of how we order our knowledge is that we can at least partly interpret, in a flash, images like that portrayed by Uccello. In this case, what allows such images to generate connotations of an upcoming, new and better order is the traditional story of martial heroism: fighting to restore or establish peace, heroes (and rebels as well) challenge the status quo. In essence, they demand a new state, ignoring the fact that to have a really new state, new people and institutions must inhabit it. If we were ever actually to encounter a situation, or an image for that matter, that were totally new, we wouldn't have the frameworks established in our minds to assess or understand it.

Importantly, one of the major ordering principles we use to connect the present to what we know of the past and to what we plan in the future is implicit in temporal constructs. That is, insofar as we learn from stories (implied or narrated), we learn from narratives that are generated in a linear structure. In other words, they are based in a forward, *seriatim* – segment by segment – linearly constructed form, the same kind of linear movement we rely on when we order time into hours, days, years and chronologies.

Time, Augustine and reading

The power of this linear form of framing is subtle. Not only does it pervade all we do, it also echoes how we read and speak, one word after another, one sentence after another: *seriatim* structures underpin what we know and how we order our knowledge. If we're not careful, however, these heuristic, rhetorical, *seriatim* structures will also lead us to believe that this is the only way we order our knowledge, or that there is only one way of thinking about something, or that there is only one cause for, say, the Battle of San Romano. Rarely are things so simple, even though we need to absorb them so simply.

The tendency to order linearly, along with resistance to the tendency, comprise one of those fundamental arcs that criss-cross western European culture. For example, if we arc back to a central writer in western European philosophy, we will find that Augustine, also known as St Augustine of Hippo, mulls over this theme in his influential *Confessiones* (The Confessions):

> Dicturus sum canticum, quod noui: antequam incipiam, in totum expectatio mea tenditur, cum autem coepero, quantum ex illa in praeteritum decerpsero, tenditur et memoria mea, atque distenditur uita huius actionis meae in memoriam propter quod dixi et in expectationem propter quod dicturus sum: praesens tamen adest attentio mea, per quam traicitur quod erat futurum, ut fiat praeteritum. Quod quanto magis agitur et agitur, tanto breuiata expectatione prolongatur memoria, donec tota expectatio consumatur, cum tota illa actio finita transierit in memoriam. Et quod in toto cantico, hoc in singulis particulis eius fit atque in singulis syllabis eius, hoc in actione longiore, cuius forte particula est illud canticum, hoc in tota uita hominis, cuius partes sunt omnes actiones hominis, hoc in toto saeculo filiorum hominum, cuius partes sunt omnes vitae hominum.

> [XI. 28 (38): 15–27: I am about to recite a psalm that I know: before I begin, (the psalm) is grasped by my expectation in (its) totality; moreover when I began, a portion of it I took from the past, my memory is stretched, and the life of my action stretches forth in memory because I recited (before) and because I expect to recite: my attention is nonetheless (in the) present, through that which was the future which will be transferred to the past. The more this is done and repeated, the briefer is the expectation and the longer is the memory until all expectation is consumed, when all of that completed action will have transferred into memory. And what goes for the whole psalm, also holds for its single elements and its single syllables – the same holds for a larger action, of which the small part is the psalm; thus also in the whole life of mortals, of which the parts are all human actions, and thus too in the entire sum of generations of which the parts are all human lives.)

Linking memory and the performance of a psalm to time, Augustine shows that although we may create images of memory, reading and time as linear and straightforward (Traugott 1985, 25–29), such images are mainly heuristic organizing devices that help us mere mortals to comprehend and come closer to the non-linear nature of the mortal world as well as to the timeless nature of the immortal world.

Augustine also conveys this idea through the *Confessiones* as a whole. Thus, rather than progressing *seriatim* through his life, he essentially selects very few, sketchily presented events in order to frame a set of meditations on God and His grace. Consequently, we don't emerge from the *Confessiones* with too firm a hold on the facts of his life, such as the following brief lines try to convey.

The Bishop of Hippo was one of the early, highly influential philosophers of the Christian Church (c. 354–430). Born in Tagaste, Africa, at the present-day location of Souk-Ahras in Algeria, he gave up the chance to earn his living as what would be the equivalent of a professor of rhetoric (surprise, surprise) to dedicate himself to the Christian Church. His numerous theological writings promulgate ideas he appropriated and modified from the ancient Greek writings of the fourth century (BCE) philosopher Plato and have shaped how Roman Catholicism has evolved. In the period under study here, St Augustine is also the subject of *vitae*, a term that literally means 'lives', but which refers to saints' lives. In the first half of the fifteenth century, for example, John Capgrave presents an English *vita*, based, for the most part, on the *Confessiones*.

Such a linearly structured list of events is at odds with the structure and focus of the *Confessiones*, which makes God's grace and love for humankind the frame and the point to which the author returns time and again. In other words, in spite of the *seriatim* structure of mortal language, Augustine builds his narrative on a circular structure, reminiscent of his attempt to memorize the psalm. Based in a neoplatonic approach to time, his narrative thereby suggests that since God is eternal and knows no change, he lives *outside* time in omnipotent, omnipresent, omniscient existence.

Experiencing a changeless present, the divine is simple, pure and constant, attributes which Augustine extols. Likewise attributable to this changeless present, God knows all that has happened, is happening and will happen all at once, in his limitless – timeless – 'present'. Indeed, time in and of itself belongs to and, actually, *defines* the mortal world, the world we live in, which is characterized by variety, complexity, constant change, mutability and lack of permanence, attributes which Augustine deems we should tame as much as possible. We can tame these attributes, he suggests, by understanding God's goodness to the best of our abilities. However, since mortal horizons are limited, we must *learn* or *come to know* whole truths by studying accurate reflections of God's goodness (like the Holy Scriptures) step by step, *seriatim*, in time. Important for our purposes here, the language we speak and in which we write also – and necessarily – exhibits this *seriatim* trait of time, since our language too is mortal.

Consequently, if we wish to demonstrate our love for God in an appropriate response to his loving creation of the universe, we would best accomplish this by reflecting Him, by acting *in imitatione Dei* (in imitation of God). Thus, we should prefer a *simple* life, act with *pure* motivation, and be *constant* in our devotion. Augustine also recommends that our language be spoken and written *in imitatione Dei*. He conveys this idea by means of meditations on language – especially in his *De Doctrina Christiana* (On Christian Doctrine) – revealing that although it must be written and spoken in a linear mode, when used *in imitatione Dei*, language may convey God's love as well. This is so, he argues, since after the fall of Adam and Eve, meaning is no longer *simple*. Meaning is no longer tied to language in a literal, one-to-one correspondence. To redeem this fallen language, a Christian is to use language's complexities and ambiguities with a pure heart to communicate a *simple* message: the love and grace of God (Colish 1968, 8–81).

From another perspective, language can also imply more than words say. It can convey a fullness in its limits, not unlike Uccello's secularly oriented *Battle of San Romano*. This is what makes language so susceptible to contexts, to audiences, to traditions. Since there is no perfect single way to convey a message, language's ambiguity and potential for variety demands that both audiences and authors participate in convention-informed partnerships. It is through this basic assumption that rhetorical and semiotic theory can help us gain perspectives on past writing. For if a text exists, it was composed by a writer whose aim was to communicate a message to some audience.

While this is true of literary systems at any time or in any place, we need, I think, to pay special attention to linguistic ambiguity for the literature of the period. Not only is any educated person's training far more linguistically and rhetorically focused than is the case nowadays (as sketched in the next chapter). In this period, it's also a given that language is imperfect, that multiple meanings may be generated by single words, that narratives will be read (aloud) multiple times, that eloquence (however it is defined) allows the value of a message to be conveyed far more powerfully than a simple statement of facts. Even when Augustine argues for simplicity, he doesn't mean simple sentences – the language may be eloquent and the narrative multiply stranded, as long as its *message* is clear and simple.

I've begun this chapter with time, since this is perhaps where we're most different from our counterparts in the period under study here – *literati* of this period had more time on their hands. They seem to reflect on time, on structure, on figures of speech, on eloquent constructions as a simple matter of course. Although clocks are found in London's St Paul's in 1286, and in Milan in 1309, they still had to be corrected against a sun-dial for quite some time. Rather than being ruled by the minutes and seconds blinking from our digital watches, people in this period were more susceptible to the division of the sun's path into, for example, religious markers. Thus, the canonical hours announced by church bells signal the day's passing and divide it into segments of about three hours each. Beginning with matins – composed of three nocturns held at about 9.00 p.m., midnight, and 3.00 a.m. – the hours continue with lauds at daybreak, prime at 6.00 a.m., terce at 9.00 a.m., sext at noon, nones at 3.00 p.m., vespers at 6.00 p.m., and compline at nightfall. These days are further grouped into periods of time marked by the feast days of major Christian events, like Christmas, Easter and Pentecost.

In this temporal framework, reading reflects the marking of time insofar as it too evolves as a communal experience. Although silent reading increasingly characterizes the scholarly world, courtly literature is still read aloud, especially during the early part of this period (Chartier and Cavallo 1999). This is something else we simply have to imagine, for reading aloud to audiences whose reactions are accessible to the performer – whether author or professional entertainer – must have generated whole levels that are lost to us now. A grimace, an ironic sneer – we have to guess at these intonations. Reading itself must have been a more leisurely activity. It simply takes longer to read aloud than it does to read privately to oneself.

The Order of the Garter

Looking at the literary system of 1337–1580, we can easily see that writers and leaders are intrigued and inspired by the idea of new approaches to the old. In the Introduction, for example, I mentioned the Order of the Garter. It's probably difficult to imagine that once, the venerable Order was actually promoted as exciting and glorious, thereby evoking associations similar to those of Uccello's *Battle of San Romano*. But the Order was indeed presented as a new manner in which to view the King and his nobles, one, ironically, steeped in tradition. In spite of the attempt to institutionalize it as quasi-eternal, however, we should keep in mind that the Order has undergone a number of changes since its inception in the fourteenth century. For example, in 1766, George III (1760–1820) changed the fixed number of members the society could honor for personal and political reasons – he wanted to accommodate his four sons (Beltz 1841, cxxxi).

Even though it has proven adaptable, if we arc forward to 1841 during Queen Victoria's reign (1837–1901), the Order is described in the following words, composed in the context of an apology for the paucity of early materials available for writing its history:

> … *this chivalrous society, having been, from its origin, placed under the sole control of the Sovereign, unconnected with the government of the state, and not subservient to the ordinary legal jurisdiction of the country,* few relative entries could be expected to appear amongst the public records; its official transactions being exclusively confided to appropriate ministers, and its statutes and ordinances authenticated by its peculiar seal. (Beltz 1841, viii, my italics)

The words here bespeak a veneration of the traditional. So much so, as the last words of this passage reveal, that analysis is suspended for belief.

Indeed, we do not have records or annals prior to the fourth year of Henry V's reign (1413–22). However, to assume that such a lacuna derives from the need for secrecy among certain ministers, as this statement suggests, belies supposedly similar needs that would have been important in subsequent years. More critically, perhaps, there are quite a few years in the Order's history when this purportedly disinterested group had much influence on what the realm did do. In other words, upon first glance, like Uccello's painting, the Order has the power to convey a single, unified image of glory regardless of contradictions or light shed upon the image from other perspectives. Steeped in the single-stranded, *seriatim* sense that the society was divinely ordained, the Order of the Garter is, actually, a remarkable public relations coup that successfully balances the old against the new.

As remarkable as this presentation is, however, knighthood itself is multiply stranded and at times deemed undesirable even by its participants. It certainly is an expensive undertaking, as suggested in a twelfth-century Arthurian narrative, the Old French *Erec et Enide*, written by Chrétien de Troyes, purportedly the first poet to put Arthurian tales into novelistic form. In this tale, for example, Enide's father is depicted as impoverished and without all the amenities that one might believe belong to knights.

> et vit gesir sor uns degrez
> un vavasor auques de jorz,
> mes molt estoit povre sa corz …
> 'Povretez fet mal as plusors
> et autresi fet ele moi.
> Molt me poise quant ge la voi
> atornee si povremant,
> ne n'ai pooir que je l'amant:
> tant ai esté toz jorz an guerre,
> tote en ai perdue ma terre,
> et angagiee, et vandue.'
>
> [374-517, Carroll's translation: (he) saw, sitting on some steps,/ an elderly vavasor,/ whose court was very poor … 'Poverty ill-treats many men,/ and likewise she does me./ It grieves me when I see my daughter/ so poorly dressed,/ yet I am powerless to change the situation:/ I have spent so much time at war/ I have lost all my land thereby,/ and mortgaged it and sold it.')

Likewise, about a century after the founding of the Order, in 1457, under the reign of Henry VI (1422–61, 1470–71), John Paston I refused a knighthood and had to pay a fine in consequence (Davis 1983, 70). And such expense continues to be a part of courtly life throughout these 250 years, as seen in the need for patronage (Lytle and Orgel 1981). Thus, in Latin (I provide only Hatch and Vos's translation here), Roger Ascham (1515–68) writes to Archbishop Thomas Cranmer in 1545:

Receiving letters from obscure and unknown men will not be a new experience for you, most accomplished bishop, but neither can the readiness to write to so prominent a man be considered presumptuous or strange in a person of my position. For as long as your great generosity stands out and shines out to challenge everyone, and so many reminders are at hand to arouse those of us who have given ourselves to learning, and as long as one is driven by poverty, another is hurried along by his eagerness to promote himself, and some – virtually all, at some point, certainly – are compelled by necessity while still others are drawn in voluntarily, certainly there can never fail to be an occasion for you to receive letters nor for us to write them. (64)

Being a knight or in the service of the monarchy was an expensive enterprise that required monetary dues along with military service, political allegiance and time.

Prior to the Order of the Garter, to be sure, there had been other knightly orders known to Edward's realm, such as Arthur's Round Table, the Oak of Navarre, and the Genet of France. These, however, were fictional. On the other hand, actual knightly orders such as the Knights Templar founded in 1119 or 1120 had, at the very least, more focus. Founded to form a religious community and to assist pilgrims attacked on the way to the Holy Land, the Knights Templar were placed under papal jurisdiction in 1139. In time, they became enormously wealthy and could boast a membership of about 20 000. Accused of heresies and crimes, however, they were destroyed in the early years of the fourteenth century. So much for Augustine's call about nine centuries prior to a simple life.

Nonetheless, even during the reign of Henry IV (1399–1413), the effect of the Order of the Garter's sense of elite nationalism elicits Arthurian responses. Thus, in 1408, a knight, John de Werchin, the seneschal of Hainault, wrote to the English King having read of the history of King Arthur as well as the Knights of the Order of the Round Table. He had heard that an English King had revived the Order and assumed that some of its traditions had been reinstated as well. He thereby offered to combat a number of the King's knights. Henry responded that the Arthur of history (note, not fiction) never allowed a number of his knights to combat a single foreign knight but, more often than not, 10 to 40 of the foreign knights would test their mettle against one knight of Arthur's. So, he allowed a single Garter knight,

John Beaufort, Earl of Somerset, to meet the seneschal at Smithfield. For the record, Werchin was defeated (Beltz 1841, liii–liv).

Arthur does seem to have inspired the Order, for around the time of its founding, in January 1344, a Feast of the Round Table was held at Windsor Castle, and nobles from many countries were invited to participate. Associating Arthur, a figure shrouded in mystery and fantastical victories, with historical veracity as Edward and the two later courtly correspondents did is perhaps unthinkable today. But if we arc forward to our own time, Arthur's appeal is still to be felt in an apparently never-ending series of films, books and computer games. While if pressed, we would probably declare our disbelief in these legends, the selfless chivalry and translation of noble ideals into courtly acts strike a chord that seems to speak even to our own culture and era. Journalists, for example, dubbed John F. Kennedy's presidency in the USA the reign of Camelot, probably referring to the sophisticated and aesthetically informed culture the Kennedys brought to the White House, but possibly also referencing Sir Thomas Malory's fifteenth-century *sobriquet* for King Arthur: *Rex quondam et futurus*, the once and future King – the King who will return.

Every era, every culture, has myths that may seem slightly ridiculous to those outside. Perhaps, readers in some not too distant future will look at our passion for sports in like vein. Not only do we make considerable financial investments in football, for example, we also accommodate a good part of our social lives to its schedule, some of us go about in a team's colors, and our public vehicles for communication – television, newspapers, magazines and the net – glorify the players as well as the sport as a sign, so to speak, of who we are. The national team is 'fighting' for the country, or so the message goes, during every FIFA-sponsored World Cup.

In a similar manner, the Order of the Garter creates the sense that a few, select knights represent the best of knighthood. While at various times in its history, foreign sovereigns or well-known knights were admitted, they all at least pledged to serve the English monarch. And everything about them, from what has become their residence (the Chapel of St George in Windsor) to their elaborate ceremonies to the special clothing they receive in installing ceremonies, all this conveys the desirability of belonging to the Order and owing allegiance to England's King.

In the Chapel itself, for example, there are two rows of stalls, each stall designated for a certain knight, whose name is inscribed on it

(Holmes 1984) – not unlike Malory's Round Table, whose much desired seats are magically inscribed with the name of its rightful inhabitant. In Malory's version, the Round Table is a gift from Arthur's father-in-law, King Leodegrance, which had been given to him by Arthur's father, King Uther (III. 2; vol. 1, 93). Later, we learn the following about the *sieges*, or seats, of the Round Table:

> So when the king and all the knights were come from service, the barons espied in the sieges of the Round Table all about, written with golden letters: HERE OUGHT TO SIT HE, and: HE OUGHT TO SIT HERE.
>
> And thus they went so long till that they came to the Siege Perilous, where they found letters newly written of gold which said: FOUR HUNDRED WINTERS AND FOUR-AND-FIFTY ACCOMPLISHED AFTER THE PASSION OF OUR LORD JESU CHRIST OUGHT THIS SIEGE TO BE FULFILLED. (XIII. 2; vol. 2: 240)

After a quick calculation, Launcelot figures that the seat would be filled the very same day, the Pentecostal feast of 454. And indeed, once Galahad appears to take the sword whose inscription states it belongs to the best knight of the world, we see that the Siege Perilous' inscription has been changed to: 'THIS IS THE SIEGE OF GALAHAD, THE HAUT PRINCE' (XIII. 4; vol. 2: 243).

Perhaps emulating the Round Table's insistence that chosen individuals occupy its seats, the Order of the Garter has a similar tradition. Upon a knight's death (or less tidy expulsion), a new knight would take his place and his name would be inscribed onto his stall accordingly. And just as the select nature of the knights is intimated by their individually inscribed stalls, so too the various ceremonies observed by the Order suggest importance. Although they might vary in any given year, the most important is that celebrated on St George's Day, 23 April, the Feast of the Blue Garter. On these days the King would preside, whenever possible, and when occasion demanded he would distribute garments to new knights of the Order, which at the beginning consisted of a mantel and the symbol of the Order, a garter – actually an ornamental representation of a Knight's sword-belt – inscribed with the words, *Hony soit qui mal y pense*, meaning, 'shame to he who thinks evil of it'.

The origin of the motto isn't actually known, a fact that nonetheless hasn't quelled stories that might explain the Sovereign's attachment to it. Probably the most commonly spread tale is the one which relates how a garter slips from the leg of a Lady, while she is dancing in Edward's court. As a chivalrous gesture, the King recovers the item, places it on his own leg, and utters the words that become the Order's motto. This particular tale seems to have been believed by a number of chroniclers. In the sixteenth century, for example, Polydor Vergil (*c.* 1470–*c.* 1555) records the Cluniac monk Mondonus Belvaleti's suspicions along these lines, as conveyed in his 1463 treatise on the King of England. Trying to locate the perhaps fictional woman of the tale, some have come to believe she is the Countess of Salisbury, Joan of Kent, based on the information provided by yet another chronicler, Jean Froissart (*c.* 1337–*c.* 1410), who conveys the information that Edward III loved this Lady, the wife of William Montacute, the Earl of Salisbury, and whose perspectives on time, by the way, are worth exploring (Zink 1998).

In addition to this explanation, during the reign of Henry VIII (1509–47), another chronicler narrates the following version of the motto's origins in the *Liber Niger* (The Black Book). While Richard I, the Lionhearted (1189–99), leads his troops in holy war against Cyprus and Acre, St George convinces the warrior to inspire his exhausted soldiers by tying a leather thong, or garter, around the legs of chosen knights and therewith honor them while inspiring others to acts of bravery. Having been successful at that battle, Richard institutes the inspired practice as a ritual. Other *literati* convey variations of this tale, suggesting that Edward III himself used his garter as a signal in battle. In still another version, the motto becomes a retort against those who object to Edward's attempts to claim the French crown.

The stories that are told to explain the origins of a motto-inscribed garter are themselves instructive. Like our earlier counterparts, we like to explain such emblems – or in semiotic terms, *signs* – and order events that seem related, even if not historically or logically accurate, into narratives. As mentioned in the Introduction, for example, that Shakespeare's birthday is unknown is a fact; yet, scholars choose to celebrate it on St George's Day. This dissonant marker is additionally notable since Shakespeare was born into an England whose religious affiliations with the Catholic Church and its worship of saints were crumbling: Henry VIII broke with the Roman Catholic Church in 1534 and named himself head of an independent Anglican Church: in 1559, Elizabeth (1558–1603) approved the Act of Supremacy that restored Henry VIII's Anglican reformation; and in 1571, the Thirty-nine

Articles defining the Church of England's framework were finalized. Article twenty-two specifically found the 'Romish doctrine' on the worship of saints 'a fond thing vainly invented' (Cross and Livingstone 1974, 1228). Thus, even though the Anglican Church has become the religious institution *de rigeur* in England, Catholic elements remain. Strands from the past weave about instances of the present to influence the future.

Perhaps the tradition of celebrating the poet's birthday on St George's Day associates him with England's patron saint and a variety of other patriotic ideas, but it also creates an arc that intimates Shakespeare (incorrectly) into Edward III's time. Such dissonant markers signal the presence of *rhetorically*-framed communication, not logical discourse. Rhetorically-impelled instances of communication, after all, seek primarily to convince.

St George

To complicate matters, the story of St George himself is multiply stranded, rather than a causally impelled, simple, linear tale. What may be historically accurate is that George of Cappadocia was born in Armorica and beheaded under Diocletian's persecution of Christians. His martyrdom is celebrated as on 23 April 303. Subsequently, his life was recorded and circulated through the auspices of the Church and found its way into the English literary system (Matzke 1902 and 1903).

In the eleventh century, for example, Ælfric, Abbot of Eynsham (fl. 1006), translated a collection of brief homiletic *vitae* into Old English to be read on the appropriate saints' days. The 14th *vita* is George's and comprises 184 lines. In this life, we learn that George is a rich noble under Emperor Dacian, who encourages people to 'deofol-gildum' (9, Gunning and Wilkinson translation throughout: devil-worship) in Cappadocia. Not able to endure such an affront, George distributes his wealth to the poor and speaks against the Emperor's paganism, exhorting people, by example, to leave the transitory and turn to the eternal (31–2). Not surprisingly, Dacian is furious. Asked who he is by the ruler, the nobleman replies, 'Ic eom soðlice cristen and ic criste þeowige' (27: 'I am verily a Christian, and I serve Christ'). (Here, by the way, 'ð', 'eth', has the value of 'th', as does 'þ', 'thorn', and when you see cheesy signs such as 'Ye Olde Cheese Shoppe', you see a modern mis-transliteration of 'þ' by 'y').

Dacian then insists that George worship Apollo; he refuses, where-upon he is tortured in various ways but remains unharmed. Dacian summons his sorcerer, who tries poisoning him, but the punishment still won't take. The sorcerer is so astonished, however, he begs to be baptized, which makes the ruler angrier still. On the second day, George is to be bound to a wheel and shoved into swords. The wheel breaks, and George rebukes the Emperor by telling him that tortures are 'hwilwendlice' (100: transitory). Not to be stopped by mere mira-cles, the ruler has a cauldron filled with boiling lead and emerses George into it. George is not hurt. Pretty much exasperated by the whole affair, the Emperor is reduced to tears and begs George to worship his gods. In response, George prays to God, who scorches the temple, thereby destroying the pagan gods along with their priests. George is then dragged through the streets, and after the saint prays again to God he is finally killed by the sword. Dacian is slain by fire from heaven and goes to hell, while George journeys to Christ.

In various stories about the saint, tortures vary, but, as Augustine recommends, the message remains *simply* the same. And St George became the patron saint of all knights throughout western Europe, probably after his more elaborate *vitae* are spread in the twelfth century. In some of these he is depicted as a dragon-killer stemming from noble stock. Yet, these *vitae* record his battle with the dragon in different terms than we might assume. He doesn't, that is, risk his life to rescue a fair damsel from a dragon-besieged tower. This tale might be most usefully summarized by reference to the best-known version of St George's life – the one spread by Jacopo da Voragine's *Legenda Aurea* (Golden Legend), a thirteenth-century collection of saints' lives and fantastical legends, hugely popular in the period under study and originally written in Latin before being translated into other languages.

The *Legenda Aurea* also depicts the Saint as stemming from Cappadocia. Riding through Libya, he encounters a town plagued by a dragon who can only be placated by daily offerings of sheep. One day, predictably, the town runs out of livestock, and it is decided that a human victim will be chosen, by lot, to feed the monster. The lot falls on the King's daughter. Having been apprised of the situation, St George mesmerizes the dragon and puts the maiden's girdle (not to be mistaken with the constricting undergarment advertised by Playtex today – more like a sash … perhaps a relative of the Order's garter) around the dragon's neck. George then tells the King and his subjects that if they are baptized in the name of God, he would slay the dragon. They agree, and St George obliges.

Perhaps it is this scene that Uccello, the self-same painter of our *Battle of San Romano*, 'comments upon' in the following painting, entitled *St George and the Dragon*, also at London's National Gallery and painted during 1455–60 (see p. 32).

On first glance, St George seems to be fighting the good fight against the dragon. However, the painting is curiously dissonant. For, as if she were taking her dragon on its golden chain for a walk, the Lady looks, perhaps quizzically, as St George heroically and valiantly kills her poor pet. In addition, the hell-mouth like opening behind the Lady might suggest that every man needs to be vigilant against the temptations of sin, which can appear in forms as innocuous as the Lady or as ferocious as the dragon. However, the storm clouds behind St George don't exactly make him seem as if he were in control of his righteous passion.

Somewhat ambiguous in these terms, the painting illustrates the need to avoid simplistic interpretations of the battle between good and evil. *If* good and evil are being portrayed in Uccello's mural, then it would seem that both the Lady and St George are not only not perfect, but that good and evil are lodged in each individual. Indeed, the need to be careful is underscored considerably, when we view Uccello's earlier version of the same theme (see p. 33).

To return to the *Legenda*: eventually St George is martyred as pagans try to kill and torture him in numerous ways, not, as in the earlier version, an easy task. Even decapitation won't hold and has to be repeated, until God is satisfied that the pagans get the message, at which time he releases the soldier from his earthly life. Herein is another illustration of the simplicity that should govern the language and writing of the Christian, according to Augustine. All the various modes of torture are examples of the multiplicity that defines the mortal realm, but they all boil down to the simple message: the wonder and miracles of God as expressed in his saints. Again, simplicity simply means clarity, not dullness.

When King Richard I, the Lionhearted, returned from the Crusades, he promulgated the idea that the saint had great power and gave his knights succor in battle (perhaps indeed the source of the Garter motto). Not long afterwards, in 1222, under the rule of Henry III (1216–72), St George's Day is included among the lesser holidays at the synod of Oxford. In 1415, in Henry V's reign (1413–22), the saint's

'St George and the Dragon' by Paolo Uccello (c. 1397–1475) circa 1460, oil on canvas in the National Gallery, London.

'St George and the Dragon', by Paolo Uccello (c. 1397–1475), panel in the Musée Jacquemart-Andre, Paris.

day becomes one of the chief feast days of the year. And, not to be forgotten, St George has *always* been the patron saint of the Order of the Garter.

By associating the Order of the Garter with St George, Edward III created a vehicle that allowed the Order to become a sign representing the country, effectively conveying national *and* religious supremacy, while functioning at the same time as a tool for political allegiances. Edward had rhetorically mastered the linguistic sign, the metaphor.

Translatio: transformation, translation, transferral and the metaphor

On the threshhold of the new, while grounded in the past, Edward III's creation of the Order of the Garter works akin to the *invention* of a new metaphor. I highlight the term 'invention,' because it has specific significance in the years under study here. In classical rhetorical treatises used and modified in this period, the term *inventio* refers to one of the five faculties that an effective rhetor must exercise: *inventio*, *dispositio* (arrangement), *elocutio* (eloquence), *memoria* (memory), and *pronuntiatio* (delivery). *Inventio* doesn't quite mean what *invention* means today, but rather, the Latin term means 'finding'; thus, a skilled rhetor wouldn't 'discover something *new*', but would *find* the right argument for the case, the perfect metaphor, a fitting mode of presentation to convey the complex idea and to reach the audience. It's a standard tenet of classical, medieval and early modern rhetorical treatises that good material must thus be found, or invented, in order to communicate effectively. And metaphors are no exception to the precept.

In Latin, the metaphor is called the *translatio*, which one of the most authoritative and popular treatises on rhetoric from classical times through the early modern period, the *Rhetorica ad Herennium*, defines as follows: 'Translatio est cum verbum in quandam rem transferetur ex alia re, quod propter similitudinem recte videbitur posse transferri' (Caplan's translation, IV, xxxiv, 45: Metaphor occurs when a word applying to one thing is transferred to another, because the similarity seems to justify this transference).

The *translatio* is more generally defined here than in common parlance today. We tend to think of the metaphor as a figure of speech that generates a comparison, without using 'like' or 'as', and that does so by means of a vehicle and a tenor. Hence, 'My love is like a rose' illustrates the simile, while 'My love is a rose' illustrates the metaphor. As such, this definition functions as a subset of the *sign*, as defined by Ferdinand de Saussure. According to Saussure, one of the two major early contributors to modern studies of semiotics, the linguistic *sign* consists of a concept, which he calls the *signified* and a sound-image, which he calls the *signifier*. Thus, the *signifier* and *signified* are more general categories in which *vehicle* and *tenor*, respectively, fit.

Nonetheless, specialized contemporary studies on the metaphor actually resemble the earlier definition. In other words, they insist upon wide applicability, a characteristic which relates the metaphor to other figures of speech such as the simile or synecdoche, through its defining principle of transferral.[1] Moreover, the metaphor not only transfers traits, it does so to achieve a *shift in perspective*. As Paul Ricoeur puts it, 'metaphor is the rhetorical process by which discourse unleashes the power that certain fictions have to redescribe reality' (Ricoeur 1977, 7).

The metaphor can consequently range in size from a word to much larger units of text, and, not surprisingly, for our writers, *translatio* has a range of applications. For example, for the Catholic Church, the term links the figure of speech with the *transformation* or *translatio* of mortals into saints as well as a *transferral* or *translatio* of the saints' remains into a holy space. The term is also, more obviously, linked to the process of *translation*, which *transfers* ideas from one linguistic culture to another (Beer 1989). Especially prevalent in our period is the *translatio studii et imperii* topos, the *topos*, or commonplace, that designates a *transferral* of culture and empire, which I'll treat below.

All these uses of *translatio* are linked, because they are generated from the *transforming* power of *transferral*, the process of *translating* one set of images or knowledge created for a particular audience into a new context for a new audience. Thus, in the Latin treatise *Poetria Nova* (New Poetics), the twelfth-century theorist, Geoffrey of Vinsauf (whom Geoffrey Chaucer will consult about two centuries later) highlights the need to pay attention to context in order to reframe the old:

> Instruit iste modus transsumere verba decenter.
> Si sit homo de quo fit sermo, *transferor ad rem*
> *Expressae similem*; quae sit sua propria vestis
> In simili casu cum videro, mutuor illam
> Et mihi de veste veteri transformo novellam.

[770–4, my italics: This way teaches how to adopt words (i.e., use a metaphor) fittingly. If a person is to be depicted by some word, then *I transfer the description to some similar thing*; when I see an appropriate garment in a similar case, I will borrow it and transform my old garment into a new one.]

The metaphoric impulse of bringing the new to bear upon the old depends upon the finding of different contexts that will cast a fresh perspective on a certain idea. The impulse stems from the continual need to create that also impels the literary system; metaphors and literature exist and are constantly regenerated in part because traditional formulae lose their 'newness'.[2]

I've spent some time here with the metaphor not only because *translatio* is one of those arcs that is critical to the period under study, as well as to the series of which this volume is a part, but also because it is a figure of speech in which the concerns of rhetoric and semiotics meet. Thus, a writer's effective *inventio* of a metaphor will not only crystallize a set of complex ideas for his or her audience, that metaphor can then become a sign for those ideas. The complex of ideas that it captures, however, can become streamlined with time. With time, that is, the metaphor acts as a simple sign, an equation, and has the value for all practical purposes of a definition. For example, whenever we see a symmetrically shaped bright-red figure on a Hallmark card, we recognize it as a heart (even though the real thing doesn't quite resemble the image), and we know it means love. At some point in time, however, when the first lover-poet told his (or her) beloved that his heart was hers (or vice versa), *this* was a stunning metaphor. And before the heart, the seat of passions was thought to be the liver. Imagine what Hallmark would have done with that.

The *translatio studii et imperii* topos

In addition to being dependent upon context for its formulation and its temporal complexities, the metaphor short-circuits expository discourse. This is, perhaps, what makes the figure of speech the poet's essential linguistic tool as well as a politician's compelling PR device. In both poetry and PR, it is essential that audiences can circumvent the linear, time-bound, *seriatim* structure of analysis and grasp complex ideas at one stroke, as it were. Thus, the associations conveyed by the Order of the Garter signify elite well-being, a tenor that might be quite difficult to substantiate if put to the task. Waging less than successful war against the Scots during the beginning of his reign in 1327, as well as against the Scottish ally, France, for a good part of his rule, Edward III is certainly in need of an emblem that suggests a unified, stable and elite England, one that would imply all is as it should be. So, too, the *translatio studii et imperii* topos, or convention, conveys similar messages, a topos well-known in the time of Edward's reign, one that describes the transferral of culture and empire from one elite kingdom to another.

While there is variation in the content of the *translatio studii et imperii* topos, in the version most relevant here, the literal level traces the ever westward transferral of imperial power and cultural superiority from fallen Troy to Rome and to subsequent European nations. Thus, the transferral of culture and empire essentially echoes the myth Vergil crafted into epic verse in his *Aeneid* into other times and places (a *translatio* in more than one sense of the word). According to that narrative, the Trojan War results in the Greeks' decimation of Troy, leaving Aeneas and his crew as the only survivors. Under the protection of his mother, the goddess Venus, Aeneas and his men take to the open sea with household gods, experience a tangled series of fantastic adventures, and arrive at last in Italy. Encountering opposition there, Aeneas and his men finally prevail in battle to found a dynasty that would eventually become the Roman Empire.

As used in subsequent narratives, the *translatio* topos is normally articulated in the prologue, by means of a list of kingdoms and heroes.[3] It thus relies on a *linear* framework to embody fortune's *cyclical* movement of rise and fall. As exemplified by the prologue of an anonymous, fourteenth-century poem, *Sir Gawain and the Green Knight*, heroes are linked to one another not only through their deeds, but also genealogically. Thus, the first 13 lines of this Middle English Arthurian narrative associate hero or founder and empire, while also linking father and heir, in naming Troy and Aeneas, Romulus and Rome, Tirius and Tuscany, Langaberde and Lombardy to arrive at Brutus before telling a tale of Arthur's court, located in the narrator's own country.

Less frequently, the *translatio* topos lists canonical poets, as, for example, Geoffrey Chaucer names them, also in the fourteenth century, at the end of his *Troilus and Criseyde*.

Go, litel bok, go, litel myn tragedye …
And kis the steppes where as thow seest pace
Virgile, Ovide, Omer, Lucan and Stace.
And for ther is so gret diversite
In Englissh and in writyng of oure tonge;
So prey I God that non myswrite the,
Ne the mysmetre for defaute of tonge …
O moral Gower, this book I directe
To the, and to the, *philosophical Strode*,
To vouchen sauf, ther nede is, to correcte…

(V. 1786–1858, my italics: Go little book, go my little tragedy … and kiss the steps where you see *Vergil, Ovid, Homer, Lucan and Statius* walk. And since there is so much diversity in English and in the writing of our language, I pray God that no-one 'translates' you badly, nor ruins your meter for lack of knowledge of English … *O moral Gower*, I direct this book to you and to you, *philosophical Strode*, although to be certain, there is need for improvement…)

Similar to the contemporary *Sir Gawain and Green Knight*'s use of the *translatio* topos, this passage lists names from ancient Greece and Rome to end up with Englishmen, John Gower and Ralph Strode. As such, this *translatio* suggests that poets are just as much *translatores* (those who transfer) as are heroic founders of countries – without the poets, heroic deeds would not be celebrated, and the whole idea fueling the *translatio* topos might not have been formulated.

Familiar with the *translatio* topos, *literati* in the period under study know its referent, the Trojan War, from various sources, some purporting to be more historically accurate than Homer, such as the accounts of the Trojan Dares Phrygius and the Greek Dictys Cretensis (Benson 1980). But it is Vergil's version that allows Troy to live on – in spite of defeat – as a sign, an emblem, of glory. By allowing his hero to escape the burning walls of Troy while carrying his father on his back, taking his son by the hand, and ensuring that their household gods are in their baggage, Vergil suggests that although Troy's enemies, the Greeks, won the Trojan War, the victory will actually belong to Aeneas and his descendants. His escape with household gods and family (*translatio studii* – transferral of culture) ends in his acquiring a new homeland, the glory of which will surpass Troy's (*translatio imperii* – transferral of empire). In other words, what at one moment in time appears to be true, an incontrovertible historical fact – Troy's defeat –

is not. What is linearly presented must constantly be revised: more strands are visible with the passing of time, necessitating a non-linear circling back, a return to prior events.

Interestingly, it is during the fourteenth century, during Edward's reign, that London is called New Troy. For example, John Gower (*c.* 1330–1408) thus names the city, while explicitly linking it to the *translatio* topos in lines excised from the Prologue, that had been dedicated to Richard II:

> Under the toun of newe Troye,
> Which tok of Brut his ferste joye,
> In Temse whan it was flowende … (37*–39*)   *Thames*

Perhaps all this is not so surprising when we look at Edward III from a writer's perspective: after all, the sovereign also created his own microcosmic *translatio studii et imperii*, with his *translatio* (metaphor) of the garter representing a *translatio studii* of England's best and a *translatio imperii* through St George, who, as a sign, narrowed to represent England after having represented all European knights.

In a very real sense, Edward's creation of the Order is a poetic as well as a PR act, one, though, that may seem less fictional than, say, Shakespeare's *A Midsummer Night's Dream*, because it is articulated in affairs of state and recorded, although only marginally, in history books. But what Edward III did was to create a structure that married traditional ideas (Arthur, the *translatio* topos) with 'new' perspectives in a 'new' context, thereby joining poetry, politics and history. While materials and audiences for these kinds of discourse usually differ, all three attempt to *invent* and invest signs with messages that communicate to a variety of audiences. This is perhaps more clear to the educated audiences of the 250 years under study here. For at that time, oratory, the writing of history and the writing of poetry were all studied and practiced in relation to the art of rhetoric.

Although learning this may strike a cynical chord among those of us who aren't persuaded by politicians' attempts to win our votes, nonetheless, to designate discourse as a 'fiction' or 'rhetorical' in and of itself does not necessarily make it a lie or morally and aesthetically repugnant. 'Fiction' stems from the Latin *fictio*, which means that which is made. The term points to the writer's craft, not to her or his craftiness. As a matter of fact, the common tag associated with the art of rhetoric is *docere et delectare*, 'to teach while pleasing' – or, from the audience's perspective – to learn from interesting narratives (Allen 1982; Olson 1982). We can tell by the variety of attempts of writers who 'spin' the *translatio* topos to their own cultural favor that this precept is widely spread – each attempts to associate his or her country not only with imperial glory, but also with cultural excellence.

However, lest you think this is a squeekily antiquated approach to history, we need only to arc forward to Edward Gibbon whose *Decline and Fall of the Roman Empire* shaped how history was viewed for some time, and the subject of which, in 1776, he saw as critical, since it 'connect[s) the ancient and modern history of the World' (Gibbon 1909, I, xli). Or, if you think that the creations of imaginative poets or dusty, out-of-touch scholars aren't really relevant, we can arc forward again, this time to the twentieth century, and specifically to Nazi Germany, where Adolf Hitler and his sinisterly adept PR team drew on the *translatio* topos as well. Apparently engaged in justifying *Das Dritte Reich* through causal links arcing back to the middle ages, a far more glorious past was proclaimed – and, hence, a right to a glorious future – than the results of the First World War would suggest. Thus, a portrait of Hitler was commissioned with the leader dressed in armor, as a knight. Likewise, the term 'Das Dritte Reich', or the third empire, referred to the third in another *translatio studii et imperii*: the Roman Empire, founded by Aeneas is the first dynasty; the Holy Roman Empire, authorized by the Holy Roman Catholic Church and ruled in a critical period of Germany's history by the twelfth-century Emperor, or *Führer*, Frederick Barbarossa, is the second; and the Nazi regime is the third – Das *Dritte* Reich. Likewise, it seems as if medieval church history was also used to effect a chilling use of signs. During the Fourth Lateran Council – held in 1215, and the largest gathering of Church officials up to that point in time – not only were many aspects of the faith, such as the sacraments, established, but other policy-defining decisions were also made. Most relevant here are two. First, Jews were not permitted to take oaths, which essentially prevented them from partaking in guilds or benefitting from the justice system and forced many of them into trade or moneylending. Secondly, Jews were forced to wear yellow patches.

Eerily and malevolently manipulating the same conventions that poets, statesmen and historians had used earlier, this particular re-'invention' of the *translatio* topos projects yet another image, whose power to influence and destroy we need not question. And the need to legitimize while stirring people to consensus has not been quelled: just check back issues of the *Guardian* or the *Times* to see how former Prime Minister Thatcher portrayed the British mission to fight for the Islas Malvinas, better known to English-speaking circles as the Falklands.

Sir Gawain and the Green Knight

Although on the surface, the *translatio* topos appears as if its sole intent is to demonstrate which empire has God-given military superiority, the topos also functions as a statement on cultural authority – and, as a result, on literary authority as well. Indeed, after *Sir Gawain and the Green Knight*'s unfurling of the list of glorious kingdoms to which Britain is heir, the *Gawain*-Poet refers to Arthur's imperial valor only then to shift to established Arthurian literary traditions:

> Ay watz Arthur þe hendest...
> As hit is stad and stoken
> In stori stif and stronge.
> With lel letteres loken,
> In londe so hatz ben longe.
>
> (26–36: Arthur was indeed the noblest; so it is set down and fixed in a bold and strong story and held in true letters; it has long been thus in this land.)

The *translatio* to Arthurian literature emphasizes the literary not only through drawing express attention to it, but also by yoking the epic-associated emphasis on military prowess to a courtly narrative.

Sir Gawain and the Green Knight is a mid- to late fourteenth-century *romance*, written in the dialect of the northwest Midlands, whose author remains unknown to us. Here, the technical literary term, *romance*, doesn't refer to the Barbara Cartland novels you can thumb through in an hour or so; the term actually derives from the French, *en romaunz*, 'in the *Roman*-derived language' or simply, 'in French'. The term as used here refers to a genre which depicts the noble class in knightly and amorous pursuits. What the term *romans* marks beyond the genre is a bit more complicated. Up to about the twelfth century, *the* language of scholarly, literary, religious and political authority, as well as of courtly culture in western Europe was

Latin. From about the twelfth century on, however, writers in various European locations began to write in their native tongues – what is known as the *vernacular* or *vulgar* languages – and to promote the use of the vernacular as just as worthy as Latin. Of course, such trends took a while to translate effectively into all walks of life.

And in what we now call England, things were more complex still. First, in the literary period commonly designated as Old English or Anglo-Saxon (traditionally beginning with the coming of the Saxons to England and ending with the Norman invasion, c. 430–1100), the literary system did include a vibrant vernacular literature along with translations of Latin texts and official documents. Interestingly, in the Old English life of St George mentioned above, George's first (and other) words in the *vita* condemn the Emperor for his pagan worship, first in Latin, then in Old English, 'Omnes dii gentium demonia dominus autem caelos fecit/ Ealle þæra hæðenra godas synd gramlice deofla' (17–18: 'All the gods of the heathen are cruel devils'). More complex still, since the Norman Conquest of 1066, French (being the language of William the Conqueror) became the language of the court and of law, evolving into Anglo-Norman, while Latin remained the language of the educated and the literary, and various dialects of English, Scots, Irish and Welsh belonged to commoners.

In any case, *romances* eventually do become in part what we now call 'romances', with an emphasis on the amorous rather than the adventurous, partly because they frequently display adventures as performed for ladies and as informed by chivalric codes. By the time the *Gawain*-Poet authors his romance, Arthurian conventions had long been established. Histories that chronicled Arthur's military prowess along with literary narratives that expounded upon the court's excellence and devotion to the chivalric had been around and modified for at least two centuries. Knights and emphases differed according to who was writing, but for the most part Arthur's knights are presented as the measure of chivalric prowess, and his court as the paradigm of luxury and sophistication.

Returning to *Sir Gawain and the Green Knight*, the poem's prologue links the glorious past to the present, just as do Werchin's references to Arthur and his court in his courtly challenge to Henry IV. Interesting, too, the poem possesses an additional, tenuous link to the Order of the Garter. Not only is a central emblem of the poem a green girdle (green being reasonably close to the blue of Edward's garter), but the poem also ends with an epilogue that features the *translatio* topos before citing the garter's motto (slightly modified), *Hony soit qui mal pense.* Written at about the time of the founding of the Order, *Sir Gawain and the Green Knight* must have appeared to the scribe who wrote these words (different from the one who transcribed the poem) to be more than a simple adventurous Arthurian romance.

The narrative of *Sir Gawain and the Green Knight* itself begins in the laughter and celebrations of the Christmas season. Set in the luxury of Camelot, Arthur is portrayed, however, as less than kingly. Almost petulantly in search of entertainment, he refuses to begin dinner without either a tale about, or an actual quest for, rousing adventure:

> Of sum auenturus þyng an vncouþe tale,
> Of sum mayn meruayle, þat he myȝt trawe,
> Of alderes, of armes, of oþer auenturus,
> Oþer sum segg hym bisoȝt of sum siker knyȝt,
> To joyne wyth hym in iustyng in jopardé to lay,
> Lede, lif for lyf...

> (93–8: a strange tale of some adventurous event, of some great marvel that he might believe, of nobles, of arms, of other adventures. Or else somebody should ask him for some trustworthy knight to joust with him, to put himself in jeopardy, life for life ...)

> (Another linguistic aside: the 'ȝ' you see in the the second and fourth lines is called a 'yogh', representing at times the sound 'y', and at times the sound 'ch' in Loch Lomand. Also, you will note that 'u' sometimes represents the sound we would associate with 'v', and vice versa.)

As if on cue, the Green Knight enters Camelot on his green horse to taunt and challenge Arthur and his court with a Christmas game: the exchange of one blow of an ax for another. Camelot is too stunned to respond to this unarmored, green-hued and -clothed interloper with rolling red eyes, until courtly Gawain, who had been sitting next to Guenevere, politely intercedes. But before he does, and in spite of Gawain's superior virtue in this opening scene, the Green Knight's mastery does force eloquent Gawain to ask for information:

> 'Where schulde I wale þe', quoþ Gauan, 'where is þy place?
> I wot neuer where þou wonyes, bi hym þat me wroȝt,
> Ne I know not þe knyȝt, þy cort ne þi name.
> Bot teche me truly þerto, and telle me how þou hattes ...'

(398–401: 'Where shall I find you', said Gawain, 'where is your home?
I never knew where you live, by Him who made me, nor do I know
you, Knight, either your court or your name. But teach me truly these
things, and tell me what you are called ...')

The Green Knight responds crisply:

'ʒif I þe telle trwly, quen I þe tape haue
And þou me smoþely hatz smyten, smartly I þe teche
Of my hous and my home and myn owen nome ...'

(406–8: 'If I (can) talk (with) you truly after I have had the tap and you
have soundly struck me, then quickly I will teach you of my house
and my home and my own name...')

Gawain takes up the challenge and beheads the Green Knight with
one stroke, causing the intruder's head to roll about the floor, which
the courtiers kick away in fear and disgust. The green body awkwardly
lurches about and picks up its severed head, whose mouth then utters
fateful words, demanding that Gawain meet him for a return blow in a
year's time. All the courtiers are appalled and saddened by Gawain's
fate.

The *Gawain*-Poet then lyrically portrays the passing of time; a year
goes by, seasons circling back to winter, and Arthur's nephew – true to
his word – sets off to find the Green Knight's chapel. Gawain's search
is an act of faith, since he doesn't have a clue where to go. Rather than
galloping straight to his destination he must roam about trying to find
it, and in doing so he suffers many hardships. Yet, the *Gawain*-Poet
only briefly mentions Gawain's fights with dragons and for ladies, to
focus instead on his inability to find the location and his suffering
from the winter cold, which seems to bring Arthur's knight to the
brink of despair. Gawain prays to the Virgin Mary, whose image is
painted on the inside of his shield, and again as if on cue, a castle
appears on the horizon. He arrives at the luxurious and festive Castle
Hautdesert of Lord and Lady Bercilak, where he is warmly welcomed,
clothed and dined, and where he catches his first glimpse of Lady
Bercilak, entering hand-in-hand with an elderly lady (whom I like to
think of as Morgan le Fay).

Welcomed by Bercilak, Gawain learns that his host knows where to
direct him:

þenne laȝande quoþ þe lorde, 'Now leng þe byhoues,
For I schal teche yow to þat terme bi þe tymez ende,
þe grene chapayle vpon grounde greue yow no more;
Bot ȝe schal be in yowre bed, burne, at þyn ese,
Quyle forth dayez, and ferk on þe fyrst of þe ȝȝere ...'

(1068–72: Then laughing, the lord said, 'Now it behooves you to remain, for I shall teach you of the place in enough time, so grieve no more about where the green chapel is located. Instead, be at your ease in your bed, sir, until late in the day, and travel on the first of the year ...')

Relieved that he will not have to break his word, Gawain settles into the joys of the castle. Echoing the beginning of the romance, Bercilak's court festively celebrates the Christmas season, and the courtiers play a game that dangles a hood precariously atop a spear. In addition, the Lord proposes a game. For what turns out to be the next three days, Gawain is to remain at the castle to recover from his energy-depleting journey, while Bercilak goes out to hunt. Upon his return in the evening, the two are to exchange the day's winnings.

The *Gawain*-Poet then alternates detailed descriptions of Bercilak's hunts that are so realistic they might well have been taken from hunting treatises, with witty descriptions of Lady Bercilak's audacious, but courtly, flirtations with Gawain in his bedroom. Consequently, at the end of the first day, Bercilak receives a courtly kiss from his guest, who refuses to name its source, while Gawain receives a deer. The two following days yield an additional kiss each evening for the Lord of Hautdesert, and Arthur's knight receives a boar and a fox. But Gawain also deceives his host on the third evening; he does not surrender a green girdle given him by Lady Bercilak, which purportedly possesses the magic that will save its wearer from all harm.

Nonetheless, after having confessed to the priest and partied in the evening, Gawain arises early on the fourth day to follow his frightened guide, who hesitantly points the way to the Green Knight's chapel which turns out to be simply an earthen mound. Sharpening his ax, the Green Knight taunts Gawain just as he had belittled Arthur's court in Camelot a year before. Gawain kneels to receive his blow, and the Green Knight swings his ax, but then stops short since Gawain flinches. The Green Knight boasts he hadn't budged at all in Camelot, to which Gawain testily retorts that he has no magic at his disposal (apparently having forgotten the green girdle). Gawain prepares himself for the next swing, and this time the Green Knight feints in order to test Arthur's knight who succeeds in remaining perfectly still. Finally, on the third swing, the Green Knight nicks Gawain on the neck, and immediately the Arthurian hero leaps to his own defense only to confront in the Green Knight the laughter of Bercilak.

The Lord reveals to Gawain that the three swings were meant for the three days spent at his castle, and the nick was intended for the small lie Gawain committed by hiding the girdle. Gawain is given the girdle as a reminder of this adventure, and abruptly, disproportionately and dissonantly Gawain blames women for their ability to ruin men (as will be looked at again in the next chapter). He then learns that the entire game was set up by Morgan le Fay to frighten Guenevere. Again encountering various adventures on the way back that are rhetorically marginalized, Gawain returns to Camelot shamed by his failure. Camelot, however, rejoices in his return, and Arthur proclaims that all his knights will wear green girdles to lessen his best knight's sense of shame.

As identified by Walter Haug, an Arthurian romance typically: (1) begins and ends in Camelot's festivity; (2) treats the battle-punctuated adventures of a single Arthurian knight; (3) arranges his adventures in a double, parallel structure, based on (a) provocation and (b) inner crises; and (4) sustains a double theme of knightly deeds and love (Haug 1985, 98–9). Even a superficial glance at this romance will ascertain that Gawain's adventures conform to the structural requirements of these traits. However, the *Gawain*-Poet's contextual modification of them is telling: rather than occurring in public spaces, Gawain's adventures occur in solitude or in private spheres, and rather than portraying love, the narrative plays with love.

As stated earlier, the *Gawain*-Poet embraces this narrative with uses of the *translatio* topos that end in laudatory references to Arthur. Arthur's public glory, however, is qualified early on, as implied not only by his insistence on a tale of adventure, but also by the Green Knight's inability to identify the worthy king from others in the throng. This is an odd juxtaposition, causing momentary dissonance as the *translatio* topos' commonplace sense of excellence seems far removed from this almost decadently portrayed court. Yet, the *Gawain*-Poet quickly shifts to excellence, displaced, through the King's nephew, Gawain.

Indeed, Gawain's legendary prowess, wisdom and courtliness are

evident in his very first act. He is the only one in Camelot not incapac-
itated by fear or surprise, enabling him to save Arthur from the Green
Knight's challenge. Further, Gawain acts with a courtesy that is especially obvious when contrasted against Arthur's hot-headed response
or the Green Knight's taunts. As Bercilak reveals at the end of the
poem, Gawain *is* Camelot's superior knight, although Arthur's
nephew himself does not feel this to be true.

Underscoring the displacement of excellence, Bercilak also reveals
at the poem's end that the object of all his games was to test
Camelot's reputation, which he does through Gawain. Here lies an
important implicit tie between Prologue and narrative beyond the
focus on dynastic excellence. Since Gawain first displaces and then
stands for Arthur in order to give meaning to the notion of Camelot's
glory, he functions as a *translatio*. Here Charles Sanders Peirce's definition of the sign fits well, Peirce being the other of the two major
early contributors to modern semiotics, and a contemporary of
Saussure:[4]

> A sign, or *representamen*, is something which stands to somebody for
> something in some respect or capacity. It addresses somebody, that
> is, creates in the mind of that person an equivalent sign, or perhaps a
> more developed sign. That sign which it creates I call the *interpretant*
> of the first sign. The sign stands for something, its *object*. It stands for
> that object, not in all respects, but in reference to a sort of idea, which
> I have sometimes called the *ground* of the representamen. (Peirce
> 1960, vol.2, para. 228, 135, his italics)

What distinguishes this definition from Saussure's is that the
addressee is brought into the foreground. The interpretant itself is a
sign, one that allows the addressee to convey meaning to him- or
herself. In other words, signs are accessible to us through other signs,
and language itself is a series of signs, or *figurative* attempts to
convey, in Peirce's terms, *objects*.

In *Sir Gawain and the Green Knight*, the narrator makes us aware
early on that we are operating in just such a figurative universe of
meaning deferred and displaced. For example, as Gawain prepares for
his journey, the narrator prepares to describe the knight's shield in
this manner:

And quy þe pentangel apendez to þat prynce noble

I am in tent yow to telle, þof tary hyt me schulde:
Hit is a syngne þat Salamon set sumquyle
In bytoknyng of trawþe, bi tytle þat hit habbez,
For hit is a figure þat haldez fyue poyntez,
And vche lyne vmbelappez and loukez in oþer,
And ayquere hit is endelez; and Englych hit callen
Oueral, as I here, þe endeles knot.

(623–30, my italics: I would like to tell you why the pentangle fits that noble lord, even though it should cause me delay. *It is a sign fixed by Solomon a while ago to designate fidelity*, to which it has a right, for it is a figure that has five points with each line overlapping and locking into another and endless everywhere. The English call it everywhere, as I hear, 'the endless knot'.)

After thus identifying the sign, its origins and its appearance, the narrator moves on to list one by one and in exacting detail the virtues which the pentangle represents, explicating the significance of the symbol and also of Gawain's relation to it. Moreover, the narrator has given the sign its name in English, drawing attention to the fact that *pentangel* and *endeles knot* are two *representamens* for the same *object*, and hence, that language too is a system of signs. This approach also accords with that of St Augustine, who wrote perhaps the first extended treatise on semiotics in western Europe, *De Doctrina Christiana*, in which he defines the sign as follows:

Signum est enim res praeter speciem quam ingerit sensibus aliud aliquid ex se faciens in cogitationem venire; sicut vestigio viso transisse animal cuius vestigium est cogitamus et fumo viso ignem subesse cognoscimus, et voce animantis audita affectionem animi eius advertimus, et tuba sonante milites vel progredi se vel regredi, et si quid aliud pugna postulat, oportere noverunt.

(II. ii: 1, Green's translation: For a sign is a thing which of itself makes some other thing come to mind, besides the impression that it presents to the senses. So when we see a footprint we think that the animal whose footprint it is has passed by; when we see smoke we realize that there is fire beneath it; when we hear the voice of an animate being we note its feeling; and when the trumpet sounds soldiers know they must advance or retreat or do whatever else the state of the battle demands.)

He goes on to distinguish between natural and given signs (*naturalia, data*), given signs being those shared by mortals, before he discusses ambiguous signs in the Scriptures and gives recommendations on how to interpret. Both Augustine and Peirce, then, focus on the readers and the 'operations' they go through to arrive at understanding.

Arriving at understanding is also a major concern of *Sir Gawain and the Green Knight*. Thus, echoing the narrator's explication of the pentangle, Bercilak as the Green Knight teaches Gawain what the three swings of his ax mean and encourages him to think about this meaning by making of the green girdle a sign that, in Augustine's terms, 'makes some other thing come to mind', that some other thing being, in Peirce's terms, 'an equivalent sign, or perhaps a more developed sign ... an *interpretant* of the first sign':

> And I gif þe, sir, þe gurdel þat is golde-hemmed,
> For hit is grene as my goune. Sir Gawayn, ȝe maye
> þenk vpon þis ilke þrepe, þer þou forth þryngez
> Among prynces of prys, *and þis a pure token*
> Of þe chaunce of þe grene chapel at cheualrous knyȝtez.

> (2395–9, my italics: 'And I give you, sir, the girdle hemmed in gold, for it is green as my gown. Sir Gawain, you may think on this very contest, when you journey among nobles of worth, and on *this pure 'sign'* of the fortune of the Green Chapel (when you're) with chivalrous knights.)

With this gift, Gawain has learned how to read and act in both Camelot and Hautdesert.

In Hautdesert's literary system, which for all practical purposes looks like Camelot's, Gawain soon finds out that it's not, and that Bercilak's turf has rules that operate on at least one other level than does Arthur's court. The *Gawain*-Poet underscores these multiple levels by juxtaposing the hunting and bedroom scenes, forcing us readers into Gawain's position, to interpret one event in light of another, to interpret, that is, *with attention to structure and parallels*. We are also thus made aware of the multiple strands that texture any single moment in time, which the *Gawain*-Poet emphasizes by juxtaposing the circular structure of the romance with the linear structure of the *translatio* topos and by marginalizing Gawain's adventures to and from Hautdesert for those in Gawain's bedroom, which convey the most lively sections of the poem.

Contextual issues

I mentioned in the Introduction how important it is for rhetorical and semiotic readings to take into consideration a variety of contexts. While I hope it is clear that contexts are important in this reading of *Sir Gawain and the Green Knight,* it might just be useful to make some of the less-overt ones explicit at this point as well.

For example, although many of us approach the Middle Ages as if it were monolithically Catholic and pious, we can see from this Middle English romance that such an approach is limiting. Although the Virgin Mary is prayed to in the poem, and her image graces the inner side of Gawain's shield, what she is prayed to for is, at least on the literal level, a mixed bag: Sir Gawain wishes to keep his word. Even if read allegorically (a mode of reading that is difficult to carry through-out the entire poem), say with the Green Knight as the devil and Sir Gawain as a St George of sorts, Gawain's prayers would then not be to deliver himself from sin, but to adhere to a promise made to the forces of evil, a dubious goal at best. And if we were to read the Green Knight as a representative of God's realm whose goal is to test our chivalric Everyman, then what do we do with Morgan le Fay and her wish to test Guenevere? The weaving of magical, Christian, Arthurian and literary themes in this poem play against a Christian backdrop, but do not generate a strictly Christian lesson.

Likewise, the poem subtly textures the socioeconomic system that dominates western Europe in the late Middle Ages and which was dubbed 'feudalism' in the seventeenth century. In principle, this system gave power to those who owned land, who distributed varying degrees of rights to those who lived on their land in exchange for taxes and services (Scattergood and Sherborne 1983). Thus, a lord of a castle, like Lord Bercilak, might have knights in his employ who would receive armor, horses and other gifts in exchange for their military talents. Young squires, who aspired to knighthood, would serve knights, who would support them in exchange for their services. Lady Bercilak would probably have been in charge of the household, keeping watch, for example, over the keys to the larder and maybe the accounts as well. If only one of the Bercilaks were literate, it probably would have been Lady Bercilak, since women were more likely to be educated in the rudiments of reading (enough Latin to read the psalter) in order to keep them focused, in theory, on the straight and narrow. Thus, for example, during the fourteenth century, Geoffrey of

La Tour-Landry wrote a book, as he says, for his young daughters, a book which clearly found resonance in the following century, since it was translated and printed by William Caxton in 1484 (*hem*, by the way, means 'them'):

> ... wherupon thei might rede and studie, to that entent that thei might lerne and see bothe good and euell ... and forto kepe hem in good clennesse ... For there be such men that lyethe and makithe good visage and countenaunce to women afore hem, that scornithe and mockithe hem in her absence. And therfor it is harde to knowe the worlde that is now ... (3, 15–21)

As Gawain too learned, 'it is harde to knowe the worlde'.

Someone like Lady Bercilak would also most likely have ladies in waiting, who attended to her needs while she saw to it that they were educated, clothed and fed. Serving these upper classes were the serfs – unpaid labor forces who did the manual work on the grounds in exchange for necessities. The Bercilaks themselves might be subordinate to nobles with larger holdings like, perhaps, Morgan le Fay, who were themselves subordinate to regents, such as King Arthur. The hierarchy of allegiances is sealed along military lines: pages to knights, knights to liege lords, lords to kings, a hierarchy often solemnized by an emblematic ritual, the dubbing of a knight as a vassal in exchange for an oath of fealty.

Although on first glance, all that occurs in the poem seems to fit in this feudal framework, there are nonetheless aspects that don't; perhaps, they are intimations of change. For example, although exchange is a key principle of the poem, it doesn't seem hierarchically based as it is in the feudal system. On the contrary, in the poem exchange seems based on the principle of equity: blow for blow, winnings of the day's hunt for winnings of the castle. Moreover, there is no emphasis on King Arthur's largesse or that of Lord Bercilak for that matter. In contrast, in Chrétien's *Erec et Enide*, for example, the generosity of the King is very much emphasized, suggesting that largesse is the glue that holds the hierarchical feudal system together:

> Or öez, se vos comandez,
> la grant joie et la grant hautesce,
> la seignorie et la richesce,
> qui a la cort fu demenee.

Einçois que tierce fust sonee,
ot adobez li rois Artus
quatre cenz chevaliers et plus,
toz filz de contes et de rois:
chevax dona a chascun trois
et robes a chascun trois peire,
por ce que sa corz miaudre apeire.
Molt fu li rois puissanz et larges:
ne dona pas mantiax de sarges,
ne de conins ne de brunetes,
mes de samiz et d'erminetes,
de veir antier et de dïapres,
listez d'orfrois roides et aspres.
Alixandres, qui tant conquist
que desoz lui tot le mont mist,
et tant fu larges et tant riches,
fu anvers lui povres et chiches.

(6610–30, Carroll's translation: Now hear, if you will,/ the great joy and the great ceremony,/ the nobility and the magnificence/ that were displayed at the court./ Before tierce had sounded,/ King Arthur had dubbed/ four hundred knights and more,/ all sons of counts and of kings;/ he gave each of them three horses/ and to each three pairs of cloaks/ to improve the appearance of his court./ The king was very powerful and generous:/ he did not give cloaks made of serge,/ nor of rabbit nor of dark-brown wool,/ but of samite and of ermine,/ of whole vair and mottled sik/ bordered with orphrey, stiff and rough./ Alexander, who conquered so much/ that he subdued the whole world,/ and was so generous and rich,/ compared to him was poor and stingy.)

In contrast, *Sir Gawain and the Green Knight*'s Arthur is depicted as almost decadently self-indulgent, while Bercilak doesn't proffer his famous and most honored guest anything above the usual hospitality.

In addition to texturing conventional notions of religion and the feudal system, the poem seems aimed at a sophisticated audience, one whose reading culture has, in a sense, objectified knowledge. I've mentioned above how Lady Bercilak parries with Gawain, particularly on the second day, playing against the traditions of courtly love literature as she does so. It is notable, moreover, that the *Gawain*-Poet has framed her coquettishly conveyed knowledge in terms of teaching:

'þou hatz forȝeten ȝederly þat ȝisterday I taȝtte
Bi alder-truest token of talk þat I cowþe ...
And of alle cheualry to chose, þe chef þyng alosed
Is þe lel layk of luf, þe *lettrure of armes;*
For to telle of þis teuelyng of þis trwe knyȝtez,
Hit is þe tytelet token and tyxt of her werkkez,
How ledes for her lele luf hor lyuez han auntered...
And ȝe, þat ar so cortays and coynt of your hetes,
Oghe to a ȝonke þynk ȝern to schewe
And teche sum tokenez of trweluf craftes.
Why! ar ȝe lewed, þat alle þe los weldez...
  I com hider sengel, and sitte
  To lerne at yow sum game;
  Dos, techez me of your wytte' ...
(Gawain) 'Bot to take þe toruayle to myself *to trwluf expoun,*
And towche þe temez of tyxt and talez of armez
To yow þat, I wot wel, weldez more slyȝt
Of þat art...
Hit were a folé felefolde, my fre, by my trawþe.'

(1485–1545, my italics: '*You have already forgotten what I taught you
yesterday "signed" in the truest language I knew* ... With all of knighthood to choose from, most praised is the true practice of love, the
texts on arms. Telling of the trials of true knights are *the "signed" title
and text of their works, how men for their true love have ventured their
lives* ... You, so courtly and charming with your vows, should want to
show a young person, *teach her some "signs" of true love's art. What!
Are you ignorant, you who wield such fame* ... I come here alone and
sit *to learn from you some game; do teach me some of what you know'*
... 'To take the trouble *upon myself to expound on true love and touch
on textual themes and tales of arms to you, who, I know well, wields
more skill in that art...*it would be a manifold folly, my lady, by my
faith.')

Of course, this is not a new idea in love's literature. The Roman poet
Ovid (43 BCE–17CE), for example, wrote ironic treatises on how to
win, maintain and escape from love and featured a narrator who
posed as someone who could teach his audiences these rules, not
unlike our 'Miss Manners' help-columns work nowadays, although
these (I think) aren't intended to be ironic. In *Sir Gawain and the
Green Knight*, however, the *Gawain*-Poet depicts his *characters* as
playing with the roles of teacher and student. One remove from the

poet-narrator who poses as a teacher of love, Gawain and Lady Bercilak play, for our 'viewing pleasure', with the literary traditions informing our literary system – the traditions and knowledge have become objectified.

And so, too, this same kind of playing with or displaying of knowledge is integrated into other sections of the poem. For example, when the Green Knight explodes into Camelot, for all his insulting remarks, he does take the time to assume the role of teacher and instruct the courtiers that he comes in peace, as indicated by his lack of armor and his spring of holly. Indeed, he demands that his audience reflect upon his explication of the sprig of holly he holds, teaching them it is a sign of his peaceful intentions. He further teaches his audience that this interpretation is supported by the argument implicit in his wearing of leisurely clothing:

> ȝe may be seker bi þis braunch þat I bere here
> þat I passe as in pes, and no plyȝt seche;
> For had I founded in fere in feȝtyng wyse,
> I haue a hauberghe at home and a helme boþe,
> A schelde and a scharp spere, schinande bryȝt,
> Ande oþer weppenes to welde, I wene wel, als;
> Bot for I wolde no were, my wedez ar softer.

> (265–71: You may be certain by this branch I carry here that I come in peace and seek no fight. For had I come in strength in fighting manner, I have a hauberk at home and a helmet too, a shield, and a sharp spear – shining bright – and other weapons to wield, I think as well; but since I wish no battle, my clothing is softer.)

In a sense, both the Green Knight and Bercilak take on the role of teacher to instruct Gawain how to arrive at the Green Knight's chapel. In the same vein, the hunting scenes are portrayed in great detail with attention focused on how Lord Bercilak has his booty correctly disemboweled, carved and distributed.

This pedagogical voice – whether aimed at explaining love, peace, an emblem or hunting – suggests not only a reading public familiar with such texts and conventions, but also the objectification of knowledge. This is not a series of treatises aimed to help people master knowledge. This is the use of knowledge and the rhetoric of the treatise to make or underscore various points in a romance. Whether this rhetorical strategy worked or not, the *Gawain*-Poet deemed his or her audience as capable of understanding this use of such passages as 'fair game', as part of the literary system of the time.

From manuscripts to printing

From an editor's point of view, *Sir Gawain and the Green Knight* has relatively few problems (although the ink is faded and at times has been blotted onto the opposite page), since it survives in only one manuscript belonging to the British Library, MS Cotton Nero A.x. The poem is bound with two Latin treatises (probably a late binding), and three other narrative poems that are clearly religious in nature: *Pearl, Purity,* and *Patience.* As hinted at above, reading was a different experience in the fourteenth century than it is now, and the binding of *Sir Gawain and the Green Knight* with the three poems doesn't necessarily mean that they are thematically linked. It probably does mean that the four poems were enjoyed by the person who had them transcribed, for they are all written in the same hand.

But again, this poem represents a relatively easy editorial task, because only one manuscript survives. Before books were run off electronically operated or even hand-run printing presses, they were prepared in a rather arduous process. Very early on they were manufactured as rolls and as joined writing tablets, which were around at least since Homer and seemed to have come to the Greeks from the Hittites. When put together as tablets, these books became known as *codices.* At least by the second century, Christians were using the *codex* to record the gospels. Eventually, books came to resemble the product we are familiar with in the twenty-first century – only, earlier, their covers were often leather-bound slabs of wood, and their sheets manufactured from treated leather.

Produced in an expensive process, books in this period were not as plentiful as they are today. For example, Chaucer introduces his Scholar from Oxford in the *Canterbury Tales* as an individual who spent his entire fortune on books:

> A Clerk ther was of Oxenford also,
> That unto logyk hadde longe ygo.
> As leene was his hors as is a rake,
> And he nas nat right fat, I undertake,
> But looked holwe, and therto sobrely.

Ful thredbare was his overeste courtepy,
For he hadde geten hym yet no benefice,
Ne was so worldly for to have office.
For hym was levere have at his beddes heed
Twenty bookes, clad in blak or reed,
Of Aristotle and his philosophie
Than robes riche, or fithele, or gay sautrie.

(General Prologue, 285–96: There was a scholar from Oxford as well, who had long gone over to logic. His horse was lean as a rake, and he wasn't really fat (either), I'd say, but looked hollow and thus sober. His outer upper short coat was totally threadbare; for he wasn't able to obtain a benefice (a church position), nor was he worldly enough to obtain a secular office. For he would rather have at the head of his bed twenty books, bound in black or red, about Aristotle and his philosophy than rich robes, or a fiddle or pleasant psaltery (i.e., entertainment).)

Although this may not seem like much to us, the time and cost of producing a book made the Scholar's collection an enviable one.

Book pages, called *folios*, were produced from the hides of cattle or sheep – the most expensive parchment, or *vellum*, being manufactured from calves. After the animals were skinned, their hides were soaked in a lye solution after which the remaining hair was scraped with a small stone-like instrument that fit in the palm of the hand. The skins were stretched out on frames to dry, and then sheets were cut from them. The resulting parchment was then prepared in various ways to be written on. In one of these methods, for example, a scribe would take two pins, insert them at the desired left and right margins of a folio, span a charcoal-covered string between them, and pop it so that on hitting the folio it would leave a straight line. Once the lines were drawn, the folios were ready for writing. Depending upon the scribe's training, the folio was sometimes divided into columns. At some stage of the process, and the practice also varies here, the sheets were gathered into bundles known as quires and sewn. Eventually, the quires were bound together, and a cover would often be attached. If the book being produced were an expensive one, not only would scribes work on the text, but also *rubricators* would write glosses, chapter headings and the like in red (*rubricator* derives from Latin *rubeo*, red), and *illuminators* would paint decorative initials, marginalia, or even full-page scenes. The cover, too, might be crafted to support elaborate and bejeweled designs.

But even if the manuscript being produced wasn't elaborate, it was expensive and frequently characterized by a frugal use of space. For example, abbreviations were often used regardless of the value or the authority of the manuscript being copied. Thus, *Ds* was used for *Deus*, the Latin word for 'God', a very common abbreviation even used in expensive manuscripts of the Bible such as the Book of Kells, the Codex Cenannensis, which was produced in Iona at about 800 by Irish monks. Up to the twelfth or thirteenth century, punctuation was also not regularly used in manuscripts. Imagine reading anything nowadays without the cues that punctuation gives us. In order to do well, readers must be very well versed in the language and its rhetoric.

But other aspects also contribute to making reading a different experience today. For example, when we read a book – say this one – anyone purchasing the same edition will be reading the same thing on any given page. Moreover, even if pagination were to differ from, say, a later printing of this book which hadn't changed the text but decided to change its format, all the words would be the same. In the middle ages, neither of these conditions prevailed. Each book developed was an individual object, often produced in a *scriptorium*, a room devoted to the production of books. Incidentally, these were frequently the only heated rooms in a monastery – to prevent inks from freezing – a pretty good reason to aspire to the profession of the scribe. Also complicating the uniformity we're so used to in our reading experiences is that narratives were bound together according to the tastes of whoever produced the codex. Thus, if ever we were to find another manuscript featuring *Sir Gawain and the Green Knight*, chances are it wouldn't be accompanied by the same pieces that are in the single extant manuscript. But perhaps most odd to us, if a scribe decided that a narrative needed improving, he or she might very well undertake to do so.

What you read today from this period is more uniformly presented than it was then. What you read has been put together by editors, who typically harmonize various versions of the text which usually varied from manuscript to manuscript. Our editors will also correct scribes (thereby following in the footsteps of medieval scribes) when they judge an error in meter or spelling has been made. Our editors also supply titles, when for a number of centuries, typically, the author or scribe had provided none. While many of these corrections are understandable, some presume a consistency that was not necessarily the overriding principle compelling the poet or scribe to write as she or he did.

*   *   *

All this attention to literature and to the production of books is not incidental to our study. The Judaeo-Christian religious system is a religion of the word: God *authored* the universe, after all, through his language, 'In principio erat Verbum et Verbum erat apud Deum et Deus erat Verbum' (John 1. 1: 'In the beginning was the word and the word was with God and God was the word'). Indeed, in ancient times Christ is depicted with a book scroll, while in later times saints and the Virgin are also portrayed in relation to books. From the twelfth century onwards, this reverence of the book proliferated. For example, in the twelfth century, Alain de Lille, a scholar-poet, depicted every human in terms of God's books, while the philosopher Hugh of St Victor described the creation as a book of God (Gellrich 1985). Of course, this metaphor and its use survived through the early modern period as well, as transformed into Shakespeare's comparison of the world to a stage.

During the 250 years under examination here, most importantly, manuscript culture evolved into print culture. Although the earliest printing was in all likelihood produced from woodblocks in Asia by the end of the second century, it was Johann Gensfleisch zur Laden zum Gutenberg (*c.* 1390–*c.* 1468), a native of Mainz, Germany, who is credited with inventing the first movable type. Following Gutenberg's successful printing operations (1450–53), William Caxton (*c.* 1422–91) began printing at Westminster in 1476, and contributed to the shaping of the literary system by means of his own editorial interventions. It is interesting to note that while Gutenberg's first book was the Bible, Caxton's first printed book in English (at Bruges) was *The Recuyell of the Historyes of Troye* (1474) – back to the *translatio* topos. Responding to the growing demand for books, Caxton also printed Chaucer's *Canterbury Tales* (1478), John Gower's *Confessio Amantis* (1483), Sir Thomas Malory's *Morte D'Arthur* (1485), along with his translation of Christine de Pizan's French *Le Livre des Faits d'Armes et de Chevalerie* (Book of Deeds of Arms and of Chivalry) (1489), and many others.

By 1492, the profession of the book publisher had firmly emerged, with three various manifestations: the type-founder, the printer and the bookseller. In addition, the first black lead pencils in England were used in 1500, and later in 1565 they began to be manufactured. Yet, even this seemingly straightforward arc is not without its tensions. Although print became an effective and widely spread medium, manuscript culture remained influential throughout these entire 250 years. Indeed, the elitism sounded in Arthurian tales, the Order of the Garter and Uccello's murals finds supportive echoes in the manufacturing of the book. Not only were elaborate manuscripts and canonical literature still valued, printers also attempted to emulate the effect of a manuscript as, for example, when they used three different forms of 's' in a single 'manuscript', as a scribe might do.

Undoubtedly, the shift from manuscript to print culture affected reading. What was once a powerfully exclusive activity became more accessible to the rising middle class. The printing press was no small accomplishment.

Notes

1. Any study on the metaphor must consider its inherent property of transferral and the goal of its transferral: a shift in perspectives, which entails past and present meanings. Older theoretical sources (Lausberg 1960, sections 558–64) tend to be more uniform than modern studies. For example, Umberto Eco argues that western tradition has looked at the metaphor through a synecdochic filter (Eco 1984, 87–129). The 'whole' which the 'part' (metaphor) represents is its synchronic effect, the 'tenor'. Jacques Derrida, on the other hand, argues that the 'whole' is its suppressed, diachronic history, which fuels his agonistic description of the metaphor, that 'can only be what it is by obliterating itself, endlessly construct(ing) its own destruction' (Derrida 1974, 71). And from a linguistic perspective, Wolf Paprotté and René Dirven propose that, '(m)etaphor is now considered an instrument of thought, and a transaction between the constructive effects of context, imagistic and conceptual representation, and general encyclopaedic knowledge' (Paprotté and Dirven 1985, ix). It is useful to read these theorists against other, more general studies (e.g., Black 1962; Lakoff and Johnson 1980).

2. Winfried Nöth examines the metaphor's relation to convention and meaning (his italics): 'the metaphoric sign departs from semiotic structure of the language system in its conventionality ... *poetic* or ... *creative* metaphors are unique. They are semantically innovative in appearing

for the first time ... Through multiple recurrence metaphors can themselves finally become conventionalized' (Paprotté and Dirven 1985, 4–6).

3. A number of studies treat this popular topos (e.g., Freeman 1979; Goez 1958; Jongkees 1967; Kelly 1978; Patterson 1987; and Vance 1986).

4. Earlier, Peirce explains 'ground' with reference to the example of blackness: '...a pure abstraction, reference to which constitutes a *quality* or general attribute, may be termed a *ground* (1. 551, 292).

2 Training, Religion and Treatises

In the course of the last chapter's discussion on the fourteenth-century romance, *Sir Gawain and the Green Knight*, I mentioned the sudden diatribe against women which served Gawain as an excuse for failing Morgan le Fay's test. Lamenting how women destroy men, Gawain utters these words:

> And purȝ wyles of wymmen be wonen to sorȝe,
> For so watz Adam in erde with one bygyled,
> And Salamon with fele sere, and Samson eft sonez –
> Dalyda dalt hym hys wyrde – and Dauyth þerafter
> Watz blended with Barsabe, þat much bale þoled.
> Now þese were wrathed wyth her wyles, hit were a wynne huge
> To luf hom wel, and leue hem not, a leude þat couþe.

[2415–21: Wiles of women have brought grief. For so was Adam on earth beguiled by one, and Solomon by many of them, and Samson too. Delilah dealt him his fate, and afterwards David was fooled by Bathsheba, who suffered much misery. Now these men were grieved by their wiles; it would bring great joy if a man could love them well but not believe in them.]

Such complaints about women's negative influence on men form another arc, whose articulations are certainly not uncommon in the centuries preceding this poem, nor, unfortunately, after.

Just beyond the years we are studying, for example, a very popular English prose pamphlet, *The Bachelor's Banquet*, was published in 1603. Actually, the anonymous collection of tales is a loose translation of *Les Quinze Joies de Mariage* (The Fifteen Joys of Marriage), probably written in the early fifteenth century, and shortly thereafter Wynkyn de Worde printed an English translation in rhyming verse in 1509. As is true with translations of this period, the French source text served more or less as a reference rather than as an absolute which had to be translated as literally as possible. Indeed, the seventeenth-century collection not only translates the original into English, but, by eliminating Catholic references, also into English culture.

The continued popularity of the collection demonstrates how widely spread the fictionalizing of treatise-related material can be, especially when concerning the anti-feminist arc. Essentially, *The Bachelor's Banquet*'s 15 chapters narrate what difficulties a husband may encounter with his wife and focus on stereotypically female concerns: gossip, clothes and status. The collection's popularity also reflects its context: from about 1540 to 1640, numerous books and pamphlets are printed in England on the subject of women's behavior. Likewise, the Church of England's 'Homily on Marriage' is read regularly in all churches from 1563 to 1640, a treatise that basically posits marriage as a way to ease the lusts of the flesh and that unequivocally places husbands as heads of the household. This Catholic view seems to have easily found its way into the Anglican context.

Vološinov's semiotic approach

It is interesting that such an arc can thrive, since a marker as general as gender hardly constitutes a uniform grouping – a whole array of cultural components divide women socioeconomically. Like St George or Uccello's portrait of Cotignola, images of women such as these attempt to simplify complexity and establish a certain perspective as authoritative. What happens to communication when authority is asserted in this manner is of particular interest to this chapter, since education and religion are social vehicles that tend to further canonical viewpoints, while treatises attempt to establish an authoritative reading. In terms of semiotics, such dynamics make the work of Valentin Nikolaevic Vološinov particularly valuable.

In mulling over prior attempts to understand the working of language, Vološinov defines two approaches. One, which he names 'individualistic subjectivism', has its roots in the romantics and had been practiced by scholars such as Karl Vossler and Leo Spitzer. According to Vološinov, they see the key to understanding language in the monologic utterance, that is, in the utterance of the individual (48–56, 83–98). The other approach is what Vološinov calls 'abstract objectivism', which has its roots in neoclassicist thought and is represented by Saussure's work, which Vološinov doesn't consider satisfactory either, finding it particularly difficult to come to terms with the Swiss linguist's attempt to objectify language and omit the individual speech act from consideration (56-82).

Indeed, beyond his breakdown of the sign into the signifier and the signified, Saussure argues that language is characterized by *arbitrariness*, meaning, basically, that signifiers have no necessary link to their signifieds. Working from this premise, Saussure observes on the one hand that no individual can change the linguistic system at any single point in time, and on the other hand that changes in language can only happen over time by some sort of general consensus. These linguistic traits of *immutability* and *mutability*, respectively, correspond to Saussure's use of *synchronic* and *diachronic* time frames. The diachronic time frame views events through a great expanse of time – it uses the line as its model. The synchronic time frame opens up a slice of time – it can be used to look at multiple strands. In terms of the *translatio*, for example, the *translatio studii et imperii* topos is a diachronically-framed text, while a *translatio* (metaphor) is synchronically framed.

Having rejected essential points of each approach, Vološinov proposes a model that incorporates while modifying both schools of thought. Thus, he includes the consideration of the individual speech act, consonant with individual subjectivism. But he also rejects the individual speech act as the basis of linguistic creativity by firmly locating it in community – the speech act means nothing for Vološinov, unless it is interpreted in the context in which it is uttered. In other words, Vološinov makes the community the basis of his ruminations. The verbal sign, as viewed in dialogic utterance, is his concern – dialogue his laboratory.

Analyzing how language works in communities, Vološinov himself was working in one in which power and authority often and forcefully modified speech acts.[1] In this context, he formulated his theory of *uniaccentuality* and *multiaccentuality*. Assuming that every sign is a 'construct between socially organized persons in the process of their interaction' (21), Vološinov argues that the sign is absolutely contingent on social conditions, on the participants as well as on their contexts. In other words, time-period and social grouping are critical factors in the creation of verbal signs, and thus every sign has an ideological base:

> In order for any item, from whatever domain of reality it may come, to enter the social purview of the group and elicit ideological semiotic reaction, it must be associated with the vital socioeconomic prerequisites of the particular group's existence; it must somehow, even if only obliquely, make contact with the base of the group's material life. (22)

Because it is a social creation, individual choices can have (and here Vološinov echoes Saussure) no meaning: '*only that which has acquired social value can enter the world of ideology, take shape, and establish itself there*' (*ibid.*, his italics). Hence, all ideological *accents* are socially based.

The next step Vološinov takes is to re-direct components of the sign. Roughly analagous to Saussure's *signified* is Vološinov's *theme* and to Saussure's *signifier* is Vološinov's *form*, whereby Vološinov's major concern is the theme (22–3, 99–106). From here, he nuances his ideas about context. Primarily, when different social interests emerge within the same social community, Vološinov argues, class struggle ensues and the sign becomes the site of the class struggle. The term he uses to describe the semiotic struggle is *multiaccentuality*,

> ... it is thanks to this intersecting of accents that a sign maintains its vitality and dynamism and the capacity for further development ... The very same thing that makes the ideological sign vital and mutable is also, however, that which makes it a refracting and distorting medium. The ruling class strives to impart a supraclass, eternal character to the ideological sign, to extinguish or drive inward the struggle between social value judgments which occurs in it, to make the sign uniaccentual [...The...] *inner dialectic quality* of the sign comes out fully in the open only in times of social crises or revolutionary changes. (23, his italics)

Although my best guess is that Vološinov intended Marxist theory as his immediate referent here, his observations are also semiotically relevant in a number of ways.

For example, it's possible to argue that the Order of the Garter has become, in our day and age, *uniaccentual*. For all intents and purposes, nobody now doubts that membership in the Order confers an elite status or that the Order represents a patriotic group, although we may argue about its definition of or approach to patriotism. In effect, the Order has become a non-issue. On the other hand, only recently the English monarchy has had to refashion itself since the *form* in which it has been appearing is wearing thin. In other words, other dialectical nodes are coming to the foreground in not so favorable perspectives: their massive wealth, for example, is now also viewed in terms of family scandals and self-centered greed. The monarchy's response to the threat of *multiaccentuality* has been to redefine the *forms* (for example, visibly public charity work by the Queen) in order to reassert the centuries-old *theme*.

As can be seen in these examples, multiaccentuality may be used to examine all struggles. But it seems especially relevant to look at the literature of this chapter in that light, since training, religion and treatises generally pronounce on areas of potential contention to establish uniaccentuality. Indeed, treatise-generated material on the fallibility of women had to be flattened into uniaccentuality for it to be so easily transferred and translated, for example, into *Sir Gawain and the Green Knight* or *The Bachelor's Banquet*.

One note at this time: for the rest of this study, I won't be using Vološinov's *forms* and *themes* as his translators do, since this use can become confusing. Instead, when I use the terms *forms* and *themes*. I will use them as they are generally understood (although there is overlap) and substitute *signifier* and *signified* for his terms.

Treatises and Sir Thomas Elyot's *The Boke Named the Gouernour*

Understood as attempts to establish authoritative discourse – to ensure uniaccentuality – treatises take a theme (as agreed, in the wider sense of the term) and demonstrate the validity of a certain position by means of precedent, example and appeal to logic – rhetoric's most effective tools. While treatises are generated throughout the Middle Ages (usually on themes concerning religion and governance), they are mostly written in Latin, and, hence, their effect is limited to those who are educated, usually through the auspices of the Church. With the success of the printing press, however, along with a growing middle class, greater numbers of people who could read, the growing insistence on English as the *lingua franca* of the realm, and the monarchy's struggle to establish legitimacy during a period plagued by the Hundred Years War, the War of the Roses and Papal insistence on Catholicism as the one true religion, treatises, too, become more fruitful and multiply.

In order to exemplify the treatise, it's probably more productive to start at the end of the 250 years since relatively straightforward examples are available in English. So, what I plan for this chapter is first to introduce a treatise that marries the issues of education and the state, before moving into educational contexts. Then, I'd like to exemplify how treatise-related anti-feminist material is modulated into two literary narratives and follow that with a look at the fictionalization of treatises in two religious narratives. I'll conclude with a glance at three treatises which treat problems of governance in different ways and in the process contextualize courtly life in the later part of our period.

Dedicated to Henry VIII, Sir Thomas Elyot's *The Boke Named the Gouernour* found favor with the King, perhaps not in small part due to its unequivocal support of the monarchy. Thus, Elyot (*c.* 1490–1548) writes:

> In a gouernour or man hauynge in the publyke weale some greatte authoritie, the fountaine of all excellent maneres is Maiestie; which is the holle proporcion and figure of noble astate, and is proprelie a beautie or comelynesse in his countenance, langage and gesture apt to his dignite, and accomodate to time, place and company; whiche, like as the sonne doth his beames, so doth it caste on the beholders and herers a pleasaunt and terrible reuerence. (II. 2; vol. 2: 12)

A very popular book for its time, *The Boke Named the Gouernour* was reprinted three times within 50 years and appeared in eight editions, the last of which emerged in 1580. Here, we'll use its first edition of 1531.

As a student of Sir Thomas More (*c.* 1477–1535) and as a scholar devoted to the classics, Elyot translated classical literature for the *literati* of his day. In 1538, he also compiled the first longer Latin–English dictionary, under the auspices of the King. Not surprisingly, this classicist's erudition is evidenced in *The Boke Named the Gouernour*, which is punctuated with Greek and Roman allusions and ideals. What may also have helped in the writing of this very long treatise was Elyot's career as a public servant. In 1527, he became the Sheriff of Oxfordshire and Berkshire and began what evolved into a long-term friendship with Thomas Cromwell (*c.* 1485–1540), named chancellor of Cambridge in 1535. Likewise, Elyot became Ambassador to the Emperor in the Low Countries and, at the same time, was commissioned to arrest the religious reformer, William Tyndale (*c.* 1494–1536), believed to reside in Antwerp at the time. With such training and experience, Elyot could well offer a synchronically detailed glimpse into a courtier's life.

However, fueling *The Boke Named the Gouernour* is a diachronically-framed idea, an arc that stretches back to the Ciceronian idea of the ideal orator and implicitly claims universal validity. The Ciceronian *vir bonus* (good man) is a citizen so noble, eloquent and virtuous that he could lead people, by means of his eloquence, to the betterment of society. And indeed, the ideal has surfaced in many treatises. Below is a faithful *translatio* of the topos from a rhetorical treatise, as conveyed by Alcuin, an eighth-century monk from York who served in Charlemagne's court:

> Nam fuit, ut fertur, quoddam tempus, cum in agris homines passim bestiarum more vagabantur, nec ratione animi quicquam, sed pleraque viribus corporis administrabant ... Quo tempore quidam, magnus videlicet vir et sapiens, cognovit quae materia et quanta ad maximas res oportunitas animis inesset hominum, si quis eam posset elicere et praecipiendo eam meliorem reddere: qui dispersos homines in agris et in tectis silvestribus abditos ratione quadam conpulit in unum locum et congregavit et eos in unam quamque rem inducens utilem atque honestam primo propter insolentiam reclamantes, deinde propter rationem atque orationem studiosius audientes ex feris et inmanibus mites reddidit ac mansuetos.

> [33–48, Howell's translation: For there was once a time, as it is said, when mankind wandered here and there over the plains very much as do wild beasts, and men did nothing through the reasoning power of the mind, but everything by sheer brute strength ... At that time a man undeniably great and wise indeed discovered what latent genius – how great a capacity for the highest things – was in the human soul if only someone could draw it forth, and by nurturing perfect it; and by force of reason he collected men into one place from being scattered as they were over the plains, and hidden in dwellings in the forests; and he assembled them together, and led them into each useful and honorable pursuit; they, at first protesting against the strangeness of it, yet finally with eagerness listening because of his reason and eloquence, were made gentle and mild from being savage and brutal.]

Virtue here means eloquence at the service of social conscience.

As is also true of Elyot's treatise, this *vir bonus* topos is the foundation of expository and prescriptive treatises composed to give advice to rulers and which are called, from the German, *Fürstenspiegel* (mirror for rulers). Important examples include John of Salisbury's twelfth-century *Policraticus*; Thomas Aquinas' *De Regimine Principium*, written in the thirteenth century; and a treatise that was to become very popular in England, *De Regno et Regis Institutione* by Francesco Patrizi (1529–97), first printed in Paris in 1518. Elyot was probably influenced by these *Fürstenspiegel* while writing *The Boke Named the Gouernour*.

Nonetheless, the abstracting idealism of his treatise doesn't match very well with what Elyot himself was to experience. From a letter addressed to the Duke of Norfolk dated 4 March 1532, for example, we learn that Elyot wasn't able to arrest Tyndale – and perhaps didn't want to – nor could he gain an audience with the Emperor, who had taken a fall from a horse. Moreover, in contrast to the King, Elyot seemed to be a conservative supporter of the Catholic Church; for example, in Nürnberg he wouldn't participate in communion because it was conducted in the vernacular. Having failed in his mission Elyot returned to England, but the Emperor, Charles V, had apparently enlisted the Englishman's help against Henry in Catherine's case. Thus, from one mud puddle into another, Elyot became unhappily embroiled in the messy divorce that would eventually enable Henry to marry Anne Boleyn.

Henry did have unexpected allies, though, in the underground Jewish community. Although Jews had been expelled from England in 1290 (the first European land to do so) and were not officially readmitted until 1655, those who nominally ascribed to Christianity – mainly expelled Spanish and Portuguese Jews who secretly worshipped their faith, the Conversos – maintained a well-ordered community in London during the 1530s and 1540s. It was here that Henry sought rabbinical interpretations to support his cause (Katz 1994). Although, given the nature of secret communities, the extent of their support cannot definitively be determined, certainly, Anne Boleyn was publicly acknowledged as Queen on 12 April 1533.

Perhaps because of his failures, perhaps because of his embrace of opinions contrary to the King's, perhaps because of the enormous expenses the office generated, and perhaps because political life didn't resemble what he had envisioned, Elyot continually excused himself thereafter from further public office. He died on 26 March 1546, leaving no children. Nonetheless, back in 1531 he had decided opinions on education and linked these to service for the state.

Consisting of three books, *The Boke Named the Gouernour* offers moral and social guidelines for heads of state along with advice on how parents might educate children whom they hope to groom as public servants, or as the title to Book I's chapter 4 would have it: 'The education or fourme of bringing up of the childe of a gentilman, which is to have authoritie in a publike weale' (28). The first book comprises 27 chapters and begins by defining what a republic is, and it continues with what the governance of a republic should be like. From there, Elyot gives advice on how a gentleman is to be educated, gives examples of prior and past gentlemen, and then describes the kinds of exercise, including dancing, in which the future servant of the realm should participate. Book II's 14 chapters discuss majesty and nobility, virtues and vices, and again provides examples. Finally, Book III, which contains 30 chapters, expounds on various virtues such as justice, faith and fortitude, as well as on vices before ending with the role of consultation.

Elyot's ideas on education are pretty detailed, idealistic and elitist. For example, concerning the child's upbringing, he considers it important that the nurse be morally fit for the job:

> Fyrste, they, unto whom the bringing up of suche children apperteineth, oughte, againe the time that their mother shall be of them deliuered, to be sure of a nourise whiche shulde be of no seruile condition or vice notable. For, as some auncient writers do suppose, often times the childe soukethe the vice of his nouryse with the milke of her pappe. (I. 6; vol. 1: 29).

We learn later that boys should be removed from the company of women at the age of seven, since being among them afterwards might encourage a tendency towards 'voluptuositie' (I. 6: vol. 1: 35). Likewise, in the section on dancing, Elyot writes:

> A man in his naturall perfection is fiers, hardy, stronge in opinion, couaitous of glorie, desirous of knowlege, appetiting by generation to brynge forthe his semblable. The good nature of a woman is to be milde, timerouse, tractable, benigne, of sure remembrance, and shamfast ... Wherfore, whan we beholde a man and a woman daun-

> singe to gether, let us suppose there to be a concorde of all the saide
> qualities ... And the meuing of the man wolde be more vehement, of
> the woman more delicate, and with lasse aduauncing of the body,
> signifienge the courage and strenthe that oughte to be in a man, and
> the pleasant sobrenesse that shulde be in a woman. (I. 21; vol. 1:
> 236–8)

Such attempts to mold and shape children into clearly defined hierar-
chies exemplify the attempt to establish *uniaccentuality*. The attempt
is also characterized in Elyot's use of direct and indirect discourse in
what Vološinov describes as the *linear* mode.

Since dialogic utterances are the laboratory for Vološinov's analyses, direct and indirect discourse become complex test cases (125–59).
When an author quotes another text directly or redacts it indirectly,
he or she incorporates the text into his or her own. Vološinov analyzes
the problem by using two sets of terms. One set is directed towards
the form (in the general sense of the term). These instances are categorized as *direct* and *indirect* discourse, but also as *quasi-direct* and
quasi-indirect discourse. The first two are pretty straightforward and
correspond to direct and indirect quotation. The second pairing refers
to the degree to which the author's *accents* contextualize the incorporated text.

The other set of terms Vološinov develops describes the relation of
the author's text to the incorporated text. The *linear* mode subdivides
into *authoritarian dogmatism* and *rationalistic dogmatism*.
Authoritarian dogmatism presents the text, in effect, as truth, while
rationalistic dogmatism reveals an even more linear disposition, since
it attempts to justify the inclusion using logic's principles. In contrast
to the *linear* mode, the *interorientation* mode infiltrates the incorporated text with commentary. This mode also subdivides into two
categories: *realistic and critical individualism* and *relativistic individualism*. In the first of these, the author comments and depicts the
incorporated text. In the second, the author essentially recognizes his
or her incorporation as subjective, and lines between the author's text
and the incorporated texts are blurred. (In giving examples of these
categories, I should add, Vološinov associates them with certain
periods of literature, generalizations that don't hold very well here.)

While in all likelihood no sustained piece of writing occurs in one
mode, Elyot's advice falls predominately into the *linear* mode, of the
rationalistic dogmatic type, and its form of incorporating secondary

texts is primarily *indirect*. For example, arguing the Platonic and Ciceronian view that *Sapience* (wisdom) is necessary to the public's welfare, Elyot sees reason as the key to harmony, a fact well-known by 'euery Catholyke man' (III. 23; vol. 2, 358), as he illustrates the importance of eloquence and erudition. This is, after all, the rationale for the book, which argues how gentlemen may become advisors to heads of state. Thus, he plainly defines such an aspirant's duties:

> This thinge that is called Consultation is the generall denomination of the acte wherin men do deuise together and reason what is to be done. Counsayle is the sentence or aduise particulerly gyuen by euery man for that purpose assembled. Consultation hath respecte to the tyme future or to come, that is to saye, the ende or purpose thereof is addressed to some acte or affaire to be practised after the Consultation. (III. 28; vol. 2: 427)

After further breaking down the component parts – his linear, rationalistic dogmatic method throughout the treatise – Elyot gives examples of important advisors such as Calchas as depicted in Homer (III. 29; vol. 2: 441–2). He concludes as follows:

> Therfore these thinges that I haue rehersed concernyng consultation ought to be of all men in authoritie substancially pondered, and moost vigilauntly obserued, if they intende to be to their publike weale profitable, for the whiche purpose onely they be called to be gouernours. And this conclude I to write any more of consultation, whiche is the last part of morall Sapience, and the begynnyng of sapience politike.
>
> Nowe all ye reders that desire to haue your children to be gouernours, or in any other authoritie in the publike weale of your countrey, if ye bringe them up and instructe them in suche fourme as in this boke is declared, they shall than seme to all men worthye to be in authoritie, honour, and noblesse, and all that is under their gouernaunce shall prospere and come to perfection. And as a precious stone in a ryche ouche they shall be beholden and wondred at, and after the dethe of their body their soules for their endeuour shall be incomprehensibly rewarded of the gyuer of wisedome, to whome onely be gyuen eternall glorie. Amen.
>
> TELOS (III. 30; vol. 2: 446–8)

In sum, Elyot's advice makes the knowledge found in Latin treatises and a plethora of literary references available to a wide readership through its use of English to convey this material. Consequently, *The Boke Named the Gouernour*'s *uniaccentual* and *rationalistically dogmatic* incorporation of a variety of sources seems to open a *multi-accentual* door to others hoping to access the halls of power ... as long as they learn how to use the same *uniaccentual* key.

Training and literature

As exemplified by Elyot's *Boke Named the Gouernour*, treatises of this period are nestled in, and reflect, the educational system which has a long history in England. Thus, in the sixth and seventh centuries, efforts by the Catholic Church to christianize England include the establishment of two types of schools: grammar schools, roughly equivalent to secondary schools, and song schools, which trained their pupils to sing Church services. There were no elementary schools as we know them today. As confirmed by Alcuin with regards to the cathedral school at York, the traditional educational program featured the seven liberal arts, comprising the language and mathematical arts: the *trivium* (grammar, rhetoric and logic) and the *quadrivium* (arithmetic, music, geometry and astronomy).

Boethius (*c.* 475–*c.* 525) provides us with the earliest treatise referring to the seven liberal arts, which continued to influence education in some form into the eighteenth century. Emphasis at the beginning of our 250 years was usually placed on the *trivium*, and specifically on grammar, which didn't then mean simply the mastery of rules. On the contrary, grammar was described as *ars recte loquendi et enarratio poetarum* (the art of speaking correctly and of interpreting the poets). A program that involved a multiply-stranded approach to texts, the *trivium* was complicated by the fact that learning, reading and writing were conducted in Latin.

By the twelfth century, schools had become more specialized, and not long after, in the thirteenth century, universities were founded. Actually, the first university had been established in the twelfth century in Salerno, but since it furthered the study of medicine the title of the first ordinarily goes to Bologna, for canon law, although Paris also makes claims, and Oxford entered the scene not long after (Paris and Oxford being devoted to theology). Schools also began to be associated with the universities, and chantry schools were founded which themselves introduced the equivalent of elementary schools. In the fourteenth century, however, the Black Death reduced the numbers of participants, including priests who could teach, and paved the way for secular inroads into the education system along with an increase in the numbers of public schools and pupils from the lower classes.

Nonetheless, a movement emphasizing elitism, of which Elyot was a part, gained force in the sixteenth century. Thus, scholars referred to as the Oxford Reformers championed the learning of Greek, philosophy, medicine and theology. Associated with Sir Thomas More (c. 1477–1535) and Desiderius Erasmus (c. 1466–1536), the *Humanists* of the Oxford School also included William Lyly (c. 1468–1523) – the grandfather of John Lyly (c. 1554–1606) – who after having studied abroad in Italy and Greece returned to become the first headmaster of St Paul's School in London, a school intended for the upper classes. Likewise, in 1547 under Edward VI (1547–53), an act was passed that in effect closed down a large number of schools, including grammar and elementary schools, so that schools became more and more dependent upon the patronage of wealthy individuals.[2]

With this concerted emphasis on pedagogy, grammar came to be perceived as simply the first stage in acquiring Latin, and grammar books which are recognizable as ancestors to our own were being produced. Thus, William Lyly collaborated with John Colet (1466–1519) and Erasmus on a new Latin grammar, which became the authoritative grammar in the English school system (after a brief battle with Robert Whittinton, which was resolved by Henry VIII himself).

While the educational system emphasized the mastery of Latin, and for the Humanists also Greek, other currents furthered the use of English in a variety of venues. For example, during the twelfth century, as mentioned in the last chapter, *literati* began to assert the value of vernacular courtly literature, with poets prefacing and ending their narratives with assertions of the educational or aesthetic value of their work and sometimes weaving the rhetorical formula *docere et delectare* (to teach while pleasing) into a defense. For example, a Middle English poem we'll be looking at in Chapter 5, *Sir Orfeo*, closes with lines that proclaim aesthetic mastery:

Harpours in Bretaine after þan
Herd hou þis meruaile bigan,

> & made her-of a lay of gode likeing,
> & nempned it after þe king.
> þat lay 'Orfeo' is y-hote:
> Gode is þe lay, swete is þe note.

(597–602: Afterwards, harpers in Britain heard about this marvel and made a lay of it that well conveyed the events, and they named it after the King. That lay is called 'Orfeo'. Good is the lay, sweet is the music.)

Lines such as these, that refer to literature, can have the effect of a mirror reflecting an object in another mirror – cascading the same image in one reflection after another. Writing of poetry in poetry, the poet creates *self-reflexive* or *metaliterary* texts that allow readers insight into the poet's concerns about the literary art.

In addition to indirect justification of the literary art, there are direct defenses as well. For example, in the thirteenth century, in a treatise called *De Vulgari Eloquentia* (On the Eloquence of the Vernacular), Dante Alighieri (1265–1321) asserts the value of writing in the vernacular (although he wrote in Latin). Just beyond the end of the period, too, we witness Sir Philip Sidney (1554–86) in *An Apologie for Poetrie* declaring that the poet can convey noble ideals more effectively than any other kind of writer. Indeed, 'Nature never set forth the earth in so rich tapestry as divers poets have done … Her world is brazen, the poets ony deliver a golden' (Shepherd 1980, 100).

Such instances exemplify the opening up of a *multiaccentual* arena. Latin no longer maintains the authority it had asserted for so many centuries, a state indirectly exemplified by Elyot's treatise which is, after all, written in English. And with more people able to read and write, there are bound to be more published opinions on what is true and correct.

As Elyot's treatise also exemplifies, however, the opening up of a multiaccentual arena does not mean that the mastery of Latin as an essential proof of literacy suddenly vanishes. Encouraging prospective public servants to master the classics, Elyot's treatise reflects others' preoccupation with literary training. And, as happens in competitive situations, 'designer imitations' meet the demand. For example, collections of tales in simple Latin are available alongside *florilegia* (anthologies of pithy sayings by canonical authors) and translations of *auctores* – Latin for 'authors', but meaning the canonically approved writers. Thus, *literati* who had some Latin, and even those who didn't, could nonetheless be familiar with the *auctores*, if not directly, then through these other means.

With increased access to classical materials, *literati* incorporate Greek and Latin material into their narratives and treatises. Indeed, one of the topoi returned to time and again *self-reflexively* testifies to the trend. Thus, the *translatio studii et imperii* topos proclaims that cultural authority descends from the classical cultures of Greece and the Roman empire. Since the topos will be referred to fairly frequently in this volume, this may prove a convenient place to summarize its mythological source here, while illustrating the *interorientation* mode in the process.

Although one of the things that's most difficult to determine is an absolute origin, let's follow one convention and set the Trojan War's inception at the wedding between Peleus, a mortal, and Thetis, a lesser goddess, a union that gave birth to Achilles, a Greek hero, who did much to decimate the forces of Troy. Unfortunately, Eris (the goddess of Discord) was not invited to the ceremony. In revenge, she rolled a golden apple, with the inscription 'To the Fairest', among Hera (the Queen of the gods), Athena (the goddess of wisdom) and Aphrodite (the goddess of love), who were, predictably, each convinced of being the intended recipient of the unambiguous message.

Wisely, the gods refused to make the judgment call, but they chose Paris, a Trojan prince, to do so. Each of the goddesses tried to bribe him: Hera promised him a kingdom, Athena promised him martial victory, but Aphrodite promised him the most beautiful woman in the world. Naturally, Paris let ration fly out the window and chose Aphrodite. When Paris saw Helen of Troy, he thought 'she's the one', so he took her – an act referred to as the rape of Helen in our literary system. This upset her husband, Menelaus, who called upon his brother, Agamemnon, to help right this wrong, and the Greeks laid seige to Troy for ten years, with Athena and Hera on their sides, being less than pleased with Paris' choice. As Christopher Marlowe (1564–93) has Dr Faustus sum it up in two stunning lines, 'Was this the face that lancht a thousand shippes?/ And burnt the toplesse Towres of *Ilium*?' (Scene 12, 81–2).

After ten years, the Greeks finally won by means of deception: upon Odysseus' recommendation they built a wooden horse taller than the gates of Troy, since, according to prophecy, Troy would fall only under certain conditions, one of which being the destruction of the arch over Troy's gates. Following Odysseus' advice, the Greeks then made it seem as if they were tired of the war and took to their ships, leaving one of their own, Sinon, behind, tied up and wailing in the vicinity of the horse. When the Trojans found him, he was able to convince them that the Greeks had left him as a sacrifice and had deserted the battlefield since the horse was a sign of Trojan victory. Of course, they believed him in spite of the warnings of one of their own prophets, Laocöon. To be fair to the unsuspecting Trojans, the prophet and his two sons were killed by giant serpents emerging from the sea right after his prophecy. The Trojans might have considered, however, that due to an old grudge, Poseidon – the god of the sea – was not on their side. In any case, fate awaits the Trojans, who destroy their own arch, drag the horse in, and are killed by Greek warriors bursting out of the wooden edifice. So much for looking a gift-horse in the mouth. The only survivors were a few women who were taken as prisoners, and Aeneas with some of his men who went on, as we know, to Italy.

Latinate vernacular

After the eleventh century, more or less, it wasn't until the fourteenth century that the English vernacular is again prominent in literary circles. The reassertion of the vernacular also found its way into other areas. For example, by the beginning of the fourteenth century, official documents are written in English; in 1362, the Statute of Pleading admits English to the courts, and Parliament is opened in English; and in 1394, the chancery court conducts most of its proceedings in English. So, too, Henry IV (1399–1413) uses English for all his government business and, after him, Henry V (1413–22) uses English not only officially but in the court as well (Tristram 1988, 60–1). Thus, even though literacy is still defined by the mastery of Latin in the English literary system of this period, *literati* also include those who read and write in the vernacular.

Indeed, the bifurcation between the educated and the literary isn't as rigid as it may at first seem. Thus, knowledge acquired from Latin treatises frequently found its way into the vernacular writer's domain, as exemplified by *Sir Gawain and the Green Knight*'s sections on hunting, as well as by Elyot's treatise. Likewise, vernacular writing from this period often exhibits a studied preoccupation with style, as old standards are now being transmitted in new forms. For example, while M. Tullius Cicero (106–43 BCE) continues to be a critical *auctor* for rhetorical studies, Marcus Fabius Quintilianus (*c.* 40–96 CE) also becomes important. His *De Institutione Oratoria* (On the Education of the Orator) doesn't differ much from Cicero's treatises in substance, but it offers more detail and emphasizes style. More tellingly, rhetorics are also being translated into English. Thus, Thomas Wilson (*c.* 1525–81) presents a very Ciceronian treatise, *The Art of Rhetoric*, devoted to the oratorical art in the vernacular.

The attention to style has interesting consequences for the vernacular, which at times takes on a Latinate flair. For example, the *Legendary* translated by Osbern Bokenham (b. *c.* 1392) from the Latin for East Anglian audiences, contains a *vita* of Mary Magdalene. Bokenham begins with his own 'prolocutorye', that includes a rhetorically elaborate display of astrological knowledge:

> The yer of grace, pleynly to descryue,
> A thowsand, fourhundryd, fourty & fyue,
> Aftyr þe cherche of Romys computacyoun,
> Wych wyth Iane chaungyth hyr calculacyoun,
> Whan phebus (wych nowher is mansonarye
> Stedefastly, but ych day doth varye
> Hys herberwe among þe syngnys twelue,
> As þe fyrste meuer ordeynyd hym-selue)
> Descendyd was in hys cours adoun
> To þe lowest part by cyrcumuolucyoun
> Of þe Zodyac cercle, Caprycorn I mene,
> Wher of heythe degrees he hath but fyftene,
> And hys retur had sumwhat bygunne.
> By wych oo degre oonly he had wunne
> In clymbyng, & drow towerd Agnarye –
> But in þis mater what shuld I lenger tarye?
> I mene pleynly up-on þat festful eue
> In wych, as alle crystene men byleue,
> Thre kyngys her dylygence dede applye
> Wyth thre yiftys newe-born to gloryfye
> Cryst, aftyr hys byrthe þe threttende day,
> Comyng from þe est in ful royal aray,
> By conduct of a sterre wych shone clere...

[4981 or 4982 (editorial error makes either line number possible)–5003: The year of grace, plainly to describe, a thousand, four hundred, forty-five, according to the Church of Rome's calculation (i.e. the Roman calendar) which with Janus (the god of the portal, for whom 'January' is named), changes its number – when Phoebus (the sun god) – which nowhere is permanently abiding, steadfastly, but each day does change his dwelling among the twelve signs (of the zodiac), as the first mover (i.e. God) himself ordained it to be – descended down in his course, to the lowest part of his circuit of the Zodiacal circle, to Capricorn I mean, of which he had only fifteen degrees in his height, and his return had just begun, by which he had only completed climbing by one degree and drove towards Aquarius – but in this matter why should I dwell longer? I mean plainly, on that festive evening on which, as all Christian men believe, three kings did apply their diligence with three gifts to glorify the new-born Christ, after his birth on the thirtieth day, coming from the East in full royal array, being led by a star which shone clearly...]

All this to say, 'on Twelfth Night 1445'. In any case, Bokenham goes on in prefatory mode to tell how on this specific night he met a number of noble women (he begins name-dropping here), one of whom asked him to write the life of Mary Magdalene in English, which he finally agreed to do. Then, he praises God and his creation before praying to Magdalene. His *prolocutorye* ends about 385 lines later.

This kind of elaborate circumlocution became a marker of eloquence among some *literati* and is often associated with John Lyly (1554-1606), whose writing gave birth to the term *euphuism*. In *Euphues: The Anatomy of Wit* (1578), the title hero, the Athenian Euphues, travels to Naples, becomes friends with Philautus, and is introduced to his friend's fiancée, Lucilla. Unbeknownst to Philautus, Euphues sues for her hand, which generates a series of combative letters between the former friends. Lucilla finally decides upon a third suitor, leaving the two nothing else to do but become friends again. Lyly continues with a long essay against love and some other pieces, all of which he reshapes in *Euphues and His England* (1580), a narrative that continues the tale of the two friends as they travel through England. But it's Lyly's Latinate circumlocutions that are most obvious in his writing. I'll not include passages here, but if you've ever watched the old BBC series, *Yes Minister,* you need not wonder about the survival of this arc.

Uniaccentual discourse

To illustrate the incorporation of treatise- and education-related material in fictional narratives, I'd like to look at Chaucer's *Wife of Bath's Prologue* and again at *Sir Gawain and the Green Knight*, which I couple here because of their use of material categorized, even in this period, as 'anti-woman.' Although the reasons for the popularity of anti-feminist material are probably complex, the heart of its *linear, authoritarian dogmatic* argument is an unfavorable interpretation of Eve, the precursor, or *antetype*, of the Virgin Mary, who is the *type* of the perfect Christian woman, just as Adam is the antetype of the type, Christ (Charity 1966). Although these pairings may seem equitable, associations gathered about women focus on their ability and desire to seduce men from the straight and narrow.

In the western European literary system, Eve's story is as ubiquitous as MacDonald's golden arches and is found not only in manuscripts of the Bible, but also in sermons, literary allusions, stained glass windows and paintings. The simplified version of her tale causally posits that since Eve tempted Adam to eat an apple (yet another story-generating apple) by means of her sweet words, language as well as a proclivity to the venial have become the weapons all her 'heirs' wield to snare men and deliver them to the devil (as if men couldn't be among her heirs – so much for logic).

This popular rendition is found implicitly and explicitly in many texts, even though it leaves out a few details. Genesis 1. 26–3.19 – as presented in the Latin Vulgate, the authoritative version since about the fifth century and pretty much throughout our period – narrates events in the following manner. After God completed his work and realized that his most excellent creation, Adam, was lonely, he formed Eve from Adam's rib. Given dominion over the earth, they were allowed to live in Eden, the earthly paradise, as long as they didn't taste the fruit from the Tree of Knowledge of Good and Evil. A talking serpent, though, successfully tempted Eve to taste the apple and to persuade Adam to do the same. Of course, God finds out. Here is the point at which it becomes interesting. When God confronts them, Eve admits to the deed, although she blames the snake for enticing her, while Adam points to his mate with the 'she-made-me-do-it' alibi. More interesting still, one of the authoritative glosses on this passage is Augustine's on the literal level of Genesis, *De Genesi ad litteram*, and his commentary on Adam's behavior is not flattering: since Adam was the head and hence the one responsible for rational behavior, he was more at fault than Eve, who represents will or desire (XI. xxxiv, 45–60).

While some of us may wish to cheer Augustine on at first, this is a knotty passage and gloss for a number of reasons. First, where is Satan in the parcelling out of blame? Next, the gloss suggests that while Adam is more to blame for the fall, women have no rational capacity. Moreover, the fall, which everyone is so upset about, is the crux of the doctrine of the *felix culpa*, or the fortunate fall, which goes something like this: if the original parents hadn't disobeyed God, they wouldn't have been ejected from the Garden of Eden, Christ wouldn't have been born in time and in mortal form, and, hence, humankind would never have had the chance to achieve eternal life. So, it *is* fortunate that the first parents did fall, that they, in other words, disobeyed God. Also difficult is God's punishment for the offense: the snake must forever after slither about on its belly, Adam and Eve are booted out of Eden, humanity must thereafter labor, and all women must bear children. One might very well argue that although Eve committed the lesser offense, she had to bear the greater burden. But the glosses have a response to that problem as well: a woman will be the mother of Christ and hence redeem all womankind.

Such questions concerned Church officials, and since the Church had amassed great wealth and power by the 250 years we're investigating, their answers had considerable consequences. But just as there is a *multiaccentual* arena jostling traditional perspectives on language, so too multiaccentual tremors are shaking up the religious sphere. Actually, absolute borders never did successfully separate religious and secular spheres. Important offices in the Church, for example, had often been a point of contention between popes and kings; castles frequently had chapels within their confines; and church officials were often accused of living a worldly life, as Geoffrey Chaucer's General Prologue to *The Canterbury Tales* exemplifies. There, for example, the narrator describes the Prioress as living quite a luxurious life and then follows with a description of the Monk:

> A Monk ther was, a fair for the maistrie,
> An outridere, that lovede venerie,
> A manly man, to been an abbot able.
> Ful many a deyntee hors hadde he in stable,
> And whan he rood, men myghte his brydel heere

Gynglen in a whistlynge wynd als cleere
And eek as loude as dooth the chapel belle ...
What sholde he studie and make hymselven wood,
Upon a book in cloystre alwey to poure,
Or swynken with his handes, and laboure,
As Austyn bit? ...

[General Prologue 165–87: There was a monk, extremely fair, an
outrider (someone who looked after a monastery's estates), who
loved hunting, a manly man, capable of being an abbot. Many a valuable horse he had in the stables, and when he rode, men could hear
his bridle jingling in a whistling wind as clear and also as loud as a
chapel bell ... Why should he study and make himself crazy, poring
over a book in a cloister, or work with his hands and labor, as
Augustine asked?]

As you can see from Chaucer's portrait and tone, the Church's relation to the secular is a *multiaccentual* arena that also engenders criti-
cism and irony. With the Great Schism of 1378 dividing the See of the
Pope between Rome and Avignon, there was, from anyone's perspective, room for improvement.

The mingling of the secular with the religious makes treatise-
related material, such as anti-feminist arguments, particularly powerful. When *uniaccentual* signs become conventional enough to find
their way into literature, they have the effect of truth. However, true to
the conventions allowing Uccello's Cotignola to strike a pose of glory
while concomitantly being glossed by less-directed knights and foot
soldiers, so too, once an idea has universal currency, it can be challenged.

Authority, multiaccentuality, and the Wife of Bath

Geoffrey Chaucer's *Canterbury Tales* depicts a group of pilgrims (a
couple of whom we've already met) on their way to worship at the
shrine of Thomas Becket (the Archbishop of Canterbury who was
murdered in the cathedral in 1170, apparently by Henry II's ambigu-
ously directed order – another interesting case of interpretation). The
pilgrims congregate at the Tabard Inn, where Geoffrey, the narrator
first encounters them. They're such an amenable group of people that
Geoffrey and Harry Bailly, the innkeeper, decide to join them. Harry

suggests that each pilgrim tell two stories on the way to Canterbury and two on the way back, the best of which will win a prize. Unfortunately, what remains to us is fragments; apparently, Chaucer never finished the project.

In any case, with such a set-up we might well expect to be reading a series of religious tales. While there are a few of these, this is, on the whole, quite a secularly-oriented group. And Alisoun, the Wife of Bath, is not only one of the most secular, she also provides one of the best examples of how religious treatise material may be incorporated into a narrative. She begins the prologue to her tale by refuting the authority of canonical texts – the basic principle, bar none, of Catholic theology – and offers experience as a truer authority. It's as if a prosecuting attorney were to argue that all legislative precedents aren't really of use and that how one feels should be the key to sentencing a murderer (this does sound familiar).

Alisoun goes on to tell the group of pilgrims about her five husbands and various lovers and to argue that even taking canonical texts into consideration, neither the Bible nor its commentators really uttered a word against multiple marriages. 'I pray yow, telleth me./ Or where comanded he virginitee?' (61–2). In *interorientation* mode of the *relativistic individual* type, but with a punch, she goes on to insist that virginity may very well be the pinnacle of human perfection, but she's perfectly content not being perfect, and besides, what are genitalia for – certainly not simply for 'purgacioun/ Of uryne' (120–1). After Alisoun argues in this manner, she goes on to exemplify what the outcome of her approach to authority might be, by regaling her audience with a more detailed review of her five husbands. She is most copious about her fifth, a clerk younger than she, who couldn't stop reading, in the *linear* mode of the *authoritarian dogmatic* kind, some of the authoritative anti-feminist treatises we've been alluding to:

> He hadde a book that gladly, nyght and day,
> For his desport he wolde rede alway;
> He cleped it Valerie and Theofraste,
> At which book he lough alwey ful faste.
> And eek ther was somtyme a clerk at Rome,
> A cardinal, that highte Seint Jerome,
> That made a book agayn Jovinian;
> In which book eek ther was Tertulan,

Crisippus, Trotula, and Helowys …
And eek the Parables of Salomon,
Ovides Art, and bookes many on,
And alle thise were bounden in o volume.
And every nyght and day was his custume,
Whan he hadde leyser and vacacioun
From oother worldly occupacioun,
To reden on this book of wikked wyves.
He knew of hem mo legendes and lyves
Than been of goode wyves in the Bible.
For trusteth wel, it is an impossible
That any clerk wol speke good of wyves,
But if it be of hooly seintes lyves,
Ne of noon oother womman never the mo.
Who peyntede the leon, tel me who?
By God, if wommen hadde writen stories,
As clerkes han withinne hire oratories,
They wolde han writen of men moore wikkednesse
Than al the mark of Adam may redresse.

[669–96: He had a book that gladly, night and day, he would always read for his pleasure; he called it Valerius and Theophrastus, a book he would always laugh at heartily. Also there were some passages by a clerk from Rome, a cardinal who was called Saint Jerome, who wrote a book against Jovinian; in it there was also Tertullian, Chrysippus, Trotula and Heloise…and also the Parables of Solomon, Ovid's *Art (of Love)*, and many a book, and all these were bound in one volume. And every night and day it was his custom, whenever he had leisure and rest from other worldly occupation, to read this book of wicked women. He knew of them more legends and lives than of good women in the Bible. For trust it well, it is an impossibility for a clerk to speak well of women, unless they speak of holy saints' lives, but of none other women a word. Who painted the lion, tell me who? By God, if women had written stories, as clerks had in their chapels, they would have written more wickedness about men than all men (those with the image of Adam) could redress.]

Jankyn's book certainly features *auctores* for the anti-feminist argument. But eventually the couple reaches an understanding. Jankyn grants Alisoun mastery in their marriage, perhaps thereby substituting *multiaccentuality* for a new kind of *uniaccentuality*. And the freshly widowed Wife of Bath goes on to let the pilgrims know she's looking for her sixth husband, before she tells her tale.

On first glance, Alisoun's words and demeanor may strike us as pretty contemporary. Yet, Alisoun is anything but an unequivocally praiseworthy character: she's depicted as a boisterous and lascivious liar and cheat. More complicated still, she's a *fun* liar and cheat. And does the fact that Chaucer was a male presenting a bumbling male narrator presenting Alisoun presenting her own story have anything to do with our understanding of what is being said about women and who's saying it? The problems erupting from the Wife of Bath's Prologue center on the problem of interpretation, a theme which Alisoun also highlights throughout her discourse. For, basically, her prologue asks the question, who has the authority to determine the meaning ascribed to a canonical text, and further, who has the power to prescribe behavior as interpreted from canonical texts?

As far as Alisoun is concerned, *in the world of the pilgrims*, broaching the theological and treatise-conveyed subject for discussion in a secular vein allows *multiaccentuality* to prevail. In other words, Alisoun rejects the Church's control of the term and offers a viable (and loud) alternative. She has, after all, successfully given her *accents* to authoritative texts. In the roughly contemporary *Sir Gawain and the Green Knight, multiaccentuality* percolates as well.

Gawain and Lady Bercilak

What is perhaps of most relevance here (regardless of what we may feel about the complex knot of gender issues) is that the tone of Gawain's rant seems to echo the whiney excuse made by Adam. Indeed, not unlike Arthur at the beginning of the poem, Gawain at the end of the romance seems a bit petulant, cranky, and literal. Thus, once the Green Knight nicks him on the neck, Gawain leaps to his own defense, like the stereotype of a lawyer, sticking (understandably) to the letter of their agreement:

> And quen þe burne seȝ þe blode blenk on þe snawe;
> He sprit forth spenne-fote more þen a spere lenþe,
> Hent heterly his helme, and on his hed cast,
> Schot with his schulderez his fayre schelde vnder,
> Braydez out a bryȝt sworde, and bremely he spekez –

Neuer syn þat he watz burne borne of his moder
Watz he neuer in þis worlde wyʒe half so blyþe –
'Blynne, burne, of þy bur, bede me no mo!
I haf a stroke in þis sted withoute stryf hent,
And if þow rechez me any mo, I redyly schal quyte,
And ʒelde ʒederly aʒayn – and þerto ʒe tryst –
    and foo.
Bot on stroke here me fallez –
þe couenaunt schop ryʒt so,
Fermed in Arþurez hallez –
And þerfore, hende, now hoo!'

[2315–30: And when the knight saw the blood gleam on the snow, he sprung forth, feet together, leaping more than a spear's length, grasped quickly his helmet, and put it on his head, jerked with his shoulders his fair shield down, drew out his bright sword and bravely he speaks – never since the knight was born of his mother was he ever in this world so happy a person – 'Cease, Knight, your blows, offer me no more! I have taken a stroke in this place without resisting, and if you offer me any more, I will readily repay you, and return (it) quickly again – and you can be sure of that – and do so fiercely. Only one stroke falls to me here – the bargain was appointed right so, confirmed in Arthur's halls, and therefore, good sir, halt!']

It is this trait of legalistic literalness that Gawain resorts to in order to assert authority in Bercilak's neck of the woods. In doing so, he is operating primarily in the *linear* mode of the *authoritarian dogmatic* variety. For it becomes clear through Gawain's sudden leap to his physical self-defense, as well as through his just as sudden linguistic leap to his moral self-defense (the one in which he blames women), that Gawain, for all his eloquence, reads and acts with a literal invest-ment in the word.

While literalness has its place, at times, it can actually lead to error. Thus, on the one hand, Gawain honorably sets out for the Green Knight's chapel at the appointed time, *bound to his word*, even though he doesn't know where to *look*. On the other hand, even in the opening scene when Gawain eloquently offers himself to be the one to take up the Green Knight's challenge, he could easily have *looked* at the scene beyond the *literal* challenge: after all, a *green* knight might very well have magic at his disposal, and consequently there might be something behind his *literal* blow-for-a-blow Christmas offer.

Likewise, when Gawain transfers to Bercilak the first of the Lady's kisses and is asked the donor's identity, he won't comply, since that wasn't part of the *literal* bargain, ' "þat watz not forward," quoþ he, "frayst me no more./ For ჳe haf tan þat yow tydez, trawe non oþer..."' (1395–96: ' "That was not agreed upon," said he, "ask me no more – for you have taken what is your due, think of nothing else..." '). Gawain's literal-leveled adherence to his word goes hand-in-hand with his attention to eloquence, attention that often makes him miss the big picture. This trait becomes most problematic when he promises Lady Bercilak he will not reveal her gift of the green girdle to her husband.

Actually, it's Gawain's encounters with Lady Bercilak that tell us most about the hero. Indeed, Lady Bercilak resembles Gawain insofar as she too generates eloquent and elegant surfaces. But she contrasts with Arthur's knight insofar as she is able to consider additional perspectives that allow her to *see* the big picture, as evidenced in her superior performance during each of their three encounters. Thus, on the first day Gawain is surprised by her sudden and somewhat bold entrance (even though, by the fourteenth century, Gawain had acquired quite a reputation as a 'lady's man'). Prepared for her visit on the second day, Gawain exchanges gallantries in the courtly manner he's accustomed to, but is nonetheless unable to anticipate her next moves. And on the third day, after an uneasy night punctuated by nightmares, Arthur's knight is put to the test. Lady Bercilak offers the green girdle with its golden trimmings suggesting its material value and its significance as a token of their flirtatious relationship. Eloquent Sir Gawain has no trouble refusing its *signifier*-related attributes; he doesn't need its beautiful surface nor its function as a sign for their daily flirts. This is his territory, and he's just not interested in the 'eloquence' of the green girdle. He cannot, however, ignore the *signified* with which Lady Bercilaks finally invests the token.

Lady Bercilak has thereby proffered the girdle as a subtly *multiaccentual* sign: recognizing the crisis in which Gawain finds himself, she creates a dialectic that enables him to *see beyond* the eloquent surface and to *accept* an unconventional, non-authoritative message. Gawain accepts the girdle as multiply significant, even though in *the world of the poem*, it actually *is* just a *literal* green girdle, since it didn't protect the hero from harm – his neck was nicked. More complex still, Gawain returns to the conventional vision when once again face-to-face with the Green Knight: his flinching suggests he didn't, at least at that moment, believe in the green girdle's magic. It's as if he had taken it in the framework of, 'Well, every little bit helps'.

When Gawain promised not to reveal the talisman to the Lord of the castle, he was, apparently, unaware that he was wrapped in a paradox – if he tells, he lies to her; if he doesn't surrender the girdle, he lies to Lord Bercilak. The *Gawain*-Poet draws attention to the deceit by having Lord Bercilak present Arthur's knight with a fox on that third day, the animal known for sly deception. Gawain has become duplicitous – he operates on two levels – even though he's not very experienced at it. Although Gawain's courtly and polite demeanor knows no parallel at Camelot, and although he can quip with Lord Bercilak in courtly fashion while hiding the identity of the donor of his kisses – in other words, even though he's mastered the rhetorical polish that enables eloquence – Gawain cannot structure this elegance into comprehensive understanding. If the sudden appearance of Hautdesert right after his prayer to the Virgin, the Christmas season, the host's knowledge of where the Green Knight's chapel is, the game with the hood on the spear, and the host's game of *exchanges* don't alert him to the 'fact' that he's treading on the Green Knight's turf, then at the very latest the green and the gold of Lady Bercilak's gift should have. Gawain needs to learn how to distinguish the truly marginal from the rhetorically marginal, to distinguish eloquent surfaces from important signs, and how to pull all this together into a multiply-stranded narrative.

The *Gawain*-Poet subtly wraps the same message for the poem's readers as well and does so in part with the use of treatise-related material. As we puzzle over how to read the hunted animals in terms of Gawain's bedroom or get distracted by what significances green may have, right before our eyes, the marginalized references to women juxtaposed to the *translatio studii et imperii* topos also generate *multiaccentuality*. Just as Gawain was given clues, we too have hints: since the *translatio* topos begins and ends the romance, it might be fairly significant. Indeed, if we isolate the two structural components of the topos, location and temporality, to look at the romance, a diagram might very well look like this:

translatio topos
  Camelot
    (journey)
      Hautdesert

(journey)

Green Chapel

(journey)

Camelot

translatio topos

Diagramming the poem in this way not only confirms the typically circular structure of an Arthurian narrative, as mentioned in the last chapter, it also enables us to see that the journeys too, while *rhetorically marginalized*, are nonetheless critical in setting up the poem's central issues.

Moreover, this structure enables us to draw large comparisons. For example, the diagram suggests that the *translatio* topos, too, can be seen as a journey, one that involves, as do Gawain's journeys, battles that will determine superiority. Pulling all the pieces together, as Bercilak in the persona of the Green Knight does at the end, we might then perceive a multiply-layered narrative that refuses to settle into simple causalities. The diachronically couched *translatio* topos and the synchronically focused journeys may well be centered in knightly and martial values, but at the same time, the poem's synchronic and diachronic presentations of women modify and texture these emphases. Indeed, we could very well modify the above diagram in the following manner:

> *translatio* topos
>   *Camelot*: Guenevere and Gawain
>   Morgan le Fay and the Green Knight
>   Green Knight and Gawain
>   (journey)
>   *Hautdesert*: Morgan le Fay and Lady Bercilak
>   Lord Bercilak and Gawain
>   Lady Bercilak and Gawain
>   (journey)
>   *Green Chapel*: Green Knight and Gawain
>   Morgan le Fay and Guenevere
>   Gawain's anti-feminist alibi
>   (journey)
>   *Camelot*: Gawain and Arthur
>   Gawain and Camelot's courtiers
> *translatio* topos

Again, what is rhetorically marginal is not necessarily thematically marginal.

Looking at the structure of the poem with women in it reveals the importance of women throughout the romance, although everything at first seems to revolve about Gawain. It is Morgan le Fay who sets up the whole test in order to frighten Guenevere (Moore 1984). It is Lady Bercilak, not ferocious warriors or dragons, who tests Gawain's virtue. And lest anyone forget, the *translatio studii et imperii* topos was set into motion for the love of Helen of Troy (or an apple). So, at first, although it appears that Gawain's diatribe against women is another *uniaccentual* confirmation of anti-feminist doctrine, it is so only *in the world of the romance*. Like Alisoun's quips, Sir Gawain's diatribe is not only *not* spoken by an authority of the Church, it is also spoken in a tone and context that robs it of its *uniaccentuality*, Indeed, *lest we miss it*, the *Gawain*-Poet gives us one last clue. On his return from Hautdesert, Gawain is welcomed heartily by Camelot even though he is embarassed by his failure. He relates his tale:

> ...and ferlyly he telles,
> Biknowez alle þe costes of care þat he hade,
> þe chaunce of þe chapel, þe chere of þe knyʒt,
> þe luf of þe ladi, þe lace at þe last.
> þe nirt in þe nek he naked hem schewed
> þat he laʒt for his vnleuté at þe leudes hondes
>   for blame.

(2494–500: ...and wondrously well he narrates, acknowledging all the hardships that he had, the adventure of the chapel, the behavior of the knight, the love of the lady, the belt at the last. The nick in the neck he bared and showed them, that he got for his disloyalty at the man's hands for blame.)

Clearly, *this* is another story, one that is recapitulated in *linear* mode. No Morgan, no Guenevere, and only a Lady Bercilak who's been incorporated into his text with his *accents*, in *authoritarian dogmatic* mode. Not surprisingly, the green girdle becomes the sign of Arthur's court, flattened into meaning 'community', after having been – in Lady Bercilak's hands – a *multiaccentual* sign of various communities.

Treatises in fictional form and multiaccentuality

In addition to narratives that incorporate treatise-related material in erudite manner, like *Sir Gawain and the Green Knight* or *The Boke Named the Gouernour*, some treatises of the period not only emulate but also argue for the special kind of simplicity that Augustine recommends. It should come as no surprise, however, that when such attempts touched upon religion, the Church, with all its power and learning, put its *uniaccentual* foot down.

For example, active for about 150 years and most popularly associated with the Oxford theologian John Wyclif (*c.* 1330–84), Lollardy attempted to 'disendow' the wealthy and powerful Church, exhorting it to return to simple ways and to its duty of serving as shepherd to its flock. Supported by John of Gaunt (*c.* 1340–99), whose dynastic interests led him to further the idea of disendowment, at least as applied to the Church, Wyclif was highly active in focusing his reform movement on lay people, rejecting papal supremacy and furthering the emulation of Christ's poverty. Thus, in his writings, he argued that the Bible should be translated into English so that lay people could learn of its treasures for themselves. Indeed, as Lollards argued, England already had a tradition of translating the Bible into the vernacular. For example, during 990–94, Ælfric, the Abbot of Eynsham mentioned in the last chapter, had already translated the Bible – in abbreviated and summarized form – into Old English.

Nonetheless, in 1378 the Pope censured Wyclif, and in 1407 Archibishop Arundel banned the translation of the Bible into English along with disputations concerning the sacrament and the possession of writings by Wyclif. Despite bans, excommunication and execution, Lollards continued articulating these demands, along with others. For example, they were against cursing and for allowing everyone, including women, to read, teach and preach. In this manner, the increasing number of trials against 'heretics' is intimately tied to book culture. Not only is the translation of the Bible into the vernacular a key point of contention, but pamphleteering for one side or the other became a norm and even included, ironically, Henry VIII's own (early) attempt to defend the Catholic faith against Martin Luther (1521).

The next two narratives we'll look at have been considered – by some of their contemporaries and modern scholars alike – to exhibit Lollard sympathies. And indeed, they do seem concerned with disseminating knowledge, using the vernacular, and conveying Christian messages to lay people. But rather than offering an expository treatise like Elyot's or using material from treatises like the *Wife of Bath's Prologue* or *Sir Gawain and the Green Knight*, these two narratives *fictionalize* treatises as they exemplify the rhetorical precept, *docere et delectare*, to teach while pleasing. To do so, both *Piers Plowman* and *The Book of Margery Kempe* play against the idea that God's language created the universe, which means that mortal history is God's story and each individual's mortal life is a vignette in this story. In the process, they offer alternatives to the Church's *uniaccentual* voice.

Although *Piers Plowman* precedes *The Book of Margery Kempe* chronologically, I'm going to start with Kempe's narrative since I want to discuss it in terms of a simpler semiotic problem. That is, I'll discuss Kempe's narrative with respect to *authorial accents* and William Langland's in terms of *interorientation*.

The Book of Margery Kempe

Probably written in the 1430s, when she was in her sixties, *The Book of Margery Kempe* depicts Margery as its central figure, portraying her in the third person as a woman determined to live a Christian life without entering a nunnery. As simple as that sounds, acceptance of her life goal was not by any means universal, and, consequently, Margery acquired quite a reputation even in her own lifetime. Perhaps it was this 'name recognition' that led Wynkyn de Worde to print a much abbreviated version of her narrative, in 1501, along with the work of other mystics. Mystics, such as Richard Rolle (d. 1349) and Julian of Norwich (d. *c.* 1415), claim a secret and direct knowledge of God, often expressing their experiences in the terminology of sensual love – maybe this was highly marketable material (Keiser 1987, Knowles 1961).

In any case, Margery's life resembles, to a limited extent, that of the fictional Wife of Bath. Like Alisoun, Margery Kempe (*c.* 1373–*c.* 1440) was a member of the middle class. Her father, John Burnham, had been mayor of King's Lynn five times, member of parliament and alderman of his guild. In addition, just as Alisoun was involved in the textile business, so too Kempe ran a brewery and a mill (although both enterprises failed), and in 1438 she was listed as a member of the

Holy Trinity Guild in prosperous Lynn, a guild which essentially ran the town (Staley 1994).

As straightforward and potentially comfortable as her conditions sound, Margery is nonetheless constantly at odds with her context. For example, her family background and her membership in a powerful guild provide her with the circumstances that would allow her a pretty good education. Yet, she claims she had to use scribal services to record the story of her life. Nonetheless, Margery, again like Alisoun, has her favorite spiritual texts, although Margery uses them for comfort and Alisoun, to excoriate clerks. Similarly unusual, Margery and her husband, John Kempe, whom she married in 1393, had 14 children in an age where surviving childbirth was not a given. This becomes more dissonant still when we learn, not even imaginable of Chaucer's character, that when Margery was about 40 she finally succeeded in convincing her husband to live with her in a celibate marriage. But beyond all these comparisons and contrasts, there is a fundamental tie between the two: Margery, like Alisoun, was determined to live her life on her own terms. Perhaps she too balked at the lists of evil women too readily available to confine individuals into a stereotype.

The dissonance that textures Margery's life emerges at the very beginning of 'her' narrative, and precisely in terms of whose narrative *The Book of Margery Kempe* actually is. It is difficult, in Vološinov's terms, to determine the author's *accents*, since the lines between direct and indirect discourse are blurred. Drawing attention to the problem, the narrative actually has two prologues. In the first of the two prologues, the narrator appears in the persona of a scribe and depicts Margery as having dictated the narrative to him. We could take this portrayal at face value, but even if we do, we should remember that, conventionally, saintly women in this literary system assume the humble pose of illiteracy. We should also consider that in Margery's time it was probably safer not to proclaim one's erudition, since the charge of Lollardy might very well be the *uniaccentual* response. Indeed, Margery was imprisoned in Leicester and put under house arrest, having been accused of being a Lollard set out to deceive the populace (I. 2624 ff.).

Not only, then, does the *uniaccentual* church and community attempt to stifle Margery's unconventional life, the question is raised as to whether the words we read in the book are hers. Is this direct or indirect discourse, and if indirect discourse, whose *accents* are we reading? The question is further problematized, when we learn that Margery had two (almost three) scribes work on her 'schort tretys' (1: short treatise). And even this incident becomes dissonant, for the second scribe initially refuses to transcribe the prior scribe's work due to its illegibility. He later feels pangs of conscience, returns to the task, and miraculously he can read his predecessor's crabbed handwriting. All this attention to the *translatio* of the narrative brings the question of *author*-ity right into the foreground. What adds to the complexity is that Margery's familiarity with religious texts and specifically with writings on lay devotion that are in circulation at the time is quite thorough – if illiterate, she's certainly not unknowledgeable. Thus, in conversation with the Vicar of Norwich, Margery,

> ... teld hym how sumtyme the Fadyr of hevyn dalyd to hir sowle as pleynly and as veryly as o frend spekyth to another be bodyly spech ... and informyd hir ... how sche schuld lofe hym ... so excellently that sche herd nevyr boke, neythyr Hyltons boke, ne Bridis boke, ne *Stimulus Amorys*, ne *Incendium Amoris*, ne non other that evyr sche herd redyn that spak so hyly of lofe of God ...

> (I. 894–902: ... told him how sometimes the Father of Heaven conversed with her soul as plainly and as truly as one friend speaks to another by bodily speech ... and informed her ... how she should love him ... so excellently as she never heard (from) a book, neither (Walter) Hilton's book (*Scale of Perfection*), nor Bridget's book (*Liber Revelationum Celestium S. Birgitte*), nor *Stimulus of Love* nor *Fire of Love*, nor any other that ever she heard read that spoke so highy of the love of God ...)

These particular texts seem to have been Margery's touchstones, as they are mentioned again much later as books read to her by a priest along with the Bible and others for seven or eight years (I. 3389–96).

Multiaccentuality, Vološinov argues, creates dichotomies, and *The Book of Margery Kempe* certainly does that. As suggested, her treatise presents a main character who is difficult to like or accept. Thus, we are told 'this lytyl tretys schal tretyn sumdeel in parcel of [Jesus'] wonderful werkys, how mercyfully, how benyngly, and how charyte-fully he meved and stered a synful caytyf unto hys love' (I. 8–10: 'this little treatise will treat some part of Jesus' wonderful works, how mercifully, how benignly, and how charitably he moved and stirred a sinful captive unto his love'). Yet, a little later we learn, 'sche lost reson and her wyttes a long tym tyl ower Lord be grace restoryed her ageyn' (I. 22–3: 'she lost her reason and her wits for a long time until our Lord by grace restored her again'). And 'Sche was so usyd to be slawndred and repreved, to be cheden and rebuked of the world ... that it was to her in a maner of solas and comfort whan sche sufferyd ... for the lofe of God' (I. 33–6: 'She was so used to being slandered and reproved, to being chided and rebuked by the world ... that it was for her a kind of solace and comfort when she suffered ... for the love of God').

Although these statements are lodged in Margery's special relation with God, they raise the possibility that she was a difficult person. And, indeed, her neighbors essentially accuse her of bearing a holier-than-thou chip on her shoulder: 'And than was sche slawnderyd and reprevyd of mech pepul for sche kept so streyt a levyng' (I. 276–7: 'And then was she slandered and reproved by many people because she lived such an ascetic life'). Later in the narrative, even Christ appears to lose patience with her, 'A, dowtyr, how oftyntymes have I teld the that thy synnes arn forgove the and that we ben onyd togedyr wythowtyn ende?' (I. 1156–8: 'Ah, daughter, how many times have I told you that your sins are forgiven and that we will be united forever?').

Importantly, Margery is aware of her unconventional behavior. At one point, for example, she asks Christ why she must wail and cry. He responds that she must do his will so that his Godhead might be seen 'in a sympil sowle' (I. 4318: 'in a simple soul'). As these words intimate, Margery is often depicted in conversation with God, Christ and the Virgin Mary, who demand various tasks of her. She usually protests that people will revile her if she carries out the request, but she is always convinced to do the right thing as occurs when God tells her she should take a pilgrimage to Rome, Jerusalem and Compostella, a journey, by the way, that mirrors the pilgrimage taken by St Bridget. Moreover:

> 'And, dowtyr, I sey to the I wyl that thu were clothys of whyte and non other colowr, for thu schal ben arayd aftyr my wyl.' 'A, der Lord, yf I go arayd on other maner than other chast women don, I drede that the pepyl wyl slawndyr me. Thei wyl sey I am an ypocryt and wondryn upon me.' 'Ya, dowtyr, the more wondryng that thow hast for my lofe, the mor thu plesyst me.'
>
> (I. 732–6: 'And, daughter, I say to you I wish that you wear white clothes and no other color, for you shall be clothed after my wish.'

'Ah, dear Lord, if I go clothed in a different manner than other chaste women do, I fear that people will slander me. They will say that I'm a hypocrite and wonder about me.' 'Yay, daughter, the more wonder that you have for my love, the more you please me')

Although from the *diachronic* perspective her white clothing and her devotion transforms this *sympil sowle* into a sign of God's love in his narrative, from the *synchronic* perspective Margery's white clothes transform her into an out-of-date metaphor, a target for ridicule.

Reading mortal against divine text in this manner reinvigorates sleeping dichotomies. And *everything* in this narrative puts readers in the position of negotiating mortal against divine texts. For example, Margery's passion is (like Alisoun's) loud and theatrical. Thus, in Jerusalem:

> And, whan the body myth ne lengar enduryn the gostly labowr but was ovyr come wyth the unspekabyl lofe that wrowt so fervently in the sowle, than fel sche down and cryed wondyr lowde. And the mor that sche wolde labowryn to kepe it in er to put it away, mech the mor schulde sche cryen and the mor lowder.

> (I. 1609–12: And when her body couldn't bear the spiritual turmoil any longer but was overcome with the undescribable love that wrought so fervently in her soul, she fell down and cried wondrously loudly. And the more she tried to keep it in or do away with it, so much more she cried and all the more loudly.)

From the mortal perspective, this is precisely the kind of behavior that gets Margery excluded from different fellowships, even though she tries to be part of them. But from the divine perspective she becomes a special sign.

This is simplicity in the sense articulated by Augustine's treatise: everything conveys the single message of God's love. And this is telling. For acting as *simply* as she did in the narrative, Margery presents an enigma to all those who encounter her, one who has to be 'read' in one way or another – as possessed by demons or as stirred by God's love – whether *in the world of the narrative* or as one of its readers, whether in the mortal or the divine realm. In other words, *The Book of Margery Kempe* fictionalizes ideas found in treatises like *De Doctrina Christiana*: the lives we live are vignettes in the story *written by God*. Consequently, mortal authorship doesn't really matter. What is important is that one's life be *authored* as purely, simply and truthfully as possible.

Piers the Plowman

The Middle English allegorical narrative by William Langland (*c.* 1330–86), *Piers Plowman*, displays some overall similarities to Margery's. For example, it seems to share some Lollard ideas. Certainly, some of Langland's own contemporaries felt so, as they cited some of its passages in support of Lollard issues. On the other hand, there are some passages that could also be used to argue against such a reading. Thus, in the first vision of Dowel we encounter Dame Studie angry that her husband, Wit, instructed the Dreamer:

> Al starying dame Studie sturneliche sayde:
> 'Wel artow wyse,' quod she to Wyt, 'suche wysdomes to shewe
> To eny foel or to flaterere or to frentike peple! ...
> The lewed aȝen þe lered þe holy lore to dispute,
> And tellen of þe trinite how two slowe þe thridde
> And brynge forth ballede resones, taken Bernard to witnesse,
> And putten forth presumpcioun to preue þe sothe.

> [XI. 4–39: Staring hard, Lady Study sternly said, 'Well, aren't you the wise one', said she to Wit, 'to show such wisdom to any fool flatterer or frantics! (It's because of such carelessness that) the ignorant dispute against the learned over holy teachings, and claim of the trinity, that two killed the third, and (then) they apply empty reasoning, claim Bernard as an authority, and presume to demonstrate the truth.']

Underscoring the importance of being more than superficially familiar with authoritative texts, Lady Study basically argues against access to knowledge without training, a position that may express some concern with Lollard practice.

Whether to be read with reference to Lollardy or not, we are made to see that Lady Study's *authoritative, dogmatic* words have something to them. For almost immediately thereafter, the Dreamer is instructed to find Dowel. Along the way, he encounters Rechelesnesse, who appears in ragged clothes and traffics in half truths. At one point, the suddenness of a series of comparisons reveals dynamics we've seen before in *Sir Gawain and the Green Knight* and the *Wife of Bath*'s Prologue, with Rechelesnesse pronouncing the following:

> Then Marie Maudelene who myghte do worse
> As in likyng of lecherye, no lyf denyede?
> Or Dauid þe douhty þat deuyned how Vrye
> Mouhte sleylokeste be slawe and sent hym to worre,
> Lelly, as by his lokes, with a lettere of gyle?
> Poul þe apostel, that no pite ne hadde
> Cristene peple to culle to dethe?
> And now beth this seyntes, by that men saith, and
> souereynes in heuene,
> Tho that worste wrouhten þe while þat thei here were.
> By that þat Salamon saith hit semeth þat no wyht
> Woet ho is worthy for wele or for wykkede,
> Wheþer he is worthy to wele or to wykkede pyne.
> *Sunt iusti atque sapientes et opera eorum in manu dei sunt.*

[XI. 264–75: Then (what about) Mary Magdalene, who might do worse than enjoy lechery and denied no man? Or, David the mighty, who figured out how Uriah might be most slyly slain, and (so he) sent him to battle, appropriately, to all appearances, but with a letter full of guile? And Paul, the apostle, who had no sympathy in choosing (which) Christians were put to death? And now there are these saints, according to what people say, and rulers in heaven, who did the worst while they were here (on earth). It's as Solomon says: it seems that noone knows who is valued for good or evil, or whether one deserves good or evil pain. *There are just men and wise men and their works are in the hand of God* (Ecclesiastes 9.1).]

The literal level of these lines argues that if so many holy people participated in sinful behavior, what's the harm for the rest of us? Langland's audiences, however, are likely to be familiar with the stories referred to here and must have seen Rechelesnesse's allusions as a breezy manipulation of authoritative texts.

In this discussion of Langland's verse narrative, I'll be referring to the latest (the third) redaction by the author, which is known as the C-Text and dated at 1387. This influential allegory survives in 51 manuscripts and some fragments. The narrative itself is divided into a prologue and two sections, labelled in Latin: *Visio Willelmi de Petrus Plowman* (The Vision of William about Peter the Plowman) and *Vita de Dowel, Dobet et Dobest* (The Life of Do Well, Do Better, and Do

Best). Each part is subdivided further into smaller units known as *passus*, a term that means 'steps' or 'stages'. With a total of 7338 lines, *Piers Plowman* comprises nine passus in section one, and 13 in section two.

An allegory like that of *Piers Plowman* presents a story with personified abstractions as characters. Allegories may seem to be straightforward, and, indeed, for them to communicate, the relation between signifying character and signified must be clear. However, allegories can become complex when the narrative encourages the reader constantly to reconsider the relation between signifier and signified. For example, if I were to write a narrative that featured Love and Lust fighting each other for Innocent's heart, then the characters Love, Lust, and Innocent would have fictional reality as individuals, but from the get-go, we would also understand them to be abstractions. The art would be to see how I could reveal that traits of Love, Lust and Innocent sometimes overlap by means of complicating the characters' relations.

Throughout the period under study here, allegory is a standard of the literary system that survives well after as well. Just beyond this period, for example, *Dr Faustus* presents an allegorically-coded scene portraying the seven deadly sins (scene 5). And the seven deadlies are even integral to the plot of a 1995 movie starring Brad Pitt, *Se7en*. Codified by Gregory the Great (d. 604) in the manifestation that has become standard, the top seven mortal failings are: pride, envy, anger, lechery, avarice, gluttony and sloth (Bloomfield 1952). Langland, too, introduces the seven vices in Passus VI and VII, among which my personal favorite is Sloth:

> Thenne cam Sleuthe al byslobered with two slimed yes.
> 'Y moste sitte to be shryue or elles sholde y nappe …
> Y can nat parfitly my *pater-noster* as þe prest hit syngeth.
> Y can rymes of Robyn Hode and of Randolf erle of Chestre …
> Y am occuepied vch a day, haliday and oþere,
> With ydele tales at þe ale and oþer-while in chirches.'

> [VII. 1–19: Then came Sloth all slobbery with two slimy eyes. 'I gotta sit to be confessed or else I'll fall asleep … I don't know my *pater-noster* as well as the priest sings it. I do know rhymes about Robin Hood and Randolph, the Earl of Chester: I'm so occupied every day, holidays and others, with useless stories at ale-houses and sometimes in churches.']

While some of you might join me in a chuckle here, it's important to note too that Langland ties even this portrait to learning and interpretation, or rather to Sloth's inability to do either effectively. More to the point, Langland presents the seven deadlies as they confess their sins in the new, ideal kingdom, thereby eliciting a pause from readers and a reconsideration of the relation between signified and signifier: what does it mean when a sin confesses itself clean?

Similar to the presentation of the seven vices, the immediate theme of *Piers Plowman* is relatively straightforward: society has too eagerly embraced material goods and become enamoured of power, necessitating a return to the path of Truth. The theme is articulated, at times, with expository clarity. For example, the ideal Christian is a person who translates theology into activity, as exemplified by Piers the Plowman, who is first introduced rather late, at Passus VII, 182–4. As the narrator states:

> Alle libbyng laborers þat lyuen with here handes
> Lellyche and lauhfollyche, oure lord Treuthe hem graunteth
> Pardoun perpetuel, riht as Peres the plouhman.

> (IX. 58-60: All living workers who live with their hands truly and lawfully, to them our Lord Truth grants perpetual pardon, right as with Piers the Plowman.)

There is very little ambiguity here.

Messages conveyed by allegorical means in Langland's story can also be pretty literal, in a figurative kind of way. For example, Pier's wife is named Worch-when-tyme-is; his daughter, Do-rihte-so-or-thy-dame-shal-þe-bete; and his son, Soffre-thy-souereynes-have-her-wille-deme-hem-nay-yf-thow-doest-thow-shalt-hit-dere-abygge (VIII, 80–3: Work-when-it's-called-for; Do-right-or-your-Lady-will-beat-you; Allow-your-lords-their-will-judge-them-not-for-if-you-do-you-shall-pay-for-it-dearly). The names are meant pretty literally, although they are intended to convey a figurative message, something like: the work-focused Christian has good habits in his or her life.

In addition to clarity in quasi-expository lines and allegorical figures, the narrative's *action* also seems relatively uncomplicated as it follows the Dreamer in his encounters with various characters. Thus, Passus I ends with Holy Church explaining the Dream experienced by Will, who happens to have the same first name as the author, but she explains it in a way that leaves the Dreamer clueless. Passus II begins with his asking her for more help, and so she instructs him to look over his left shoulder. There he sees the richly dressed, beautiful Lady Mede (Lady Reward). She is to be married to Fals Faythlesse (False Faithless) the very next day, but as the next two passus reveal, the marriage is hindered, mainly by Theology, the King and his two advisors, Conscience and Kynde Wytt (*Kynde Wytt* meaning something like 'innate intelligence').

Conscience and Kynde Wytt finally defeat Lady Mede, who is chastised by the King for encouraging lawyers to manipulate language for their own ends. Lady Mede simply doesn't get it, though. She can't help using her charms and wealth to win people over to her side, somewhat in the manner of Mae West lasciviously uttering, 'Oh, why don't you come up and see me some time, big boy.' For example, even while on trial, Lady Mede displays her alluring powers:

> Mede in the mot-halle tho on men of lawe gan wynke
> In signe þat thei sholde with som sotil speche
> Reherce ther anon ryhte þat myhte Resoun stoppe.

(IV. 148–50: Meed in the council hall then began to wink at the men of law to signify that they should there make some subtle speech right away so that Reason might be stopped.)

And even though she is defeated, she leaves with two officials of the Church – a *sysour* (an assize-man) and a *somnour* (summoner) – who, we can guess, will have few defenses against her seductive ways.

I won't treat the second section in detail here, which essentially recapitulates the same themes in different forms. *Dowel* comes to mean knowing what kinds of questions can be asked without blathering on and on about subjects for which one only has partial knowledge. The Dreamer's glimpse of Piers the Plowman in Passus XV suggests the epiphany that Truth allows and emphasizes again the importance of the active life (*activa vita*) allowed through God's gift of free will (*liberium arbitrium*). Christ's life is recounted, as well as the history of the Church, with the admonition that Truth must always be pursued. And in the last passus, Langland brings the vision up to fourteenth-century England, depicting his country and his times as a land beset by Anti-Christ, the seven deadlies, and corrupt friars.

As simple as the narrative action may be, *Piers Plowman* also treats and conveys the ambiguity that defines the mortal realm. For example, *per se*, Mede does nothing evil, even though she traffics in material reward and thus easily slips into the mores of the worldly, as evidenced in the court scene just mentioned. This kind of ambiguity is actually referred to after her wedding plans are ruined, when the King tries to cheer her up by suggesting that she marry Conscience, who, however, vehemently opposes the match. She retorts with words from Solomon, which essentially praise generosity, and Conscience responds to her attempt in this manner:

> Thow art lyk a lady þat a lessoun radde,
> Was *omnia probate*, þat plesede here herte;
> That line was no lengur and at þe leues ende.
> Ac hadde she loked in þe luft half and þe lef turned
> A sholde haue y fonde folynge felle wordes aftur,
> *Quod bonum est tenete*, a tixst of Treuthes makynge.

> [III. 487–92: You're like a lady who read a passage, which was, 'Try everything', which pleased her heart; the line was no longer and at the page's end. But had she looked on the left side (after having) turned the page, she would have found the following harsh words thereafter, 'Hold on to that which is good', a text composed by Truth.]

Showing how Lady Mede's ambiguity stems from partial knowledge, Conscience expresses this idea through *metaliterary* terms *in the world of the narrative*. But Langland also demonstrates the same message *for his readers*, also through Conscience, just about 140 lines earlier:

> That is god the ground of al, a graciouse antecedent.
> And man is relatif rect yf he be rihte trewe:
> He acordeth with Crist in kynde, *Verbum caro factum est* ...

> [III. 353–5: God is the foundation of all, a gracious antecedent. And man is in direct relation to Him, if he will be truly correct: he is in harmony with Christ in gender, (Christ who was) 'The Word made flesh' (John 1: 14).]

On the narrative level, this seems a dubious reason not to marry an attractive woman, especially since the King thinks it's a good idea. We can surmise that what is meant is that a good conscience can never function well when money's in the picture. But why the terminology of grammar? *In the world of the narrative*, a figurative analogy is drawn which translates into something like this: a mortal is like an adjective which should be in harmonious relation to Christ, both of whom are preceded by the antecedent God. Not only does an allegorical figure speak figuratively here, but this message doesn't seem to fit the situation.

Conscience's use of the Bible in both quotes functions *on the narrative level* pretty much in Vološinov's *linear* mode of the *authoritarian dogmatic* variety. He wants to win the argument. *For Langland's readers*, however, the use of a grammatical analogy in conjunction with the biblical text seems to function (at first) pretty much in *interorientation* mode of the *realistic and critical individualistic* kind. Conscience depicts God's relation to humanity and then supports the depiction by recourse to Scriptures. Since God created the universe by means of his language, and since humanity is made in God's image, we are not only instances of his language, we also have mortal language with which to create.

When, according to Augustine, Adam and Eve disregarded God's words and tasted the apple, they were not only ejected from the Garden of Eden – everything changed, and language no longer corresponded one-to-one with meaning. Language became more diverse still when pride overcame Nimrod the Hunter who thought he would challenge God by building a great tower from which he could strike at the Creator. However, the Tower of Babel was never completed since God dispersed communication by creating various languages, and the workers could no longer understand one another (Genesis 11, 1–9). When Christ entered time and the mortal world, things changed once again. Not only were mortals able to enter Paradise and redeem themselves if they followed Christ's example (lived *in imitatione Dei*), language, too, was redeemed. Christ spoke in parables which made use of language's ambiguity and the mortal tendency to demand variety to bring home the message, 'love God'. And just as Eve is the antetype to the Virgin, so too the Tower of Babel is the antetype to Pentecost which celebrates the moment when the Holy Spirit descended upon the disciples after Christ's crucifixion, and no matter what language was spoken all understood the message.

Like Gawain, we are nudged to go beyond what we see in the present moment to get the big picture. A marriage of Conscience to Lady Mede would not only corrupt moral judgment *per se*, in any individual's case it would also skew the basic relation between mortal and God, a relation created by language. Indeed, this marriage would influence a mortal to live in his or her special kind of ambiguity, the ambiguity of the world, where only half the truth is known, where only the surface is taken into consideration, where only one page is read without continuing on to the next. Such a relation would prevent us, then, from understanding how to interpret (grammar, part II: *enarratio poetarum*), because the basic relations are not put together correctly (grammar, part I: *recte loquendi*).

By returning to the Prologue to *Piers Plowman*, we can see that this is one of Langland's major themes from the beginning. The Prologue presents Will, a persona for the author, narrating a dream vision he experienced in spring. Dressed as a hermit – although without good deeds to his credit and hence suggesting that appearances deceive – the narrator relates:

> Ac on a May mornyng on Maluerne hulles
> Me biful for to slepe...
> And merueylousliche me mette, as y may telle,
> Al þe welthe of the world and þe wo bothe
> Wynkyng, as hit were, witterliche y sigh hit;
> Of treuthe and tricherye, tresoun and gyle,
> Al y say slepynge, as y shall telle.

> (Prologue, 6–13: But on a May morning, on Malverne's hills, I fell asleep...And marvelously I dreamed, as I will tell, of all the goods of the world and the woes as well, with sleeping eyes, as it were, truly I saw it; of truth and treachery, treason and guile, all I saw sleeping, as I shall tell.)

In the east, he sees the Tower where Truth abides, and in the west, a darker scenario where Death rules. In between the two there is 'A fair feld ful of folk... Of alle manere' (Prologue, 19-20: A fair field full of people... of all kinds). In relating this vision, the Dreamer also records the first of many barbs aimed at Church officials who've become much too interested in the world:

> I fonde þer of freris alle þe foure ordres,
> Prechyng þe peple for profyt of þe wombe,
> And glosede þe gospel as hem good likede...

> [56–8: I thus found friars of all the four orders (Dominicans, Franciscans, Austin friars and Carmelites), preaching to the people

for profit of their bellies, and glossing the gospel as they well pleased...]

But he also meets Conscience and Kynde Witt along the way. Kynde Witt introduces an analogy about a 'route of ratones' (Prologue, 165: 'group of rats'), who are determined to bell the cat. A mouse, however, advises that even if they do succeed, another cat will come along, so that it's best – in today's idiom – to let sleeping dogs lie.

Ordinarily, a prologue is articulated in the persona of a poet addressing his or her readers. Frequently, it will begin with a *sententia* (a proverb), it might tell who or what circumstances inspired the narrative, and it almost always – directly or indirectly – lets readers know how talented the poet is. Here, the Prologue begins, as we might anticipate, with the poet speaking to his audience. However, already in the first five lines we see that the poet has slipped into another persona, that of a hermit who hasn't actually done the things a hermit is supposed to do (live like an ascetic, pray and worship). Rather than presenting material in expository manner, this persona for the poet creates another fictional world and, in that fictional world this persona is a fraud. That world in and of itself generates another world, as the poet as Dreamer depicts himself in a dream meeting *allegorical* characters – Conscience and Kynde Witt – who, in the waking life of the narrator, are traits belonging (presumably) to the narrator himself. Finally, that dream world generates yet another world, when Kynde Witt introduces talking rats and mice who wish to better their lives.

Here, Langland uses various literary conventions in a space where expository discourse is anticipated. In doing so, he creatively introduces the themes that will occupy Will, the Dreamer, for the entire 22 passus: the corruption of the world, the need for Conscience and Kynde Wytt to guide society's relations, the necessity for Truth to win over Death, and the importance of a fair government (as suggested by the plight of the rats and mice). More subtly, Langland implies that the dream world and our actual world are not as distinct as we might think, as we will learn, in large part due to Lady Mede's alluring ways. If we are asleep to what God offers mortals, we might paraphrase, we are living in a dream. The substantial world is that which we cannot see, but which will outlast the transient stage upon which we act out our lives ... a key tenet of platonic and neoplatonic thought so critical to the literary system stemming from the Middle Ages (Wetherbee

1972). And the theme is introduced again at the very beginning of the first passus:

> What the montaigne bymeneth and þe merke dale
> And þe feld ful of folk y shal ʒou fair shewe.
> A louely lady of lere in lynnene yclothed
> Cam doun fro þe castel and calde me by name
> And sayde, 'Wille, slepestou? seestow þis peple,
> Hou bisy þei ben aboute þe mase?
> The moste party of this peple þat passeth on þis erthe,
> Haue thei worschip in this world, thei wilneth no bettere;
> Of othere heuene then here thei halde no tale.'

[1–9: What the mountain means and the dark dale and the field full of people, I shall show you well. A lovely lady of learning clothed in linen came down from the castle and called me by name, and said, 'Will, are you sleeping? Do you see these people, how busy they are about in the maze? (For) the greater part of these people that live on this earth, if they have honor in this world, they don't want anything better; of other heaven than here they take no account.']

Not only is meaning, underlying meaning, the explicit concern of the Dreamer, as seen in line two, the lovely lady – who is introduced some lines later as Holy Church – draws attention to these lines insofar as it seems she will offer the explanation.

But in doing so, Holy Church transforms the flow of individuals into a scene which she invests with *indexical* value. According to Peirce, who was introduced in the last chapter, there are many different subdivisions for a sign or *representamen*. The one that has become most popularly associated with the American philosopher is the trichotomy of *icon*, *index* and *symbol*.

> An *Icon* is a sign which refers to the Object that it denotes merely by virtue of characters of its own, and which it possesses, just the same, whether any such Object actually exists or not ... An *Index* is a sign which refers to the Object that it denotes by virtue of being really affected by that Object ... A *Symbol* is a sign which refers to the Object that it denotes by virtue of a law, usually an association of general ideas, which operates to cause the Symbol to be interpreted as referring to that Object. (Innis 1985, 8–10)

Peirce gives the following examples to clarify what he means: a pencil streak representing a nonexistent line is an *icon*; a bullet hole is an *index*, and any speech utterance is a *symbol*. While there may be areas of overlap, this trichotomy becomes useful particularly when looking at *indices*.[3]

Thus, Holy Church transforms the scene into a sign by using index-laden words that point to specific instances: 'seestow þis peple,' 'Hou bisy þei ben,' 'on þis erthe,' 'in *this* world.' Since these *indices* are also speech utterances, of course, they are also symbols. But, more importantly, they exhibit the three traits Peirce argues belong to all indices, but which no index has absolutely: they do not significantly resemble their objects; they refer to specific objects, whether individual objects or groups perceived as a single grouping; and the signs direct attention to their objects (Innis 1985, 13). The effect of the *index* is to focus a reader's attention.

Within this heightened scene, Holy Church also uses a metaphor – *þe mase* – to suggest that people who live in the world live in confusion. In other words, at any single point in time and space, individuals may think they are travelling along the right path, but if they're not careful, like Gawain, they will lack the overview that would allow them to understand they are trapped in a maze and consequently kept from reaching their true goal.

Thus, looking at many different individuals who don't belong to anything as coherent as an image or a narrative, Holy Church transforms them into an *index*, grouping them into a single, simple, meaningful unit and then shifts perspectives on this index, by means of a metaphor, a shift that in effect generates a narrative. In doing so, Holy Church foreshadows Conscience's grammar-centered analogy for a mortal's proper relation to God. For God created the universe through language; each mortal is an instance of that language, and in its totality humankind will tell the same story, in another version, that the Bible tells, the story of God's creation. What else could Holy Church see but this story?

Also illustrating the same point, Langland blurs these series of fictional worlds and stories through the narrator, whose waking and sleeping states are difficult to keep apart. In this dream, for example, he meets Holy Church, who explains – during his dream – what his dream means. In Passus II, moreover, after Holy Church indexically instructs the Dreamer to watch what happens to Lady Mede, the narrator reports, 'Thus left me that lady lyggynge as aslepe/ And y say how Mede was married, metyng as it were ...' (II. 53–4: 'Thus that lady left me lying in my sleep, and I saw how Mede was married, dreaming as it were'). Not only does Holy Church explain in his dream what Will has seen, but Will also sees himself sleeping, having his dream. Likewise, at the beginning of Passus V, the Dreamer records, 'Thus y awakede...' (V. 1: 'Thus I awoke'), only then to engage – presumably in his waking state – in a conversation with a character called Reason. Just as complexly, the following lines in Passus IX, which record the moment when Piers the Plowman reads the pardon, the Dreamer is suddenly present, as a character who pops in alongside a priest:

> And Peres at his preyre the pardon vnfoldeth
> And y byhnde hem bothe byheld alle þe bulle
> In two lynes as hit lay and nat a lettre more,
> And was ywryte ryhte thus in witnesse of Treuthe:
> *Qui bona egerunt ibunt in vitam eternam;*
> *Qui uero mala in ignem eterum.*
>
> [IX. 284–9: And Piers, at his asking, unfolded the pardon, and I behind them both beheld the entire bull; in two lines as it was laid out and not a letter more, and it was written right thus in witness of Truth: 'They who've done good will walk in eternal life; those who've done evil in eternal fire'. (Athanasian creed)]

The lines here cascade language's ambiguities into all levels of the narrative. And if we hadn't begun to wonder about the blurring of levels by now, at this point the narrator tells us how the priest and Piers argued over their words so loudly they woke him and caused him to ponder his dream (IX. 294–303).

Like *The Book of Margery Kempe*, *Piers Plowman* fictionalizes treatise-related themes. Illustrating rather than declaiming, both authors allow for *multiaccentuality*, and in their own ways encourage the *relativistic, individualistic* decomposition of authorial context. Using fictional forms to convey their multiaccentual ideas, these treatises are openly religious and perhaps covertly political. The final three treatises to be briefly introduced here – *The Mirror for Magistrates, Speke Parott* and *Report and Discourse of the Affaires and State of Germany* – share their predeliction for using fictional forms to convey treatise-related material, but they do so overtly confirming the political, and sometimes hiding the religious, *accents* of the time.

The Mirror for Magistrates

This narrative presents a collection of tales that illustrate what goes into making a good monarch, thereby in effect fictionalizing the tenets associated with *Fürstenspiegel*, such as Elyot's *Boke Named the Gouernour*. First printed in 1559, *The Mirror* seems to have been composed by various writers. Although the printer addresses William Baldwin (fl. 1547) as the principal contributor, other known contributors include George Ferrers (*c.* 1500–79), Thomas Chaloner (1521–65), and Thomas Phaer (*c.* 1510–60). Its presentation of the divine right of kings as both an ecclesiastical and political necessity fits well into its times, but *The Mirror* had its influential predecessors as well, such as *De Casibus Virorum Illustrium* by Giovanni Boccaccio (1313–75), which was loosely translated by John Lydgate (*c.* 1370–1449) as *The Fall of Princes* via a French translation of the Latin original. Presenting exemplary stories of 'princes', the tales in these collections in effect allegorize or universalize the historical and the particular – they appropriate texts with a clear notion of what is worthy of emulation and what isn't. Indeed, *The Mirror*'s first preface begins with this tradition-rich admonition:

> Plato among many other of his notable sentences concerning the government of a common weale, hath this: 'Well is that realme governed, in which the ambicious desyer not to beare office'. (63)

Thus, *The Mirror* begins in *interorientation* mode, of the *realistic and critical individualistic* kind, to comment on Plato's good sense.

Commentary becomes a framing motif in this narrative as, between the stories, 'intermezzos' occur between an editor and a reader who chat about the presentations. Thus, during these exchanges the *interorientation* mode slips into a kind of *relativistic individualism*, as boundaries between narrative and authorial context are blurred. For example, in the second part of the tale collection, which is focused on exemplifying the malevolent machinations of Richard III, the two comment on the story of Lord Hastings, before the reader asks the editor if he possesses the tragedy of the murder of Edward's two sons:

> No surely (quoth I) The Lord Vaulx vndertooke to penne it, but what he hath done therein I am not certayne, & therfor I let it passe til I knowe farder. I haue here the duke of Buckingham, king Richardes

chyefe instrument, wrytten by mayster Thomas Sackuille. Read it we pray you sayd they [the readers]: with a good wyl (quoth I) but fyrst you shal heare his preface or Induction. (297)

As if conversing in a private library, the two *literati* invite readers to partake of their *literary* perusal of historical figures of the near-contemporary English past. Thus, the tale the editor refers to here begins with a meditation on the turning of the seasons, before it proceeds to its subject, the fall of princes or peers (pieres), the seasons and the turning of fortune's wheel thus being brought into association with each other and the way of the world.

> That musing on this worldly wealth in thought,
> which comes and goes more faster than we see
> The flyckering flame that with the fyer is wrought,
> My busie minde presented vnto me
> Such fall of pieres as in this realme had be:
> That ofte I wisht some would their woes descryue.
> To warne the rest whom fortune left aliue. (300: 64–70)

The tale then begins with its narrator meeting a withered woman full of woe and dressed in black, the goddess Sorrow, who will guide him to see the fates of the powerful.

Led by an allegorical figure, the tale's narrator comes to a hideous hole of endless depth, where he sees various figures like Remorse and Dread, along with conquerors like Pompey, Priam and Hector. The narrator is particularly struck by Troy's fate, 'But Troy alas (me thought) aboue them all,/ It made myne iyes in very teares consume' (313: 435–6). Those who suffer most are those imprisoned on Fortune's wheel, and first among them is Henry, Duke of Buckingham (317: 533). After declaring how difficult it is to tell the Duke's tale, he nonetheless does, with the clear message that siding with a tyrant such as Richard III was the worst possible path the Duke could have taken.

Reminiscent of Dante's *Inferno*, the characters met by this narrator are forced to tell their stories to him. Thus, *in the world of the narrative*, the narrator-pilgrim listens to utterances encouraged by *dialogue* and aimed at moving him to sorrow while admonishing him on the importance of ethos over policy. *For readers*, however, what is witnessed are instances of *quasi-direct* discourse, since although we get the tale from the teller's mouth, so to speak, *authorial accents* are easily detectable. For instance, in the intermezzo preceding Richard III's tale, our narrator declares it important to relate his story, awful as it is, and he *instructs* the reader: 'For the better vnderstanding whereof, imagine that you see him tormented with Dives in the diepe pit of Hell, and thence howlinge this that foloweth' (359). After this instance of *interorientation* of the *realistic and critical individualistic* variety, Richard III begins the tale as follows:

> What hart so hard, but doth abhorre to heare
> The ruful raygne of me the thyrd Rychard?
> King vnkindely cald though I the crowne dyd weare,
> Who entred by rigour, but ryght did not regard,
> By tyranny proceding in kyllyng kyng Edward,
> Fyft of that name, ryght heyre vnto the crowne,
> With Rychard his brother, prynces of renowne. (360: 1–7)

Richard III's tale, moreover, is focused on the murder of the children and on his desire for power and battle, before drawing the appropriate conclusion at Bosworth:

> My body it was hurryed and tugged like a Dogge,
> On horsebacke all naked and bare as I was borne.
> My head, handes, & feete, downe hanging like a Hogge,
> With dyrt and bloud besprent, my corps al to torne,
> Cursing the day that ever I was borne.
> With greuous woundes bemangled most horrible to se
> So sore they did abhorre this my vile crueltye. (370: 281–7)

Richard ends by declaring himself, univocally, an example of how not to rule:

> See here the fine and fatall fall of me,
> And guerdon due for this my wretched deede,
> Whych to all prynces a myrrour nowe may be
> That shal this tragicall story after reede,
> Wyshyng them all by me to take heede,
> And suffer ryght to rule as it is reason,
> For Time trieth out both truth and also treason. (370: 302–8)

Like Elyot's treatise, a clear lesson is articulated about the use and

abuse of power, but like the narratives of Margery Kempe and William
Langland, this is accomplished through the vehicle of fiction.

Interestingly, this second section of *The Mirror* also appropriates
anti-feminist treatise material, but unlike *The Wife of Bath's Prologue*
and *Sir Gawain and the Green Knight*, it confirms the *uniaccentual*
position in two negative examples: Dame Eleanor Cobham, the
Duchess of Gloucester, who is portrayed as having exercised witch-
craft, and Jane Shore, who is portrayed in shades of Eve. Placing
herself in the framework of the powerful, she seems at first, however,
to offer a tale that positions her as *equal* to the men who grasp at
fortune's gifts:

> Among the rest by Fortune overthrowen,
> I am not least, that most may wayle her fate:
> *My fame and brute abrode the world is blowen,*
> Who can forget a thing thus done so late?
> *My great mischaunce, my fall, and heauye state,*
> Is such a marke whereat eche tounge doth shoote,
> That my good name is pluckt vp by the roote ...
> In Fortunes frekes who trustes her when she smyles,
> Shal fynde her false, and full of fyckle toyes,
> Her tryumphes al but fyl our eares wyth noyse,
> Her flatteryng gyftes are pleasures myxt wyth payne.
> Yea al her wordes are thunders threatnyng rayne.
>
> (373: 1–14, my italics)

But upon listening to her tale, we learn that her access to power is due
to her appearance, the fact of which persuaded her parents to marry
her off too early:

> But cleare from blame my frendes can not be found,
> Before my time my youth they did abuse:
> In maryage, a prentyse was I bound,
> When that meere love I knewe not howe to vse.
> But wealaway, that can not me excuse,
> The harme is mine though they deuysed my care,
> And I must smart and syt in slaundrous snare. (377: 106–12)

Moreover, she became the King's mistress through the same 'virtue',
and was thus able to influence him to do her will (even though she
often did so for the benefit of others):

Yf iustice sayd that iudgement was but death,
With my sweete wordes I could the kyng perswade,
And make him pause and take therein a breath,
Tyl I wyth suyte the fawtors peace had made. (379: 176–9)

In the end she died in poverty, without support and without her
beauty: 'What fall was this, to come from Princes fare,/ To watche for
crummes among the blinde and lame?' (385: 358–9). Although there is
no explicit comparison to Eve, using her body and language to influence men's actions marks Jane Shore as one of Eve's 'heirs'.

Like the narratives presented by Margery Kempe and William
Langland, *The Mirror for Magistrates* continues to hammer home a
straightforward message in fictional guise. It is the shaping of the
surface, the *delectare*, that makes the *docere* palatable. The same
could be said for John Skelton's *Speke Parott*, which uses a talking
parrot to comment on his immediate contemporaries.

John Skelton's *Speke Parott*

John Skelton was born around 1460, maybe in Yorkshire. Having
received a laureate (either a university degree in grammar, rhetoric
and versification or an honorific title) in 1488 from Oxford (about
which he wrote in *Garland of Laurel*), in 1492 from Louvain
University, and in 1493 from Cambridge, Skelton was considered one
of the intellectuals to note during his lifetime. If known to readers
today, however, it is usually for his 'skeltonic' verse, highly alliterative
short, rhymed lines. Nonetheless, he also tutored Prince Henry from
about 1496–1501, and from about 1503 until his death on 21 June 1529
he was rector in Diss, Norfolk.

Skelton was a scholar, poet and playwright influenced by the literary system of the late middle ages, but one, like the authors of *Mirror
for Magistrates* or Thomas Elyot, who wrote on political themes as
well. For example, while Henry VIII besieged French Thérouanne in
1513, France's allies, the Scottish, were defeated and King James IV
killed at Flodden Field by English forces under the command of
Thomas Howard, Earl of Surrey. To celebrate the victory, Skelton
wrote *A Ballade of the Scottysshe Kynge* and the more detailed *Agaynst
the Scottes*. With at times a very heavy hand, Skelton appeared deeply
concerned about the political and cultural events of his times,

concerns which emerge in his satirical *Speke Parott*, composed in autumn 1521, and introduced here as found in British Library MS Harley 2552.

The poem's 520 lines center on a brightly colored parrot, taught to speak in several languages. Alternating among the voices of the parrot-narrator, an omniscient narrator, and the lover-parrot of Galathea, the poem contains phrases in a number of languages: Greek, Latin, French, German, Italian and Spanish. Moreover, it alludes to various poets, among them, Ovid and Boccaccio: Ovid's *Amores* (II. vi) also features a pet parrot, Psittacus, and in Boccaccio's *De Genealogia Deorum* (IV. xlix), Psyttacus appears as the son of Deucalion and Pyrrha (the couple who survived the flood in the first book of Ovid's *Metamorphoses*). In this parade of learning, Skelton even refers to himself, '*Secundum Skeltonida famigeratum*' (231: 'according to the famous Skelton').

Beginning harmlessly enough, the parrot introduces himself and describes how people encourage him to speak, hence the title of the poem, 'With, "Speke, Parott, I pray yow", full curteslye they say' (13). He goes on to claim that he was blessed by Lady Philology – an allegorical figure whose name means, 'love of knowledge':

> My lady mastres, Dame Phylology,
> Gave me a gyfte in my neste when I lay,
> To lerne all langage and hyt to speke aptlye. (43–5)

'Dropping' pearls of wisdom throughout the poem, the parrot also quotes people who speak to him:

> '*Que pensez-voz*, Parrot? What meneth this besynes?'
> *Vitulus* in Oreb troubled Arons brayne;
> Melchisedeck mercyfull made Moloc mercyles. (58–60)

On the literal level, these lines allude to the Old Testament book of Exodus (22. 1–24), which records how the Jews, leaving Egypt for the promised land, lost faith. On Mount Horeb ('Oreb' in the poem), Aaron collected their gold to make an idol, a golden calf (*vitulus* meaning 'bull-calf'), which angered God and led him to punish his people. The third line above also refers to the Old Testament (Genesis 14. 18–20). Melchizedek is a priest-king who was used by Skelton in *Agaynst the Scottes* to refer to Henry VIII, while Moloch is a pagan bull-god (I Kings 11. 5 and II Kings 23.13). According to the notes of John Scattergood's edition, both Aaron and Moloch refer to Cardinal Wolsey (c. 1475–1530), who allied himself with the Emperor against the King. The former reference stresses his neglect of religious duty and the latter suggests that if Henry VIII isn't more careful, Moloch/Wolsey will prevail. Indeed, Skelton mentions the bull-calf again later in the poem, in lines that express the hope that the King will not be wrongly ruled (347–52). In other words, with strong authorial *accents*, Skelton does what Elyot admonishes statesmen to do: advise the monarch.

Although a political thread thus appears in this poem, what seems to occupy Skelton most insistently here is the newfangled approach to pedagogy furthered by the Humanists. Indeed, the poem ends with a dialogue between Galathea and Parrot about the sorry state of learning in the country (447–8). Likewise, commenting on the parrot's use of Greek, the narrator expresses reluctance at the energy expended in the academy on the learning of this language (*Greci fari*), which puts the learning of Latin (*Latinum fari*) and logic's syllogism (*silogisari*) at danger, not to mention the *trivium* and *quadrivium* (tryvyals and quatryvyals):

> In *Achademia* Parrot dare no probleme kepe,
> For *Greci fari* so occupyeth the chayre,
> That *Latinum fari* may fall to rest and slepe,
> And *silogisari* was drowned at Sturbrydge Fayre;
> Tryvyals and quatryvyals so sore now they appayre,
> That Parrot the popagay hath pytye to beholde
> How the rest of good lernyng is roufled up and trold.
>
> (162–8, his italics)

Concerned with the worsening (appayre) of learning and how it's messed up (roufled, trold), the narrator extols the type of learning that had set the agenda for centuries.

Indeed, alluding to grammar's *auctores*, Donatus and Priscian, along with others (169 ff.), he mourns the neglect of the oldies but goodies. But Skelton also disrupts this simple message. For example, in what appears to be an ironic tone, two stanzas are devoted to the parrot's mystification of the obvious (190-203), which functions as a shield (*pavys*) to protect him: '*metaphora, alegoria* withall,/ Shall be his protectyon, his pavys and his wall' (202–3, his italics). Likewise, in line 233, Galathea and Parrot begin speaking of love, conveying the 'juicy bits' in Latin (269), before the narrator sends four envoys (messages), intercalated with multilingual comments, even though, usually, only one envoy ends a poem to send it on its way to a hopefully happy fate.

As may be surmised from this overview, the bulk of this multiply-stranded treatise in fictional form incorporates material in *interorientation* mode of the *realistic and critical individualistic* variety. The authorial *accents* are clearly satirical and univocal: as an example of satirical political allegory, *Speke Parott* attempts to squash any other possible viewpoint. In contrast, Roger Ascham's report on Germany also treats directly contemporary events, but does so in the language of expository prose. Its prose, however, makes stories out of recent events, and foreshadows a number of traits we tend to associate with journalism.

Roger Ascham's *Report and Discourse of the Affaires and State of Germany*

Roger Ascham (1515–68), the scholar quoted in the last chapter in need of patronage, is probably best known for his *Scholemaster*. A Tudor Humanist, he was also Queen Elizabeth's tutor and personal Latin secretary and wrote admiringly of her erudition. Although he tried to put to practice the classical precepts for being a good statesman, Ascham was not, apparently, very successful. He was a scholar first and a courtier second.

The Report and Discourse of the Affaires and State of Germany was written in 1553, but it was not printed until after Ascham's death in about 1570. It is framed as a letter written in response to John Astely's request for information on affairs abroad. And while it has some of the features of an epistle, it actually more prominently conveys the concerns of a *Fürstenspiegel*. The main difference is that *The Report* uses contemporary events to illustrate the traps and problems of governance, the vicissitudes of fortune, and the need for ethical advisors. For example, we learn by means of a principle and its exemplification that France acts without honor. Thus, while reporting of the Prince of Salerno's sudden enmity to the Emperor, Ascham 'digresses' on the principle that a generous monarch should win the hearts of his people and not over-tax them, finding support in classical authorities and history, in the *linear* mode of the *authoritarian dogmatic* species. He then exemplifies, 'And therfore haue I heard wisemen discommend the gouernement in *Fraunce* in makyng theyr people almost slaues' (141). The inference is pretty clear.

Ascham evinces a similar open distaste for *anything* the Pope does, along with only slightly veiled dissatisfaction with the Emperor, who, Ascham avers, hears only what he wants to hear (137). Indeed, at times, the Emperor appears to be a ninny, a self-centered brute, and an indecisively myopic policy-maker. Thus, Ascham has this to report regarding the Pope's manipulation of the ninny Emperor (aiming at two birds with one stone), 'The Emperour good man yet agayne trustyng him who so spightfully had deceaued hym' (139). Likewise, with regard to the Prince of Salerno's enmity, Ascham gives the self-centered brute the blame: 'I haue heard some in this Court say, which loue the Emperour well and serue him in good place, that their master hath done the Prince so much wrong, as he could do no lesse then he dyd' (140). So too, the Emperor's indecisive and myopic rule does more harm than good: after informing the Protestant Duke John Frederick by writ that he was to be executed – in hopes of convincing the Duke's followers to turn to Catholicism – the Emperor is surprised to learn of the Duke's cool response, who continued with his chess game, 'as though he had receiued some priuate letter of no great importance', and consequently, 'The Emperour (I doubt not) chiefly moued by God: secondly of his great wisedome and naturall clemency, when he vnderstode his meruelious constancie chaunged his purpose and reuoked the write' (154).

In portraying such negative examples of statesmanship, Ascham makes Livy, whom he and Astely had read together, his guide, stating, 'we concluded both what was in our opinion to be looked for at his hand that would well and aduisedly write an history: First, point was, to write nothyng false: next, to be bold to say any truth, wherby is auoyded two great faultes, flattery and hatred' (126). Drawing on classical *auctores* and biblical references, Ascham goes on to point out that an analysis must be scrupulously conducted to include the 'causes, counsels, actes, and issues in all great attemptes' (*ibid.*). But it is most important to evaluate and not simply list what causes are just and what aren't, which counsels are wise and which are rash, which acts are courageous and which are not, and finally, with regard to the issue or outcome, what lesson is to be noted. Likewise, accuracy in chronology is important as is the lively description of places along with the inner and the outer disposition of persons. The style should be plain, yet higher and lower as fits the material. Moreover, the depiction should be realistic: 'A man shal thincke not to be readyng but present in doyng of the same' (*ibid.*). Ascham then praises the writing of several writers for displaying such traits, considers Livy the best, and states, 'Syr *Thomas More* in that pamphlet of *Richard* the thyrd, doth in most part I beleue of all these pointes so content all men, as if the rest of our story of England were so done, we might well compare with *Fraunce, Italy,* or *Germany* in that behalfe' (*ibid.*).

These lines which occur at the beginning of the report convey treatise-like recommendations. Moreover, Ascham's report, his modesty to the contrary, does follow the advice he gives, as he conveys his material colorfully and especially conveys his own judgments about people and events. For example, he argues that contrary to those who believe that religion and liberty are the root causes of all the stirrings depicted, he actually believes the single cause to have been unkindness, alluding to Sir Thomas Wyatt (*c.* 1503–42) for support, who 'wrote to his sonne that the greatest mischief amongest men and least punished is vnkyndnes' (128).

After announcing his thesis, Ascham then backs up to begin when he first came to the imperial court in 1550, when the Emperor was 'in peace with all the world' (129). Shortly thereafter, after having learned of the Turks' preparations for warfare, the Emperor sent one of his commanders to conquer a Turkish stronghold. The Turks requested the return of the town, which the Emperor had agreed to but not done. So, in the following year the Turks attacked Malta and Tripoli, making Sicily and Naples easily accessible to them along with the coasts of Italy and Spain. Moreover, because the Emperor had played falsely, the general who won Tripoli 'put old & yong, man, woman, and child to the sword sauing two hundred of the strongest men to be their Galley slaues for euer' (130–1). This unkind act was answered with another similar act in Hungary during the next year. Ascham comments, 'it is pitie that mans nature is such, as will commonlie commend good thynges in readyng and yet will as commonly follow ill thyngs in doyng' (131). And these deeds are followed by another pair of cruel deeds. The Turks tie a Roman to a pillar and cut out chunks of his flesh to feed to starved dogs before letting them loose on his remains. Thereafter, the Christians follow the same script with boars on three Turks – boars, by the way, since the Turkish eat no pork. Ascham sums up, 'For these foule deedes I am not so angry with the *Turkes* that began them as I am sory for the Christen men that follow them' (132).

In this manner, Ascham follows his own advice, selecting events that illustrate his thesis that unkindness caused the Emperor's problems. Ascham then goes on to report of the Emperor's increasing woes, as others begin to turn on him as well. These problems, however, seem to emerge from the Emperor's alliance with the Pope, thereby subtly conveying the message that while unkindness may be a root cause of current troubles in Europe, the Emperor's own lack of judgment certainly doesn't help.

Towards the end of 1550, for example, Octavio, the Duke of Parma, turned against the Emperor because he would not support his cause against Don Ferranto Gonzaga, governor of Milan, who had killed Octavio's father. The feuding families 'hath stirred vp such a smoke in *Italy* betwixt the Emperour and *Fraunce*, as is not like to be quenched but with many a poore mans bloud' (133). Octavio then went to Julius III of Rome for help, and the Pope, wishing to gain leverage against the Emperor, advised Octavio to put himself under the protection of the French king. Upon the Emperor's command, however, the Pope excommunicated Octavio and then besieged Parma, leading to the French King's falling out with the Emperor.

Matters get more complex still when in the summer of 1551 the French King declared war against King Charles of Spain, even while his ambassador was successfully explaining to the Emperor that these were simply rumors of war. His assurances, of course, proved false, and the Emperor was again craftily manipulated by the Pope to give up his siege of Mirandula, making the French only stronger, and to move the battle to Lorraine and Picardy. Even on the day Ascham was writing, 25 June 1553, news came to Brussels that the Pope had yet again wrongfully advised the Emperor to give up another siege, this one of Siena, leaving this town too to the French, who then fortified it to such an extent that the Emperor was not likely to recover it.

In linking these latter events to the Emperor's alliance with the Pope, Ascham subtly suggests, essentially, that this monarch is not a good ally for England. With such implied advice along with examples of bad leadership, *The Report* thereby functions as a *Fürstenspiegel*, while at the same time giving treatise-like advice on how to write an effective political history.

*   *   *

While treatises and treatise-related material appear in a variety of forms throughout this period, their aim is generally to establish or to respond to *uniaccentuality*, as they incorporate discourse from a variety of authoritative sources. In the next chapter, the period's dramatic literature will be surveyed. As I hope will become clear, drama provides another arena for semiotic theory, as it materializes the author–audience relation and generates a different level of signs.

Notes

1. Vološinov was not well-received in the former Soviet Union, although in the 1920s and 1930s he and M. M. Bakhtin both worked on semiotics, especially through the prism of dialogue. Indeed, some have claimed that *Marxism and the Philosophy of Language* is actually the work of Bakhtin, although the study's translators are convinced that it is Vološinov's work, and in deference to them I accept the argument.

2. Information on the liberal arts and educational systems is available in a number of sources (e.g., Baldwin 1972; Caplan 1970; Curtis 1965, 1–109; Irvine 1994; Lanham 1976; Reiss 1997).

3. Comparing this against Augustine's definition of the sign, as given in the last chapter, you'll notice the similarity to Peirce's much later definition of *index*. For your information, though, many contemporary semiotic approaches to this period's literature are articulated through structuralist models of language as articulated by A. J. Greimas (e.g., Vance 1986). His taxonomies (Greimas 1966) come from what I would call a grammatical rather than a rhetorical perspective, since they examine the functions and properties of linguistic units and marginalize the audience.

3   Drama

One of the fascinating aspects of the 250 years under study here is the concomitant growth of national identity and national literature. As discussed earlier, Edward III's Arthurian-influenced founding of the Order of the Garter serves as a sign of this twin growth, not only to us, but to 'readers' of the time as well. So, too, the *translatio studii et imperii* topos, intertwining the transfer of culture and imperial power, offers another sign of the same. Indeed, the fact that English *literati* call London 'New Troy' demonstrates their awareness of the closeness between national identity and the literary system.

At the same time, the Peasants' Revolt of 1381 yields another inter-twined strand, also articulated in public and literary fora, but communicating the crumbling of feudal structures. Although the leaders Wat Tyler and Jack Straw are killed and the rebellion quelled, disgruntlement with taxing policies and with the moral state of the country are nonetheless expressed, along with the egalitarian ideals articulated by John Ball, in an attempt to establish new relations with the nobility and the clergy. With the Catholic Church's dissipating hold on power, both religious and secular; Henry VIII's dissolving of monasteries in the 1530s and the accompanying need for the poor to find help elsewhere; continuing battles and expeditions to expand empire and taxes to fund them; outbreaks of the Black Death; the growing middle class; the Englishing of the nation's multiple vehicles of communication; the success of Caxton's printing press; and the increase in numbers of those who could read – with all this, England is caught in a period of strident and multiply-stranded transitions. Small wonder that those dominating nation and church often evoked, relied upon and revived the traditional. Nonetheless, as seen in *Piers Plowman* as well as in other literary narratives, critique is part of this period's national literature as well.[1]

Among the many transitions of the period is the emergence of an increasingly secularly-oriented literary system, most obvious, perhaps, in its drama. Indeed, maybe more than any other literary genre, drama obviously reflects wide-ranging changes. Written for and presented to members of a range of socioeconomic classes in the vernacular, drama opens up a whole new 'trade'. Visually and in public spaces, drama suggests that apparent dichotomies emerging from *multiaccentual* discourse actually do belong to a whole. Thus, members of different socioeconomic classes are depicted in interaction on the same stage, and, just beyond the 250 years studied here, women are translating and writing drama as well (Cerasano and Wynne-Davis 1996).

Quintessentially rhetorical, drama's visceral address of the audience allows it unusual power to effect change and influence concepts of what it means to be English, power that is not to be underestimated. Indeed, again just beyond the period under study here, Robert Devereux, the Earl of Essex, commissioned a performance of Shakespeare's *Richard II*, presumably for its very powerful deposition scene, and shortly thereafter led a group attempting to depose Elizabeth – an attempt for which, in 1601, he was executed. In spite of its failure, the attempt suggests that the Earl of Essex judged he could persuade public opinion through the stage.

Keir Elam's semiotic approach to theater and drama

Keir Elam's semiotic analysis of plays underscores the multiply-stranded mode of communication defining drama, by separating the *performance* from the *dramatic* text, whereby, simply put, the *performance text* is produced *in* the theater, and the *dramatic text* is produced *for* the theater. Thus, the *dramatic text* is more or less constant, while the *performance text* varies in crucial aspects, from theaters to staging to acting. Although our knowledge of acting troupes, performances and staging during this period is sketchy, especially for the early half, it is still useful considering this complexity of dramatic texts to envision the play, whenever possible, as it might have been performed.

Envisioning a *performance text* takes into account drama's ability to actualize the different worlds created in just about any piece of literature. You may have noticed how in Chapter 2, I italicized the phrase 'in the world of the narrative' and the like. I did so to emphasize this particular literary trait. While there is a good deal of overlap in how non-dramatic and dramatic texts create worlds, nonetheless, drama's worlds have their own, additional ways of signing. According to Elam,

> Dramatic worlds are hypothetical ('as if') constructs, that is, they are recognized by the audience as counterfactual (i.e. non-real) states of affairs but are embodied *as if* in progress in the actual here and now. (102, his italics)

The world of any text relates to the world we live in insofar as 'our' rules and conventions are observed. Sometimes, they seem to overlap completely. For example, since Ascham's report on Germany concerns actual events, there seems to be no distinction between reported and actual worlds. Yet, Ascham is still *portraying* only a selection of events and putting them together from his own perspective with certain goals in mind – in this sense, he is creating a *fiction* (remember the Latin root of the word). The important thing to keep in mind here is that the worlds of a text convey *relations* to what we commonly call our world. And this holds true for drama as well.

> Being mimetic rather than strictly diegetic – acted rather than narrated – the drama does not lend itself to a distinction between *narrative* order [*sjuzet*, or the plot as it's presented] and the structure of events [*fabula*, storyline, or the events in their logical, chronological order]. None the less, the *sjuzet/fabula* distinction holds good for the drama...to the extent that the actions and events supposedly occuring [in the world of drama] have to be inferred from a representation which is non-linear, heterogeneous (some events are 'seen', others not), discontinuous (the plot passes from one line of action to another...) and incomplete (not everything ... will be explicitly shown or described: years may pass, large 'gaps' may appear between incidents and have to be filled by the spectator). (119–20, his italics)

Moreover, in the *performance text*, semiotic factors are intensified. For example, as Elam argues, every single aspect of an actor has significance in our viewing of a play:

> The audience starts with the assumption that every detail is an intentional sign and whatever cannot be related to the representation as such is converted into a sign of the actor's very reality – it is not, in any case, excluded from semiosis. (9)

Likewise, everything on the set, actors included, exhibits what Elam calls connotations, which are basically a sign's secondary meanings. In the fourth act of Shakespeare's *Richard II*, for example, the mirror that the monarch uses in the moment he is to be deposed does not simply signify all mirrors, but a whole complex of secondary signs, including these: tragedy brings an individual to self-reflection, kingship is merely an image, and life is a shadowy reflection of greater forces. In Peirce's terminology, though, connotation belongs to the dynamics of a sign: a representamen's or sign's *object* will create another sign, or *interpretant* in the mind of the receiver, and since an interpretant is a sign, this series of reflections can go on, theoretically, *ad infinitum*.

For drama, Elam situates the concept of connotation in a relation; thus, everything on the set 'is governed by the denotation–connotation dialectic' (11). He goes on to suggest that the theater is the perfect place to demonstrate Peirce's trichotomy of the sign. Roughly, when similar to the object being signified *in a general way*, everything on the set may function like *icons* – somewhat akin to the *denotation* of objects. For example, trees painted on a backdrop signify trees in general, not the one in my backyard. In addition, *performance texts* are replete with *indices*. For example, if a director decides to make Richard II first appear with a crown atop his head, the crown is an *index*, signifying he is king. When the actor playing Richard II later actually points to the crown, however, he refers to it, thereby marking it as a sign and performing what is known in philosophical discourse as *ostension*.

Symbols are the difficult category, and Elam here suggests that in the theater, the whole performance is symbolic in Peirce's sense, since it is governed by conventions (27). The *symbol* in Peirce's scheme *is* a wobbly category, exacerbated by Peirce's choice to use the term 'symbol', which has a more figurative application in general usage than what Peirce grants the term. Probably using the term as intended in math or logic, Peirce (who was a philosopher) posits that symbols are constant, like '*a*' or '*x*' in an algebraic formula, or the word 'the' in any sentence. Although a performance is symbolic in the widely used, figurative, sense of the term, I don't think it is in Peirce's sense. Symbols in theater would be the same, I think, as Peirce himself exemplifed: the actual words used are symbols, the constants around which we build meaning. As such, symbols are theoretically important – they function as a foundation – but for purposes of critical analysis, they are less interesting.

What is significant about objects is that when they appear in different contexts they may acquire a variety of signifieds, a semiotic state which is often referred to as *over-determined*. Thus, the girdle in *Sir Gawain and the Green Knight* is over-determined, beginning as an item of luxury, becoming quickly a love token, transforming into a magical amulet and, finally, functioning as a sign of community. None of the meanings are replaced or lost over the course of the narrative, although at times one of the meanings may be emphasized over the others. Just a reminder: a sign is *multiaccentual* when meanings are engaged in dialectical exchange. Thus, while a multiaccentual sign is *over-determined*, not every case of over-determination is multiaccentual. In any case, the theater is highly conducive to over-determination, since the visual dimension makes viewers see every object as intentional, especially when they are *foregrounded*, or made to seem critical.

Plays with religious themes

In medieval western Europe, drama probably began under the auspices of the Church, whereby the liturgy as performed in the tenth century by priests and choir easily lends itself to *performance* coding. From the liturgy to drama, plays of the fourteenth and fifteenth centuries are probably performed first in the Church, moving then outdoors to the front of the edifice and then in some central area or in the streets, for which temporary stages are specifically assembled. At times, plays are sponsored and performed by guilds, as exemplified by the London Drapers' Company, in existence since at least 1438, which would produce plays on various occasions, but regularly for its own annual company feasts (Lancashire 1993).

In addition to such centrally located performances (mainly in East Anglia and southeast England), especially the north witnessed performances of Corpus Christi cycles. Basically staged to celebrate the feast of Corpus Christi, cycle plays present guild-sponsored episodes or *pageants* from biblical stories, spanning from Lucifer's ejection from Heaven to the end of the world. The feast of Corpus Christi had been initiated by the Church in 1215, but actually realized in 1311, to occur 60 days after Easter and to assert the validity of transubstantiation (against which the Lollards took issue). Various cycles are extant, like the Towneley (32 pageants) probably performed at Wakefield in

Yorkshire, and the N Town cycle (43 pageants) probably performed in Lincolnshire or Norfolk. Some cycles are performed on movable wagons, whereby each wagon would present a pageant along a pre-established route. Thus, at each of the stopping points, or stations, each wagon would perform its piece, and the audience gathered there could enjoy the entire cycle.

What may be difficult for today's audiences to adjust to is that religious plays often contain bawdy humor or material that seems sacrilegious. For example, in the *Second Shepherds' Pageant* (in the Towneley cycle), which is set at the birth of Christ, Mak and Gill exchange some sharp and saucy quips as they try to hide Mak's theft of a lamb from the shepherds who will eventually be *those* shepherds who honor the birth of the Christ child. Also very different, Christianity is glorified at times by the use of anti-semitic barbs aimed at Jews and Moslems. Roger Ascham in his report on Germany may be able to distinguish thus: 'the great *Turke* him selfe (Religion excepted) is a good and mercyfull, iust and liberall Prince, wise in makyng and true in performyng any couenant, and as sore a reuenger of troth not kept' (132). Although slanted, even this degree of tolerance is not the norm for religious drama of this period. Nonetheless, plays with overtly religious themes are often composed, it seems, along Augustinian lines, training the ambiguity of language and actions defining the mortal realm to focus on the single message of God's love. Even when ribald or anti-semitic scenes are presented along with solemn ones, their juxtaposition tends to communicate the variety found in 'our world' and at the same time texture themes of the dramatic world.

Of specific interest here is the staging of allegory. When *Piers Plowman* depicts Holy Church, a certain edifice which we call a 'church' is not of primary importance, but rather that sign's *interpretants*, which gather significations of religious community, adherence to Christ's precepts, and love of God. When allegory is translated into a *performance text*, additional dynamics come into play. For example, if we decided to stage *Piers Plowman*, Holy Church would at first seem an *icon* for some woman. Probably by her gestures, clothing and other *indices*, we'd assume she were more the Mary rather than the Eve type. Once we learn that she is Holy Church, the *connotation–denotation* dialectic would be set into motion, and perhaps the *relations* between worlds would be highlighted, more so than in a text intended for reading alone. Although we might be inclined to view her as part of the narrative, the *over-determination* struck at that initial moment of recognition is a potentially creative tool for generating multiple levels of meaning.

For when allegory is used to visualize religious thought in a performance text, the viewer can shift attention from where the story is going and instead become involved in what happens at various moments in the story. In this respect, allegorical drama is not unlike Indiana Jones movies. Identified by his hat, whip and safari look, we know the Harrison Ford character to be the ultimate hero, who in the end will defeat evil and 'get the girl'. With the suspense removed from the narrative's direction, viewers can get lost in special effects and also experience, comfortably, the chills and spills created by Indy's narrow escapes.

Such involvement in the 'how' grants a 'space', wherein, for example, voyeuristic horror at seeing the hero struggle in a pit of snakes can be encouraged. But involvement in the 'how' also allows for a self-reflexive guffaw when Indy battles a tall sword-slinging Arabian not by meeting the enemy on his turf and proving superior in the mastery of swords, but by taking out his pistol and just shooting him. Such *self-reflexive* moments take the viewer out of the world of the narrative and telegraphically allow an additional, critical glimpse, here, at the implausibility of the 'karate-killer' genre – a world which furthers such duels (even in Arabian guise). In this period's religious drama, the highly traditional subject matter allows for a 'base line' that encourages similar kinds of participation. Here, we'll look at *Everyman* to exemplify how an allegorical *performance text* can allow audiences to get involved in the 'how', before turning to the Digby *Mary Magdalene* to see how *self-reflexive* moments can be generated from a very well-known story.

Everyman

Probably composed at the end of the fifteenth century, *Everyman* survives to us in four printed editions, dating from 1508 to 1537. The play has a close relative in *Elckerlijc*, a Flemish version of the play which was first printed in 1495. Not a typical religious play for its time, being so focused on the coming of Death and lacking comic elements, *Everyman* nonetheless conveys typical themes of its literary system and expresses sentiments that can be linked to the reform movements brewing at the time. For example, the play echoes precepts of the treatises on the *ars moriendi* (art of dying) that were written to enable Christians to face death (Duclow 1983), while it also contains critiques of the clergy for abusing Christ's doctrine.

Although there are no stage directions to help us envision *Everyman's performance text*, the *dramatic text* suggests a stage on which God is seated above and with some kind of trap door that allows the central figure to enter his grave. Written in verse, *Everyman* begins with a Messenger who frames the play for the audience, before we witness God lamenting the lack of reverence displayed by mortals, who are 'Drowned in sinne' (26) and given to 'the seven deedly sinnes dampnable' (36). Thus, the world in which God is a reality and can use metaphors such as 'drowning in sin' is juxtaposed already, at the beginning of the play, to an allegorical world which includes the seven deadlies.

Alluded to only verbally, the reference to the seven vices probably has the effect of simple signification, since by the time of the play they are so conventional they've probably lost some of their original allegorical punch. But at least God's presence on stage is a signifier of a different world, one which has relations to ours, even if it is one we generally consider to be invisible.

We learn soon that God is determined to 'Have a rekeninge of every mannes persone' (46), since if He were to leave things as they are, people would 'become moche worse than beestes' (49). Here, the use of 'every man' works as a *symbol*, in Peirce's sense, not yet as an *icon* or *index*. So, God sends for his messenger, Death, who responds in this manner (marginal translations to the right are Bevington's throughout):

> Lorde, I will in the worlde go renne over all,   *run everywhere*
> And cruelly out-serche bothe grete and small.
> Every man will I beset that liveth beestly
> Out of Goddes lawes, and dredeth not foly. (72–5)

Our relation to Death is distinct from our relation to God, although both signs in 'our world' *index* something not exactly of this world nor out of it.

Death's allegorical function in the *performance text*, however, levels some of the distinctions between God and Death, since they interact in the same performance world. In effect, God becomes colored with allegorical shading. But if the *dramatic text* is foregrounded in the *performance text*, say, through the set's emphasis on death as a phenomenon, then the dramatic text's message may gain in significance. Thus, we could see Death's entrance on the stage as a *metaliterary* message, whereby we begin at the ending (death) and hence are made aware of the play's circular structure, or we could also interpret such a heavily-coded sign as a theological message, whereby in the Christian system death is the beginning of immortality.

Once Death responds to God's request, Everyman enters, thereby *over-determining* what was until now only a verbal sign. In addition to signifying people in general, the actor adds *at least* one additional signified: *each individual*. In the process, the playwright also generates another *connotation*; that is, the exchange with Death makes Everyman seem foolish:

> *Everyman.* What desireth God of me?
> *Death.* That shall I shewe thee:
> A reckeninge he will nedes have   *he must have*
> Without ony lenger respite.   *any longer*
> *Everyman.* To give a reckeninge, longer laiser I crave!   *leisure*
> This blinde mater troubleth my witte. (97–102)   *obscure*

Everyman responds in what can be perceived as a flip manner, partly because the dialogue offers an instance of *dramatic irony*, whereby the audience is more informed than at least one character on stage.

Dramatic irony has the ability to draw audiences closer to the authorial perspective, which is characterized by being able to generate an overview. As a result, the audience's superior knowledge has the effect of demarcation – the stage, so to speak, is held in *ostension*. Thus, dramatic irony enables the audience to pay attention to the 'how', here, to observe just how foolish the character's response is. Indeed, the playwright actually defers the moment of Everyman's recognition, making the 'how' more intensely the focus. When Everyman does learn that God's messenger is Death, he responds in a manner that confirms the dramatic irony, 'O Deth, thou comest whan I had thee leest in minde!' (119).

Everyman then attempts to bribe Death, but in spite of his pleading and whining, Death remains adamant and forces Everyman to take a long journey whereby he must record all he's done in his accounting book, good and bad. The allegorical aspect of this demand can be intensified in the performance text, should the director have the Everyman character walk about, *as if* on a journey and carry a book, that *represents* the accounting book. In the world of the performance text, his walking and the book would then function as *icons*, first, but whose interpretants, secondly, would *not* be 'walking as activity' or 'book as object,' but other *interpretants*, generated by the allegorical framework. Thus, the *relation* between 'our world' and both the walking and the book is not located in the actions themselves, but in these signs' interpretants, life and deeds, a relation based on the premise that a mortal may live *in imitatione Dei* or not.

Death does give Everyman permission to take along anyone who would be 'so hardy' (157) as to accompany him. Wishing he had never been born (189), Everyman approaches Fellowship, Kindred, Cousin and Goods who all prove to be fair-weather friends. He then encounters Good Deeds, who's so weakened by his sins that she can't even stand. Upon her advice, Everyman approaches her sister, Knowledge, who leads him to Confession. Having benefitted from their interchange, Everyman scourges himself, and Good Deeds rises to accompany him to his judgment.

Although in the *performance text*, Everyman's encounters with his acquaintances and friends may have a continuity encouraged by the actions and gestures of the actors, insofar as the *dramatic text* is *foregrounded*, different worlds within the allegorical world may emerge. Thus, Fellowship, Kindred and Cousin represent people and their relations; Goods represents objects with which these relations are enhanced or not; Good Deeds represents actions; and Knowledge represents a part of an individual's non-tangible acquisitions as well as a society's non-tangible acquisitions. On the allegorical level, then, Good Deeds and Knowledge, although of different qualities in their relations to an individual, are signs existing in *ostension* to Everyman, and hence are *indices* in the performance text, while in 'our world', the words are *symbols*, in Peirce's sense of the term.

Like Indy's pit of snakes, our hero is now entangled in a complicated situation with only his wits to help him out. Thus, Knowledge gives Everyman a garment of contrition to wear, and then Beauty, Strength, Discretion and Five Wits are called on, again in allegorical ostension, to accompany him along his way. Everyman receives extreme unction (opening up a relation that mirrors 'our world' more closely); Beauty leaves him, and shortly after, Strength, Discretion and Five Wits do as well. Good Deeds alone walks with Everyman, although Knowledge remains on stage after the pilgrim sinks into his grave to announce the joy at Everyman's soul having been received by Heaven, followed by an Angel's praise. At this point, Knowledge ceases to have the individual character assumed by proximity to Everyman and becomes *over-determined* insofar as Knowledge now represents something like omniscient knowledge.

The play ends again closer to the dynamics of 'our world', with the words of a Doctor, who makes the message clear should anyone have missed it – and a message often used to characterize the middle ages – one should live *in memento mori* (in remembrance of death), or to put it in the words beginning the play, in the words of the messenger, who directly addresses the audience:

> I pray you all give your audience,
> And here this mater with reverence,   *hear*
> By figure a morall playe: *In form*
> *The Somoninge of Everyman* called it is,
> That of our lives and endinge shewes
> How transitory we be all daye. (1–6)   *always*

Beginning and ending, in *all* worlds generated by this *performance text*, have reality only for those who forget that death is *not* an ending. For death, in the Christian system, is the beginning of eternal life, whether in heaven or hell.

In this manner, the play conveys theological commonplaces in vernacular dramatic form. In doing so, it visualizes lessons that might easily form the text of a sermon. Indeed, among Everyman's last words are these:

> Take example, all ye that this do here or se,   *hear*
> How they that I loved best do forsake me
> Excepte my Good Dedes, that bideth truely. (867–9)

Perhaps not quite as exciting as watching our hero escape a snake pit, this performance text nonetheless allows audiences to focus on *how* Everyman (with his aversion to death) – like Indiana Jones (with his aversion to snakes) – extricates himself.

The Digby *Mary Magdalene*

The Digby *Mary Magdalene*, which was probably written in late fifteenth century East Anglia, survives in one manuscript, the MS Digby 133. Although extant in only one manuscript, fortunately, it contains a number of stage directions. Viewers are likely to have seen the play on the village green or in the town square, where platforms (of an uncertain number) represent the forces of Hell, the World and Heaven, which, as indicated in the *dramatic text*, are spread out among 19 locations. On and between these platforms, about 50 characters interact in a time span of about 60 years. Special effects are also part of the play: hell's fire is represented in some form, and a ship enters the playing space in order to take Magdalene on a journey. In sum, this is the most elaborate *performance text* of a religious play we have extant from this period, making it, in a sense, a religious Indiana Jones movie – action and special effects promise a spectacular adventure for the central figure, who will, in the end, escape harm.

The central figure, Mary Magdalene, is indeed well-known to audiences of this period; she is, for example, the subject of one of the lives written by Bokenham, mentioned in the last chapter. Simply put, Magdalene is both Eve and Mary in one. Moving from sin to redemption, she is also, in effect, another Everyperson, even though she is deemed to have been a historical figure as well, a contemporary of Christ. Apocryphal tales and information evolved about the saint, as they did for other biblical characters, such as the idea that she was wealthy and of noble descent. Pulling together various bits and pieces of information about different Marys from the Bible and the *Legenda Aurea* (also a source for St George's life), Magdalene is identified as the one who washes Christ's feet with her tears and hair; as one of the three Marys who come to Christ's tomb only to find the stone rolled away, his corpse no longer present; and as one to whom an angel explains that the son of God has risen. Likewise, she is the Mary to whom Christ first appears, although at first she mistakes him for a gardener, an encounter commonly referred to as the *Hortulanus* (Gardener) scene.

Written mainly in four-stress verse (with three- or two-stress bob-and-wheel stanzas) the play brings all these vignettes in Magdalene's life together and orders them in a linear manner, although the playing space is probably arranged in a semi-circle or, more complex still, in a circle.

The beginning of the play is firmly fixed in the world, as on their separate platforms Tiberius, Pilate and Herod vaunt their power, while on another platform the ruler Cyrus – Magdalene's father – demonstrates his love for his three children: Mary, Martha and Lazarus. The first imperial trio's fixed determination to dominate others puts them on their guard when they hear news of Christ's birth. Cyrus dies, and an allegorical scene takes place: the World, the Flesh, the Devil and various attendants brag about their power (echoing the emperors) and then plot to seduce Magdalene. Lady Lechery is sent to accomplish the mission. She befriends Magdalene, saddened by her father's death, and the two enter a tavern where Curiosity seduces her to accompany him to a garden bower, which delights a bad angel and the devil.

Asleep in the bower on one platform, while Simon prepares a banquet for Christ on another, a good angel appears to Mary. Christ dines with Simon, and Magdalene comes to him, begging him for forgiveness, weeping and washing his feet. Upon her redemption, hell is devastated. Martha and Lazarus welcome Mary home, Lazarus dies, and Christ raises him from the dead.

At this point, other regents perform on a platform, the King and Queen of Marseilles, whose blustery language at first echoes the language of the first imperial trio, except that these regents are also in love with each other. A devil then announces that Christ has escaped death, and the next scene we witness is at the sepulchre where the three Marys discover the absence of the corpse, so that two of the Marys leave to inform the disciples that Christ's body has been stolen away. Alone, Magdalene weeps, and Christ appears to her. The two other Marys join her, and all three go to tell the good news to the disciples.

The King and Queen of Marseilles are next shown with their pagan priest and his less than respectful assistant, sacrificing to an idol. Pilate, Herod and Tiberius are enraged by the news of Christ's empty tomb. Magdalene is then shown to be Christ's favorite, before she enters a ship and converts the regents of Marseilles by promising to fulfill their wish for a child in a very long scene that includes a contest with the pagan priest along with a procession in light. After that, she takes various journeys, their child is born, the Queen seems to die and is revived before, finally, Magdalene is depicted after having fasted in the wilderness for 30 years, and angels take her into heaven. A priest ends the play with praise.

The multifarious strands running through the play are all connected in the figure of Magdalene, since everything and everybody are *dramatically* and *theatrically* subordinate to her. For example, Christ appears in the playing space only during the following Magdalene-focused occasions: at Simon's dinner, to forgive her (614 s.d.–704); at Lazarus' death, to resurrect her brother as well as her faith (846–924, n.b. 891–2); in the *Hortulanus* scene, to resuscitate her faith once again (1055–95); in a scene in which he praises the Virgin and sets Magdalene a task (1349–75); at two occasions to assist her (1587–99, 2004–19); and, finally, to bring her into heaven (2074–81). Although her life is depicted as dependent upon and interwoven with Christ's, not unlike Margery Kempe, she is nonetheless rhetorically *foregrounded*.

While we could walk through the play as we did with *Everyman*, I'd like to focus here instead on some of the play's *self-reflexive* material. More specifically, physical movement seems to link both dramatic and performance texts, as yoked in the commonplace metaphor of life as a pilgrimage. Thus, prior to her decision to turn to Christ, Magdalene doesn't move much, thereby echoing the rulers of the world who are securely ensconced on their mortal platforms. However, after both Magdalene and the King of Marseilles experience conversion, they emulate Christ, who moves throughout the play. Thus, the King makes an 'actual' pilgrimage with Peter through the stations of the cross (1848–51), a journey underscored by the parallel 'spiritual' pilgrimage taken by his supposedly dead wife, who reports she was accompanied by Magdalene (1904–11). Thus, mainly by means of the *performance text* as read against the literary system, the Digby playwright suggests that life in Christ means development, while life in the world means stasis and stagnation.

Moreover, in the performance text, the pilgrimages function as *icons* for pilgrimages *per se*. They also function in both performance and dramatic texts as *metaphors* for life. In addition, since the journeys 'walk' the play's pilgrims through the stations of the cross, they further serve as *icons* for Christ's path to his crucifixion, which metaphorically suggests that Christians should follow this path *in imitatione Dei*. Following this series of *interpretants* makes all levels cascade into one another. For, if mortals are instances of God's words since they are part of the Book He's authored, then all mortal creations – such as literature, pilgrimages that represent Christ's life, and actors in plays – are tales within tales, plays within plays.

The deeper significance of *divine* language, then, can become evident through working out *mortal* language's various levels in time and space, dimensions important to performance texts. As the Digby playwright suggests, the blustery commands of the rulers 'go' nowhere, whereas Christ's command that Magdalene *return* to God, '*Revertere*', unleashes a chain of events that keeps her in motion and defeats the underworld, as is further underscored in the play's Edenic allusions.

Watching Magdalene move to the arbor allegorically implies how the biographical Magdalene may have fallen into a life of sin: saddened by the loss of her father she loses faith in the invisible and turns towards the visible, tangible, mortal world. The arbor, however, is not simply a neutral playing space in the performance text. By the time of the play, arbors have acquired associations with gardens of fleshly delights, an earthly version of the Garden of Eden, and hence also with the Garden of Eden, as well as – by means of typological extension – with the heavenly paradise. These *connotations* would have been underscored more forcefully in the performance text, when later Christ teaches Magdalene how to read by indirectly *over-determining* the arbor. That is, in the *Hortulanus* scene, upon Magdalene's surprise at having mistaken her Lord for the gardener, Christ answers:

> So I am, forsothe, Mary;
> Mannys hartt is my gardin here.
> Therin I sow sedys of vertu all the yere;   *seeds*
> The fowle wedes and vicys, I reynd up by the rote.   *rend, tear*
> Whan that gardin is watteryd wyth teris clere,
> Than spring vertuus, and smelle full sote. (1080–5)

The lesson here, that Christ redeems Eden, builds upon the typological dynamics that link Eden and paradise by taking the common vehicle – the garden or arbor – and literalizing it into *verbally portrayed* action (sowing, weeding, watering). Moreover, later we see that Magadalene understood the actual lesson conveyed here as she successfully converts the Rulers of Marseilles. Thus, through his clearly signified analogy of the garden, Christ teaches Magdalene how to read in 'Christ-speak', in parables that figuratively equate a short narrative with an underlying message.

By making journeys and movement a determining *signifier* of the play, the Digby playwright *self-reflexively* transforms the theater into a book, as suggested when Christ attempts to teach the disciples to *read* and *interpret* his actions through his resurrecting of Lazarus: 'of my deth shew yow I will' (856). And, further, the deepening of Magdalene's understanding through her journeys comments upon how a play works, as is underscored by her reference to the Pentecost shortly before she is to board ship for Marseilles, 'Of alle maner tongges he gaf us knowing,/ For to undyrstond every langwage' (1343–4). As implied by the juxtaposition of Pentecost to her journey, this text suggests, paradoxically, that the negation of *signifiers* – the part of language that causes confusion – along with the refusal to stay or dwell in any mortal space enables understanding. For a pilgrimage in *God's dramatic text* is a journey to paradise, one which is success-fully staged only when mortals refuse to remain in mortal space and thereby translate His *dramatic text* into a *performance text.*

Plays with secular themes

In the sixteenth century, the subject matter of plays tends to change, shifting from religious to political and social issues (Bevington 1962). With strands reflecting the objectification of knowledge mentioned in earlier chapters, some English plays begin to mingle typically medieval and classical subjects and approaches. One example of such mingling is *The Tragedy of Gorboduc,* a particularly elaborate court production written by Thomas Norton (1532–84) and Thomas Sackville (1536–1608) as a Christmas play for the Inner Temple. Presented to the Queen on 18 January 1562, the play's classically-influenced five acts shape the medieval material of *Fürstenspiegel* into a tragic warning against civil strife. Thus, *Gorboduc* portrays how a king attempts to abdicate and divide his kingdom between his two sons. Porrex, however, murders Ferrex, although he doesn't get very far since he is killed by his own mother, an act resulting in an uprising, the murders of the king and queen, and the subsequent instability of the realm.

Hard to imagine, *Gorboduc* was written for a single performance, staged elaborately, and then probably circulated in manuscript form to be enjoyed basically as a *dramatic text.* Like *Gorboduc,* humanist plays of the sixteenth century do seem to emphasize the primacy of *dramatic* over *performance* text. For example, humanist plays closely associated with More and Erasmus are performed mainly in grammar schools, though these performances eventually lead to the formation of boys' companies that would provide entertainment for the court during Christmas and Shrovetide. In any case, by 1576, drama had become a well-defined profession, with adult players and permanent theaters emerging as its popular markers.

While some troupes enjoy the privilege of playing at court during this period, public squares or inns are more common venues for acting companies. In the fifteenth century, companies begin to seek licensing through some lord who would provide them with the protection to travel and perform. Censorship is nonetheless a frequent enough reaction to such wandering troupes' search for patronage, a reaction which in turn probably helped to fuel the building of the first permanent playhouses. The first, the Red Lion, was built in 1567. Not to be challenged by such responses, in 1574 the Common Council of London restricted performances in London's taverns to those that were licensed and to plays that had already been censored.

Robin Hood plays

It should be noted that although religious plays dominated the fifteenth century, secular drama was also performed even then. The productions may not have been as elaborate as those of the following century, but they too reflect the multiple strands of transition criss-crossing this period. Associated with May Games, for example, the Robin Hood plays are written in the vernacular, and they code rebellion as a positive act. Apparently, they were very popular.

Actually, tales about Robin and his men had already circulated in ballads since at least the thirteenth century. We know that they had become popular by the fourteenth century, since we have the reference in *Piers Plowman*'s description of Sloth, as cited in the last chapter. Indeed, the legend is so well-known by this time that the phrase 'Robin Hood in Barnsdale stood' is used in legal contexts to mean a well-known fact. There is also a Scottish version of Robin's adventures, and apparently, his name is frequently used or given as an alias in chronicles and civic records. As well-known as the legend must have been, early references to Robin do not provide a detailed portrait. What we can garner from various sources is that Robin is said to have lived during the late thirteenth century in Barnsdale, as well as in the royal forests near Carlisle, Nottingham and South Yorkshire.

Couched in anti-authoritarian and anti-Church sentiment, both the Robin Hood ballads and plays seem to appeal particularly to the socioeconomically lower classes, even though Robin is essentially portrayed as a robber, murderer or a leader often defeated in hand-to-hand combat. Part of the reason may be that the plays feature tradesmen, while Robin himself is identified as a yeoman. By the 1590s, however, plays, masques and other literary endeavors transformed the hero into an aristocrat, usually the Earl of Huntingdon, who had been deprived of his land and whose nobility is not only of the inherited variety (Knight 1994). As certain as Indy wins in the end, so too in these later plays, Robin is sure to regain his land and heritage when the good king returns.

But it's the plays of the fifteenth century that are of interest here. The play called *Robin Hood and the Knight* or *Robin Hood and the Sheriff*, for example, is a brief piece, a little over 40 lines long. It may be incomplete, although it's also possible that most of it existed in *performance text* alone. The play begins with a knight promising a sheriff he will capture Robin. The knight meets the hero and challenges him to several contests – shooting arrows, throwing stones and wrestling. Robin wins in each of the three cases, so the knight decides to blow his horn to signal for help, at which point, Robin kills him. Robin then dresses himself in the knight's armor and bears the defeated man's head in his own hood. Meanwhile, the sheriff has attacked Robin's men, one of whom meets his leader. Robin rushes to the scene. And this is where the text ends in the single manuscript written in about 1475.

This is the kind of play which makes a reader beg for a *performance text*. Even so, it's not hard to imagine that actors dressed as *icons* of knighthood and law in this particular narrative might cause authorities to become a tad nervous. In addition, Robin's victories over the knight occur in contests that are not associated with a nobleman's sports. Thus, for audiences of the time, one message communicated by his victories could even suggest that the feudal hierarchy isn't one that had to be endured. In 1562, the Robin Hood plays were banned by Mary Queen of Scots and attacked by the Protestant clergy as well. Short as these pieces are, they clearly elicit strong reactions.

Another example, this one aimed at the clergy, may be found in the play called *Robin Hood and the Friar*, which is about 120 lines long and which was printed in about 1560. It begins with Robin telling Little John how a friar fought with him and robbed the leader of his purse. Little John promises to bring the scurrilous churchman to his leader. We are then made privy to Friar Tuck's chortling to Robin's men in the next scene:

> *Deus hic! Deus hic!* God be here!
> Is not this a holy worde for a frere?
> God save all this company!
> But am not I a jolly fryer?
> For I can shote both farre and nere,
> And handle the sworde and buckler,
> And this quarter-staffe also ...
> I am come to seke a good yeman.
> In Bernisdale men sai is his habitacion,
> His name is Robyn Hode;
> And if that he be better man than I,
> His servaunt wyll I be, and serve him truely;
> But if that I be better man than he,
> By my truth, my knave shall he be... (22–44)

Apparently Robin's men leave, and he seizes the Friar by the throat. In their struggle, Robin lets Friar Tuck know he never loved friars, 'For he that meteth a frere or a fox in the morning,/ To spede ill that day he standeth in jeoperdy...' (63–4). Friar Tuck is made to carry Robin over the stream, whom he then throws in, and they scuffle again. Robin tricks the Friar into allowing him to blow his horn, which summons his men. The Friar then whistles, and his men appear. Impressed, Robin asks the Friar to join him – for his service he'll get gold and a woman, to which the Friar happily agrees.

As with the first play, this one too might easily upset the authorities. From the outset, the churchman is depicted as one not overly fond of virtue. When Robin lets Friar Tuck know his distaste for friars in general, Tuck is positioned by our forest hero as an *icon* for religious men. When Robin admits him into the fellowship of the forest, though, we learn that Tuck isn't like the 'bad' churchmen. He's just one of the guys, who can rob, fight, drink and whore with the best of them. Although this acceptance into the group serves as an example of *over-determination*, it also illustrates Vološinov's *multiaccentuality*. as well. What a good friar is differs according to one's relation to ecclesiastical power.

Ralph Roister Doister

The play often considered to be the first English comedy is *Ralph Roister Doister*, written by Nicholas Udall (*c.* 1505–56), and performed first in about 1553. Modelled on Roman comedies of Terence and Plautus, the five-act play focuses on a braggart, Ralph Roister Doister. He is encouraged in his erroneous good opinion of himself by Matthew Merrygreek, a 'needy humorist' who lives from the generosity of others. Smitten – on the day portrayed in the play – by Dame Christian Custance, Roister Doister proceeds to make a fool of himself in his badly executed pursuit of her. Within this comic plot, Udall includes *self-reflexive* scenes that comment on *performance text* dynamics.

Act I begins after a Prologue, with Merrygreek in soliloquoy, informing the audience how the shameless flatterer mooches from everyone he can, especially Roister Doister, who believes, 'If any woman smile, or cast on him an eye,/ Up is he to the hard ears in love by and by:/ And in all the hot haste must she be his wife...' (58). True to this description of his companion, Roister Doister eventually confides in Merrygreek of his love for Custance, even though, as Merrygreek informs him, the widow is betrothed to Gawin Goodluck. Hearing only what he wishes to hear, Roister Doister is sure he will win her love:

M. Merry. But now to your widow, whom you love so hot –
R. Roister. By Cock, thou sayest truth, I had almost forgot.
M. Merry. What, if Christian Custance will not have you, what?
R. Roister. Have me? yes, I warrant you, never doubt of that:
I know she loveth me, but she dare not speak. (67)

Off to fetch musicians, Merrygreek leaves Roister Doister to wait for Custance, whose servants happen to come along. Providing 'homespun' humor, the servants chat, sing and dance to Roister Doister's delight – they *perform* for him – but he proves not to be their match. We encounter Custance in scene five, receiving a letter sent to her by Roister Doister via one of these servants, which she refuses to read.

Act II continues in the same vein, and in Act III Custance explains to Merrygreek that she loves her betrothed Goodluck, a merchant, and leaves it up to Merrygreek to convey the message clearly to Roister Doister. But communication fails here, as Roister Doister is knocking

at her door again. Upon his insistence, Merrygreek reads Custance
Roister Doister's love letter, *self-reflexively* pausing at all the wrong
places, so that its meaning is totally transformed:

> Sweet Mistress, where as I love you nothing at all,
> Regarding your substance and riches chief of all;
> For your personage, beauty, demeanour and wit,
> I commend me unto you never a whit.
> Sorry to hear report of your good welfare,
> For, (as I hear say) such your conditions are,
> That ye be worthy favour of no living man... (111)

We see here the importance of effectively acting out a *performance*
text, since Custance, as audience, is not impressed and leaves. Udall
underscores the message by having Roister Doister angrily send for
the Scrivener. He, however, defends himself, pointing out that it was
Roister Doister himself who copied the letter and in reading it, paused
faultily. The Scrivener shows how the epistle should be read:

> Sweet Mistress, whereas I love you; nothing at all
> Regarding your riches and substance; chief of all
> For your personage, beauty, demeanour, and wit,
> I commend me unto you; never a whit
> Sorry to hear report of your good welfare;
> For (as I hear say) such your conditions are,
> That ye be worthy favour; of no living man
> To be abhorred... (119)

The Scrivener concludes, 'Then was the fault in reading, and not
in writing' (120). Thus, Udall underscores the interrelationship
between *dramatic* and *performance texts*, suggesting that no matter
how well a *dramatic text* is written, it's the actors who will determine
its success.

After being highlighted in this fashion, the *metaliterary* messages
begin to multiply more overtly. Thus, Act IV introduces the captain of
a ship, friend to Goodluck, who is to check up on Custance.
Merrygreek and Roister Doister, of course, enter just at that moment
and with their forward and premature remarks make it seem as if
Custance had encouraged their attentions. Here's a case of bad timing
ruining the message Custance wishes to convey to the captain,

namely, that she *is* constant to her betrothed. After the captain leaves, moreover, Roister Doister is determined to read her the letter again, correctly, but she refuses to allow him, causing the suitor to burst out, 'I command you to love me! wherefore should ye not?' (128), all the while spurred on by Merrygreek. When he finally understands she will not have him, he threatens her with violence, causing Custance to seek help.

At this point a dissonant twist surfaces, one that underscores a *self-reflexive* tendency that had been part of the play from the start. That is, Merrygreek returns to Custance with Goodluck's friend, Tristram Trusty, and all three leave the paths suggested by their roles. That is, instead of depending upon and acting out Roister Doister's wishes, Merrygreek takes over the role of a director while he also acts out the role of Roister Doister's ally. Instead of performing his role as Goodluck's friend, Trusty assumes the role of peacemaker 'in another play'. And instead of defending herself with the help of friends, Custance agrees to act the role of the beleaguered damsel in distress. In other words, all three join forces and *metaliterarily* stage a fight:

> M. Merry. If occasion serve, taking his part full brim,
> I will strike at you, but the rap shall light on him.
> When we first appear –
> C. Custance. Then will I run away,
> As though I were afeared.
> T. Trusty. Do you that part well play,
> And I will sue for peace.
> M. Merry. And I will set him on... (136–7)

The battle ensues as planned, complete with a call to arms in St George's name (141), and Roister Doister exits a coward. Act V brings Goodluck to Custance, with some complications stemming from the captain's report, and the play ends in song.

In this comedy, the *metaliterary* episodes featuring the letter and the staged fight elicit critical responses from the audience, responses that balance type against individual and thereby reflect upon the dynamics of *performance texts*. Such dynamics are present even in the names of the characters. For when characters are identified by tags that combine conventional names with general, allegorical types, like 'Ralph Roister Doister' and 'Gawin Goodluck', the characters constantly oscillate between *denotation* and *connotation*, between literal and figurative representations, between types for humankind and individuals.

More complexly but in the same vein, when Merrygreek and Roister Doister draw attention to the love letter, a series of *connotations* and levels of meaning percolate into the text's literal-level meaning. Thus, the letter, presented *in ostension*, depicts knowledge as a commodity, objectified to the extent that a pompous and myopic man of means can purchase a document that will enhance his 'type'. Moreover, when he has Merrygreek read the letter for him, while he's standing there, Roister Doister unintentionally reveals his staging of the lover-poet *type*, staging done rather poorly, since, according to tradition, if a lover-poet is to use a go-between, he really shouldn't be present at the same time. Semiotically, Roister Doister presents himself along with an *icon* of himself in Merrygreek and an *index* of his love in a purchased letter.

The *metaliterary* strands introduced by the letter complement the staging of the battle, which also shows the importance of knowing what roles, what types, an individual can effectively play – Roister Doister proves to be as ineffective a lover-poet type as he is a warrior type. The staged battle also makes clear what Merrygreek has been doing all along – directing, staging, acting, writing – transforming the relation between himself and Roister Doister from one of dependency into one of control. Thus, Udall's play encourages a multiply-stranded, *metaliterary* interpretation, and in doing so further reflects the dependency–control relationships among playwright, actors and audiences.

The Historie of the Tryall of Chevalry

The Tryall of Chevalry is a five-act play, probably written some time between 1599 and 1603, and performed by the Earl of Derby's men by 1605, just a bit beyond the limits of our period. Nonetheless, I would like to include a brief discussion of the anonymous play here, since it illustrates a number of the themes and arcs discussed so far.

Not well-known and certainly not often anthologized, *The Tryall of Chevalry*, as is suggested by the title itself, articulates a desire to return to old values, not unlike the same desire that led the Lollards to portray idealized relations between church and worshippers in terms of the past. The play depicts the efforts of two warring countries which try to achieve peace by means of arranged marriages. They are almost thwarted, but succeed in the end. The success of their venture, which is of primary interest here, is achieved by the energy and virtue of an English nobleman. The most striking scene in the play involves the English knight's challenge to all who pass by to joust with him in honor of his friend. It is this trial of chivalry, a tournament, that allows the *performance text* to comment on the play's themes most powerfully while also evoking the past.

Originally, tournaments were arranged battles in which two teams met in a free-for-all, a sport that probably began in France. Richard I (1189–99) licensed tournaments in 1194, which gave him more control over the popular activity while also endowing the sport with more significance. It's as if the Queen were to become the major stockholder and CEO of Manchester United. Due, however, to a few tournaments that went awfully awry, complete with deaths, they were cancelled for a while, revived again during Henry III's reign (1216–72) and furthered in the reigns of Edward I (1272–1307) and, not surprisingly, Edward III (1327–77). Eventually, the old mélée style of tournament faded into oblivion, and one-on-one jousts became popular. For the record, jousts lent themselves very well to *performance text* codes, as exemplified in 1362 when seven knights jousted against all comers at Cheapside as the Seven Deadly Sins. Although in England tournaments ended, for all practical purposes, with Henry IV (1399–1413), well into the fifteenth century, very expensive, full-scale jousts were still conducted in France and Burgundy (Barber and Barker 1989). All this information suggests that jousts were part of the antique past when *The Tryall of Chevalry* was written, even though the performance text's central actions revolve around them.

The play, however, doesn't start as if it's going to dwell in the past. Moving briskly, *The Tryall of Chevalry* begins with Louis, the King of France, ready to make peace with the King of Navarre, whose kingdom is located in northern Spain, since their children are engaged to be married. Philip, Louis' son, is to marry Bellamira, Navarre's daughter, and Ferdinand, Navarre's son, is to marry Katharina, Louis' daughter. However, Katharina's feelings do not incline to Ferdinand, but to Ferdinand's best friend and appointed go-between, the English Earl of Pembroke. More problematic still, the Duke of Bourbon loves Bellamira.

As you've probably guessed, these elements threaten the tenuous peace made between Louis and Navarre, and a sub-plot involving soldiers and their loyalties doesn't make the situation less brittle. The third act witnesses the total dissipation of the peace process, with Bellamira's face being disfigured by acid thrown at her by the scorned Bourbon; Louis and Philip swearing enmity for the wrongs done their children; and Ferdinand fighting his best friend, Pembroke, resulting in each having wounded the other so badly that once they recover, each believes the other to be dead. All is, of course, eventually ironed out.

And, importantly, all is ironed out by Pembroke. In Act IV he disguises himself in armor and erects a shrine to his best friend, and – this is where the jousts come in – he challenges all those who pass to fight in honor of his friend's glory. While these actions are handled in just a few lines in the *dramatic text*, the *performance text* must have been impressive. The usual suspects pass by, and each is defeated in single combat. Even Philip fights Pembroke and must forfeit his shield. Finally, Ferdinand too rides by, challenges Pembroke's assertion, and the two fight, only to recognize each other just before it's too late.

This scene is rhetorically and semiotically central in a number of ways. First, it achieves a dissonant texture since it is different from all other scenes in the play. It seems located in a distant past. It seems to allude to *literary* narratives, like those celebrating Arthur in which knights who had been defeated surrender their shields or perform other homage to the victors. It is also, strictly speaking, not necessary to the action of the play. Indeed, the scene actually seems to slow down the play which until this moment had been hurtling forward into battle. In addition, the scene must have seemed emblematic to its audiences. Dressed in armor in front of a tent, the display of older chivalric times – whether in image or only in language – must have evoked *interpretants* of a 'better', 'more honorable', time, not unlike how John de Werchin must have imaged Arthur, in 1408, when hearing of the establishment of the Order of the Garter. This particular evocation of Arthuriana, however, is yoked to the idea that while chivalry is the only ethical modus acceptable to a nobleman, love – whether between friends or lovers – is what fuels chivalry.

This is pretty astonishing, considering chivalry's origins and its practice in 'the old days'. The term *chivalry* derives from the French *cheval*, meaning 'horse', originally used to refer to those soldiers who ride on horseback. The use of the term became glamorous with time, in part through depictions of worthy knights such as Sir Gawain.

Although loyalty and other virtues are critical components of these chivalric codes, obeisance and courage as pledged to one's liege lord is at its fundament. For example, in 1484, William Caxton translated and printed *The Order of Chivalry* from a French version of the original Catalan by Ramón Lull (b. *c.* 1235). The treatise argues the view that a knight is not just an armed warrior but, ideally, a literate soldier who owes allegiance to Christ, to his worldly lord, and to the people of his worldly lord.

The playwright of *The Tryall of Chevalry*, however, doesn't recognize this socioeconomic base at all. In fact, Pembroke's setting up a tent to gather shields has no relevance to dynastic concerns whatsoever. Moreover, chivalry can be performed by anyone in any class. Thus, the fourth act begins with Pembroke's words to a Forester who has helped nurse him back to life:

> I thank thee, Forrester, whose rough grown walks,
> Wild in aspect, afford more courtesy
> Then places smoother for civility. (319)

While these lines recognize the Forester's chivalric behavior, the play clearly presents the view that nobility sits best in those of noble blood. Thus, later, when Katherina comes to the memorial, she learns from Pembroke how noble and chivalric Ferdinand 'was':

> He was the very pride of fortitude,
> The house of vertue, and true friendship's mirrour.
> Looke on his picture…
> He lookt so lovely…
> See with what courage he indur'd the combat,
> Smiling at death for all his tyranny. (323)

Through Pembroke, then, Katharina is made to see the error of her ways, finally loving the man she ought to love, Ferdinand. And then the pace picks up again. Bellamira's face, we are told, will be healed by herbs. In the last act, Pembroke, Ferdinand and Philip are displayed on the battlefield – perhaps in *ostensive* relation to the rest of the iconically represented armies, but certainly with *connotations* of chivalry accumulated through the jousting scene – justice is meted out, and the parents are made to comply with the younger generation's demand for peace and marriage.

Although this isn't a history play, *The Tryall of Chevalry* may actually have historical touchstones. For example, England had vital interests in both France and Spain. Moreover, Navarre was a very important territory during Elizabeth I's reign (1558–1603), since it not only controlled the main pass into Spain, but was also a major stopover on the much travelled pilgrimage route from the north down to Santiago de Compostela. Likewise, Elizabeth I had to fend off many suitors who made court to her hoping to secure various degrees of peace. Perhaps most interestingly, the play's overall messages of chivalric peace through marriage alliances are, critically, dependent upon Pembroke, who, however, remains single, chivalrously superior to any of the other characters in the play, and married to England as much as he is to virtue. Thus, Pembroke's last longer speech directed to Louis of France contains these words:

> ... know Pembroke is an Englishman
> Highly deriv'd, yet higher in my thoughts;
> And for to register mine acts in brasse,
> Which all-devouring time shall ne're race out,
> Have I through all the Courts of Christendome
> In knightly tryall prov'd my vertue sound,
> Raisd England's fame aloft ... (354)

The last two lines cited here suggest that Pembroke envisions himself as a sign, signifying chivalric, noble England. As such, he presents himself in *ostension*, an image to be examined. Perhaps these words are intended somehow to evoke Elizabeth, even if the play had been first performed in 1605, two years after her death. After all, Elizabeth was master of the image and of creating a strong sense of English identity. Indeed, consider her response to the Commons' petition that she marry, as recorded by William Camden (1551–1623):

> 'Yea, to satisfie you, I have already joyned my self in Marriage to an Husband, namely, the Kingdom of England. And behold...the Pledge of this my Wedlock and Marriage with my Kingdom.'
> (And therewith she drew the Ring from her Finger, and shewed it, wherewith at her Coronation she had in a set form of words solemnly given her self in Marriage to her Kingdom.) (Camden 1970, 29)

Notes

1. This is a difficult area to analyze, as the texts that are transmitted to us are mostly written by those in authoritative positions. As two studies in the *Transitions* series make clear, cultural materialist and Marxist analyses create a fuller picture of how literature fits in social networks (Brannigan 1998; Haslett 1999). And while some studies have teased out readings from literary narratives by accessing historical studies and official documents (e.g., Aers 1988), we are reading in a highly sophisticated rhetorical literary system and any depiction of those without access to media is likely to undergo distortion and filtering (e.g., Greenblatt 1980). What can be gathered about early drama from records can be valuable for contextualizing, if we take into account their limits as well. (e.g., Braunmuller and Hattaway 1990; Briscoe and Coldewey 1989).

4   History and Literature

At the end of the last chapter, you caught me hypothesizing about a relation between a fictional text, *The Tryall of Chevalry*, and historical reality, Queen Elizabeth I, mainly on the basis of a report finished in 1615, a few echoes I heard reverberating between the texts, a predeliction for zeroing in on rhetorically significant passages, and a hunch. Maybe more often than not, history, the genre we tend to equate with truth and reality, is just such a mix. This is a claim that needs to be considered here, since *literati* of the period seem to have had more than just a mild obsession with the writing of history.

The proliferation of histories was probably encouraged when, in 1505, Henry VII (1483–1509) commissioned the Italian Polydore Vergil (*c*. 1470–*c*. 1555) to write a new, lavish history of England. It is also during this period that Latin depictions of England like Vergil's give way to vernacular histories, as evidenced by Edward Hall's *Union of the Noble and Illustre Families of Lancaster and York* (1542) and Raphael Holinshed's *Chronicles* (1577), to name but two. Linking the Latin and English versions, and in contrast to many of our histories today, writers during this period tend to arrange otherwise isolated pieces of data in the imaginative framework of a story, a *history*.

As a matter of fact, the Latin word from which the term derives, *historia*, not only means 'history' as understood today, but also 'fiction', as is the case with Middle English *storye*, Modern German *die Geschichte*, and Modern French *l'histoire*. In the sense understood in English today, *historia* refers to 'narrative', to a *historia rerum gestarum*, 'a story of things done.' And although writers during this period understand that there are differences between fictions and histories, there is no separate training for the different genres (Breisach 1985; Partner 1977; Patterson 1987; Spiegel 1993). In mastering rhetoric, a student learns to structure language into effective narrative arrangements – history or poetry – by means of models from both historical and fictional writing.[1] As Roger Ascham's report on Germany admonishes and demonstrates, the criteria for writing a good history differ only slightly from those for writing a good story. Considering the rhetorical basis of historical writing, which aims to persuade some audience with a particular arrangement of data, it becomes useful at this point to consider what Umberto Eco has to say about interpretation.

Umberto Eco's *Limits of Interpretation*

A major focus of Umberto Eco's theoretical work is the analysis of semiotics in terms of rhetorical systems, as his relatively recent work on interpretation demonstrates. In rhetorical systems, as we know, the interchange between addresser and addressee is critical and presupposes common grounds that enable some degree of understanding. 'Even the most radical deconstructionists', Eco points out, 'accept the idea that there are interpretations which are blatantly unacceptable' (6). Rejecting the propensity of especially recent critical readers to see in every text a world of infinite possibilities, along with the attempt of other readers to find the single, original intent of an author, Eco occupies a space in between these two positions. Thus, Eco argues that texts may have multiple, but not infinite, meanings. Contexts and interpreters reduce the possibility of infinitude.

Since, in Eco's estimation, those who argue for infinite possibilities have dominated critical discourse in recent years, he coins a term, *hermetic drift*, to discuss their activity, describing it as

> ... the interpretive habit which dominated Renaissance Hermetism and which is based on the principles of universal analogy and sympathy, according to which every item of the furniture of the world is linked to every other element (or to many) of this sublunar world and to every element (or to many) of the superior world by means of similitudes or resemblances. It is through similitudes that the otherwise occult parenthood between things is manifested and every sublunar body bears the traces of that parenthood impressed on it as a *signature*. (24, his italics)

Eco goes on to compare this idea with Peirce's notion of *unlimited semiosis*, whereby, at least theoretically, each *interpretant*, in itself constituting a sign, can infinitely produce others. In Peirce's system, however, the interpretants become more and more determined, *not* loosely associative – somewhat like the path scientists have taken in trying to determine the smallest particle imaginable: always another possibility, but always more defined.

In other words, Eco proposes that a text generates interpretive limits along with its Model Readers, who may respond on two levels, *semantic interpretation* and *critical interpretation*. Semantic interpretation describes, to use terms already introduced here, the kind of response that a reader has when she or he basically accepts the relations between *the world of the text* and 'our world'. In contrast, critical interpretation, again in our terms, is used when a reader responds by exploring, along formal lines, various relations between these worlds. In discussing the responses of Model Readers, Eco points out that we are caught in the *hermeneutic circle*, a concept introduced here (unlabelled) in the opening pages of Chapter 1. That is, any reader's act is dependent upon prior learned frameworks.[2] In Eco's words, 'the text is an object that the interpretation builds up in the course of the circular effort of validating itself on the basis of what it makes up as its result' (59).

Histories generally elicit *semantic interpretation* and discourage *hermetic drift*, mainly by means of an omniscient narrator, the reliance on details and dates, and expository markers that explain cause and effect. But while positing him– or herself as authoritative, the writer of historical narratives has also, obviously, *read* and *interpreted* data, and done so, we can assume, from the perspective of a reader in search of original, *authorial intentions*. Indeed, in readings that resemble my interpreting Elizabeth as a touchstone for *The Tryall of Chivalry*, no doubt about it, there's some *hermetic drift* to be found. The question of how much drifting is finally 'allowed' into a history is determined by the literary system's *codes*.

Importantly, the codes for historical writing today do not encourage readers to participate in *critical interpretation* – if you're presenting the truth, you don't really want your readers to challenge the rhetorical structures that convey it. The narratives discussed here, however, do draw attention to their rhetorical elements and, as Ascham suggests, are in part judged by them. In order to make these issues clear, I'm going to start with what we would probably call a fictional narrative, although it has some markers of a history, Sir Thomas Malory's *Le Morte D'Arthur*.

Sir Thomas Malory's *Le Morte D'Arthur*

It may seem odd to begin a chapter introducing history with a text that we would nowadays clearly categorize as a fiction. But as we saw in Chapter 1, response to King Arthur is frequently *semantic* rather than *critical.* Thus, Edward III is able to author a new emblem for the kingdom, whose *semantic* response can be measured in readers like John de Werchin. Likewise, later in the period, when Polydore Vergil's *Anglica Historica* (English History) basically scoffed at the Arthurian legends, it generated aggressively nasty barbs aimed at the Italian historian in *semantic* distaste. As a final example among many, in 1542, John Leland, who compiled all data known about Arthur, *semantically* identified Cadbury Castle as Camelot.

And by Malory's time, the genealogy leading to *Le Morte D'Arthur* is not inconsequential, although his narrative probably redacts only English and French narratives. The earliest extant narrative that refers to a figure who probably serves as a *locus* for Arthur is Gildas' *De Excidio Britanniae* (On the Destruction of Britain), a history written in about 540, in which the leader is called Ambrosius Aurelianus. Perhaps the first narrative to mention Arthur by name is the Welsh *Gododdin*, written in about 600, which contains a series of laments for the British nobles who fought against the Angles. In Nennius' *Historia Brittonum* (History of the Britons), written in about 800, Ambrosius Aurelianus is called a *dux bellorum* (leader of battles), whose victory at Mount Baden is celebrated as the culminating event of his career. In about 900, the *Spoils of Annwfn* relates the adventure of Arthur's acquisition of a magic cauldron, while another Welsh narrative – this time of the historical genre – mentions the deaths of Arthur and Medraut at Camlann, in about 960, a narrative called the *Annales Cambriae* (Annals of Wales). An early mention of Arthur as the great King of the Britons occurs in 1019, in the prologue to a life of St Goeznovius, *Legenda Sancti Goeznovii.* Two Latin histories, written in the 1120s, mention Arthur as well: William of Malmesbury's sceptical account in the *Gesta Regum Anglorum* (Deeds of the Kings of Britain) and Henry of Huntingdon's *Historia Anglorum* (History of the English), which records 12 of Arthur's battles along with the observation that still, some Britons refuse to believe in Arthur's death and so await the return of their leader. Geoffrey of Monmonth's Latin *Historia Regum Brittaniae* (History of the Kings of Britain), written in around 1136, contains the first full version of Arthur's life. As you can guess, the numbers of extant narratives increase as we proceed in time, so I'll mention only two more, which were probably important for Malory: the Vulgate cycle, a massive French prose narrative starting with the early history of the Grail and ending with Arthur's death, composed in about 1215–35, and the *Alliterative Morte Arthure*, written in about 1390, in Middle English verse.

Little is known about the *Morte's* author; possibly, he is the Sir Thomas Malory (Maleore) of Newbold Revell in Warwickshire (d. 1471) who soldiered at Calais under Richard Beauchamp, Earl of Warwick, and witnessed the decline of the Lancastrian fortunes. This individual apparently had been in prison for armed assault, rape and a number of other derelict activities. Here, we'll be reading William Caxton's 1485 edition of Malory's *Morte*, which modifies the narrative a bit, but which also provides a preface that incorporates the responses of an interested reader.

In his preface, Caxton writes that he is printing, 'the noble histories of the said King Arthur, and of certain of his knights, after a copy unto me delivered, which copy Sir Thomas Malory did take of certain books of French, and reduced it into English' (Preface; vol. 1: 5). Earlier, Caxton tells his readers that he often thought he should write about the story of the Sangrail (the Holy Grail) and of the most famous Christian King, Arthur, one of the world's nine worthies (Preface; vol. 1: 3). So, upon King Edward IV's request, he decides to print this narrative, noting

> ... that divers men hold opinion that there was no such Arthur, and that all such books as be made of him be but feigned and fables, because that some chronicles make of him no mention nor remember him nothing, ne of his knights. (Preface; vol. 1: 4)

Hedging his bets, Caxton later states, 'but for to give faith and believe that all is true that is contained herein, ye be at your liberty. But all is written for our doctrine' (Preface; vol. 1: 6).

Vacillating between *semantic* and *critical interpretation*, Caxton demonstrates some discomfort with Malory's narrative, even though Malory does use the rhetoric of chronicles. Thus, after Arthur's mighty battle with 11 kings, we learn that his advisor, Merlin, journeys to his own master, Blaise, to tell him all that transpired:

> And so Bleise wrote the battle word by word, as Merlin told him how

it began, and by whom, and in likewise how it was ended, and who had the worse. All the battles that were done in Arthur's days, Merlin did his master Bleise do write; also he did do write all the battles that every worthy knight did of Arthur's court. (I. 17; vol. 1: 41–2)

Here is the authority for some of the tales' validity – enough reason for Caxton to squirm into *critical interpretive* mode.

But the quantity alone of material in the *Le Morte D'Arthur* has the effect of lulling *critical interpretive* sensibilities, even though there are places where such awareness actually seems elicited. The following such site, for example, encourages the question, when does the rhetoric of chronicling give way to allegory and bleed into fiction? Thus, early on (I. 19–20; vol. 1: 45–8), before he marries Guenevere and receives the Round Table as a present from her father, King Leodegrance (III. 1; vol. 1: 92–3), Arthur is visited by Margawse – Sir Lot's wife – the mother of Gawain, Gaheris, Agravain and Gareth; Margawse is also Igraine's daughter, and thus, also Arthur's sister. She consents to Arthur's advances, stays a month, and Mordred is conceived.

Then we learn that although not knowing he had committed incest, Arthur dreamed that griffins and serpents were destroying his kingdom, and in trying to defend his people against the monsters he is killed. He awakens and decides to go hunting after a hart, is wearied by the chase, and rests. Hearing what sounds like 30 hunting dogs, Arthur sees a beast, whose belly, it turns out, was making the horrific noises which were silenced once it drank. The king sleeps again, and a knight who is following the beast arrives upon the scene. He asks Arthur for his horse since his has died of exhaustion. Arthur wants the quest instead, but is refused; the knight takes his horse, Arthur challenges him, and is told:

> ' … seek me here when thou wilt, and here nigh this well thou shalt find me,' and so passed on his way.
> Then the king sat in a study, and bad his men fetch his horse as fast as ever they might. Right so came by him Merlin like a child of fourteen year of age, and saluted the king, and asked him why he was so pensive. (I. 20; vol. 1: 47)

Merlin plays with the befuddled king, first as a child and then as an 80-year-old man. As a child, the sorcerer tells him not to waste his time thinking about what just happened – 'thou art but a fool to take thought, for it will not amend thee' (*ibid.*). He goes on to inform the King that Uther Pendragon and Igraine were his real parents. Arthur is not pleased, the 'boy' leaves, and Merlin returns as an old man to confirm what the boy had to say and to add that the king has slept with his sister, which will result in a child that will destroy the realm. Merlin finally reveals his true self, tells Arthur he is to die in battle because of his sin, and that in contrast to the king Merlin himself will suffer a shameful death, bewitched by his passion for Nimue (in IV. 1; vol. 1: 117–18). Arthur's horse is returned, and the King sends for Igraine to learn the truth. By the way, at the end of the prior chapter we had learned that the knight who was following the Questing Beast was Pellinor, and after Pellinor died Sir Palomides took up the chase.

Thus, the episode lopes along from one event to another treating each of them as if they had equal truth value. The site's major obvious concern is, ironically and *self-reflexively* for a historical narrative, to learn the truth. In addition, creating dissonance regardless of the disguise Merlin appears in, his rhetoric elicits the responses of a *semantic* reader, although he 'knows' that the *fictions* he uses (his disguises as the boy and the old man) to house the truth will also elicit rejection and questioning of the form – they call for a *critical* reader. Nonetheless, even though Merlin plays with Arthur's abilities as a reader, he also sets limits – the king is not to engage in *hermetic drift* and worry about Pellinor's hunt for the Questing Beast, he's to focus instead on the central issue. And as a reader, Arthur does interpret here as a *critical reader*: he responds sceptically to the boy, to the old man and to Merlin as well – after all, he sends for Igraine to learn the truth. He himself rejects hermetic drift once he learns of the importance of the issue at hand.

But all this metaliterary activity occurs *in the world of the narrative*. In 'our world', we readers are encouraged, it seems, to leave the confines of authorial intention and semantic interpretation to drift along hermetically, albeit in limited fashion, and to the tunes of critical readership. Merlin's *ostensive* admonition *not* to pay attention to the Questing Beast of course draws our attention to it. It's difficult, besides, to ignore all those barking dog sounds. And how in the world did Pellinor get away with treating Arthur like that? While seeking the truth is the metaliterary problem presented in *this* world of *historia* (history or fiction), it cannot be the focus for us readers, since dramatic irony gives us the edge over Camelot's ruler. Not only do we know, from the narrator's information, that the boy and the old man are Merlin in disguise, but the beginning of the entire *Morte* gives us the data to 'confirm' Merlin's information. It has survived in our Model Readerly memory as 'how the whole thing began', a readerly type of response that is essential to the appreciation, as well as the creation, of historical narratives.

To return to the beginning then. In 21 books, Malory relates the story of Arthur, starting from Uther Pendragon and ending with the death of Sir Launcelot. Book I begins with Uther's attempt to reconcile with the powerful Duke of Tintagel, in Cornwall, whom he had sent for along with his beautiful wife Igraine. Uther's passion for Igraine leads her to insist that the couple leave prematurely, which Uther then seizes as an excuse to wage war on the Duke. In the course of besieging Terrabil, while Igraine is left in the safety of Tintagel, Uther avails himself of Merlin's magic. He is transformed to resemble the Duke so that the passionate King can enter Tintagel safely and be with Igraine. The Duke is killed in battle just before Uther lies with Igraine (hence, technically, Arthur is not conceived in adultery). Uther's barons insist he marry the widow, and the regent agrees. Later, when Igraine hears of when her husband died, 'she marvelled who that might be that lay with her in likeness of her lord; so she mourned privily and held her peace' (I. 2; vol. 1: 12). The two are married, and King Lot of Lothian and Orkney marries Margawse (yes, Igraine's daughter), and King Nentres marries Elaine. Morgan le Fay is placed in a nunnery where she learns the arts of magic, and later she is married to King Uriens.

Thus, by the end of the second chapter of the first book, the scene is set for Arthur. For reasons never explained nor even intimated, Merlin demands that Arthur be raised by Sir Ector and his wife. Upon Uther's death, the Archbishop of Canterbury, again upon Merlin's advice, calls all the nobles of the country to gather at Christmas in the greatest church in London, 'whether it were Paul's or not the French book maketh no mention' (I. 5; vol. 1: 15), and there, in the courtyard, rests a stone inscribed with the message that whoever can remove the sword is England's rightful king. All try, none can even budge it, and a New Year's Day tournament ensues with Sir Kay, Sir Ector's son, having lost his sword. Arthur resolves to find his brother another weapon, sees the sword in the stone, and takes it to him. After a feeble attempt to claim the monarchy, Kay tells the truth and Arthur demonstrates to his foster father what he had done. He then demonstrates the same for the rather upset lords, time after time after time – at Twelfth Day, Candlemas, Easter and Pentecost – until the Archbishop of Canterbury finally declares 'enough' and crowns the boy, the King.

Like Merlin's messages as a boy and an old man, the stone clearly 'relates' the truth, albeit in unconventional form, but nonetheless garners quite a bit of disbelief. Thus, at first, a number of powerful lords won't accept Arthur's regency, and no less than 11 kings join forces to challenge him (I. 14–17; vol. 1: 31–43). The battle proves his valor, and after many die – 15 000 remain of Arthur's original 60 000 men (I. 17; vol. 1: 40) – Merlin intervenes, demands that Arthur make a truce, and reassures him he won't be attacked by them for another three years anyway, since Saracens are ravaging their lands. Besides, Merlin adds, two great knights will avenge Arthur on them all in one day, Balin le Savage and Balan his brother (I. 18; vol. 1: 44).

In this indecisive and excessively bloody battle, we encounter the martial ethos that will dominate Malory's narrative in a variety of forms and which is applicable to either side of a conflict. Thus, Merlin praises the enemy, 'there were never men did more of prowess than they (Arthur's men) have done today, for ye have matched this day with the best fighters of the world' (I. 17; vol. 1: 41). Likewise, time and again, tournaments and skirmishes are waged where this martial ethos determines the worth of a knight, especially after Book III which begins with Arthur's marriage to Guenevere, the gift of the Round Table and his establishment of the knights of Camelot, among them Sir Tor, son of King Pellinor, and Gawain, whose adventures along with those of King Pellinor focus this book in the fellowship of Camelot. Indeed, battles, marvelous adventures and individual encounters multiply after this, through which knights will 'prove their worship', their reputation and value, by fighting others. Again, like Arthur's request to hear the facts from Igraine's mouth, a secondary report won't suffice – other, more immediate, proof is required for the *critical interpreter*, whether it be an original statement or actual deeds.

Not only must Arthur's knights be the best that military prowess has to offer and loyal beyond question to their king, they are to be courteous, especially to ladies, and hold to their word. But even when they do all that is required by chivalric *codes*, sometimes conflicting values or events nonetheless culminate in tragic outcomes. Thus, Book II begins with an odd analogue to Arthur's early years. Preparing to do battle with King Rience of North Wales, who had attacked Arthur's lands, Camelot is visited by a maiden sent by Lile of Avelion. She has a sword girt about her, which may only be drawn from its sheath by a knight good enough for her quest. None of King Rience's men could do so and neither could men of the Round Table. However, a badly neglected, poor knight, one who had killed another, was among the court. Sir Balin (one of the two Merlin had predicted would avenge Arthur on the 11 kings) is finally allowed to attempt the task; successful, he is anxious to pursue the adventure, even against her warning. Arthur apologizes to Balin for his former treatment of the knight, apparently not having registered Merlin's prophecy and claiming not to have known of his worth. For Arthur, who's 'been there, done that', the young knight's success at pulling the sword demonstrates valor. At least for now.

Because now, the trouble starts. A Lady of the Lake comes to court and demands either the head of the knight who won the sword or that of the maiden who had worn it. Balin had slain the Lady of the Lake's brother, and the sword-adorned Lady had caused the death of her father. Arthur asks her to reconsider, but she refuses. On his way out to begin his quest, Balin sees and recognizes her as the one he had been searching for for three years, learns that she asked for his head, and then, because it was she who caused his mother's death, in one fell swoop he decapitates her. Arthur is appalled and demands that the knight leave. Balin gives the head to his squire who is to return it to Northumberland, *as proof,* and he sets on his way.

A proud knight, Lanceor, wins Arthur's approval to avenge the Lady of the Lake. Meanwhile, Merlin arrives to reveal that the maiden with the sword is treacherous and that the sword will be the worthy knight's doom. Later, Merlin adds to the prediction: Balin will kill the truest knight now living and hence cause the fall of three kingdoms. Shortly thereafter, Lanceor is killed by Balin (is this the truest knight?). Lanceor's beloved appears out of nowhere and kills herself out of grief. Balin meets his brother, Balan, to whom he confides that he will attack King Rience at Castle Terrabil (the former Duke of Cornwall's stronghold) to regain Arthur's favor. They deliver King Rience to Arthur, with Merlin prophesying again, this time that the two brothers will win even greater fame for Camelot's King. Then, King Arthur besieges Castle Terrabil, and Balin and Balan join him to win the day. King Lot, having been deterred by Merlin, arrives late on the field, and although Gawain's father fights bravely against Arthur's forces, Pellinor, the Knight of the Questing Beast, kills the King. Ten years after he was made a knight, Gawain, we are told, kills King Pellinor in revenge (II. 10; vol. 1: 76).

We learn in the next chapter that 12 kings are interred as a result of this battle – and thus one of Merlin's predictions concerning Balin and Balan is fulfilled. Later, we learn, another of Merlin's prophecies is fulfilled, as Balin – in fair combat with King Pellam whose brother was slain by Arthur's knight – 'smote him passingly sore with that spear' (II. 15; vol. 1: 83), bringing the castle down with the 'Dolorous Stroke'. This, presumably, is the truest knight living. Or is it? Because another (or the same) prophecy comes true, as – unbeknownst to each other – Balin fights his own brother, Balan, and each die of their wounds in battle (II. 18; vol. 1: 87–90). Balin's sword is recovered by Merlin, who buries the brothers in one tomb and inscribes it with letters of gold. He then predicts that the sword can be wielded only by the best knight of the world, which will be either Sir Launcelot or his son Galahad (II. 19; vol. 1: 90).

I've spent some time with these tales within the tale, partly because they have some affinitites with *The Tryall of Cheualry* discussed in the last chapter, partly because they flow directly out of *Morte D'Arthur*'s opening, but mainly because they foreshadow the passage depicting Merlin's appearance to Arthur, disguised as a boy and an old man. The beginning of the *Morte*, after all, describes what Merlin is trying to reveal to Arthur so that he can understand that the King did, truly, commit incest. In all likelihood, we readers will recall the striking beginning of the narrative and hence experience double dramatic irony when we come to the boy–old man site. But associating this site with the narrative as it rolls into the Balin episode seems to smack of *hermetic drift*.

Nonetheless, each of the episodes just described *is* about truthful interpretation *in the world of the narrative*. The only purpose of the sword-in-the-stone adventure is to determine who the true heir to Uther's throne is. The 11 kings don't believe the stone's authority and are willing to test out their own interpretations in battle, just as all worthy knights need to 'prove their worship' through deeds. Likewise, when the maiden arrives – dissonantly girt with a sword that like all the swords up to this point are used to demonstrate truth of knightly valor – the need to arrive at truthful interpretation and to be able to judge becomes manifest with dizzyingly intense alacrity.

For example, the maiden is sent by Lile of Avelion, which seems to be a good thing, 'Avalon' having positive connotations, although

Merlin later tells us it's not. Likewise, Balin gives instructions to his squire to take the head back home, suggesting a tale of adventure, but none emerges. Similarly, the added information that Balin's mother was not only killed, but burned because of the Lady of the Lake, seems to demand another story – after all, burning is not your everyday killing in the world of the *Morte*. Could the Lady of the Lake have been virtuous after all, and if so why wasn't her murder avenged? And why is there more than one Lady of the Lake? In similar vein, we're made to understand that Lanceor is haughty, suggesting a flawed knight. But can a flawed knight be so loved that his beloved would kill herself for his sake? And what about Merlin's warning of the sword-wearing maiden's treachery? Moreover, what are we to do with this: at the battle against the 11 kings, the King Lot who was killed by Pellinore, Knight of the Questing Beast, was the King Lot who married Margawse when her mother married Uther, after Uther had besieged the Castle Terrabil to destroy Igraine's husband, the self-same castle that Arthur is now besieging. With so many coincidences, surely there's an underlying message here.

Such a series of adventures that reveal links can cause a reader to drift hermetically quite quickly and afar. And besides the links peeping out between the narrative's actions, there are apparent inconsistencies to deal with as well. What do we do, for example, with the battle of 11 kings and the interring of 12? Which prophecy came true, or are they all versions of the same prophecy told differently? Why can't Merlin warn Arthur *before* trouble begins? My guess is that even the most devoted *semantic* reader can't help but be nagged by at least one of these or similar questions. The apparent links and incon- sistencies elicit our *readerly* participation in a *writerly* fashion, to make narratives of our own that make sense. This is, at the same time, the historian's dilemma. For events may follow one another like pearls on a string, but it is an already predisposed vision that sees the pearls on a string, or even only one string. Actually, the strings connecting events are multiple and not necessarily causally formed – frequently it's just a question of being at the right place at the right time.

Being aware of multiple arcs linking events is *not*, however, how histories are generally written. What Merlin does is. The so(u)rcerer reveals causes, he indicates endings, and he isolates important themes. Thus, what is presented in the *Morte* juxtaposes what the historian does (through Merlin) with a representation of a much more complex world (through the adventures that appear to forge links with others). In inducing readers to perform acrobatic interpretations, Malory generates exactly the question that challenges historians and writers of fictions: how do you select the critical data and in what relations do you present them?

Malory's inclusion of bits and pieces that seem to lead directly into other related adventures, only not to, makes his narrative a tale that needs to be told again and again by writerly readers. In the remainder of his narrative, he presents the events leading to Camelot's destruction in a manner that highlights the theme of re-writing as well.

After Arthur conquers Rome and is named emperor in Book V, he begins to get squeezed into the margins, and even sometimes when he does appear, in disguise, he is unhorsed (for example X. 69; vol. 2: 144–6; X. 73, vol. 2: 151–4). While the King subsides into the margins and apparently loses his touch, Sir Launcelot du Lake is introduced as the hero, who 'passed all other knights' (VI. 1; vol. 1: 194). His many knightly deeds and adventures interlace with those of other knights and ladies, along with his affair with Guenevere, for the rest of the *Morte*. It is in this weaving of tales that re-writing becomes high-lighted: jousts and tournaments, demonstrations of piety, demonstrations of impiety, and characters' predicaments recur again and again, suggesting that after Arthur secures the kingdom, he attempts only to 'write the same story' rather than to begin another one.

The repeated motifs have the additional effect of emphasizing the existence of those multiple, visible strands that link events. For example, before Merlin was imprisoned in stone by Nimue in Book IV and consequently dropped out of the picture (IV. 5; vol. 1: 124), Arthur's sorcerer attributes the end of Camelot to Arthur's incestuous fathering of Mordred. While this is in one sense true, Launcelot's adulterous and treacherous relation with his Queen additionally contributes to the ultimate destruction, as counterpointed and at times echoed in the parallel love triangle involving Sir Tristram, in love with Queen Iseut, the wife of his uncle, the sinister King Mark of Cornwall, which too can be interpreted as having contributed to the end. Indeed, beginning in Book VIII, Launcelot and Tristram are constantly referred to as the best knights of the land, a pairing that Merlin had foretold earlier as well (II. 8; vol. 1: 71), thereby suggesting crucial links. From an entirely different perspective, Launcelot's son contributes to the tragedy too.

When Launcelot is tricked into sleeping with Elaine, King Pelles' daughter, Galahad, the knight who will achieve the Sangrail, is conceived (XI. 2; vol. 2: 190–2). While from this point on Launcelot is depicted as in and out of trouble with the Queen, so too, increasingly, the vision of the Sangrail enchants a number of Arthur's knights to take the holy quest. Inspired by Galahad, Arthur's knights, including Launcelot, try to commit themselves to the greater kingdom with varying degrees of success. The Round Table no longer signifies unified chivalric fellowship, thereby also signalling the end.

After demonstrating his purity countless times, Galahad, along with Sir Percival and Sir Bors, is entrusted with the Sangrail which is to be returned to the city of Sarras – a reverse *translatio studii et imperii*, so to speak (XVII. 20; vol.2: 366). Galahad does so, is proclaimed king, and finally is brought to God by Joseph of Arimathea (XVII. 22; vol. 2: 370). The markers of the saint's life, as seen in the previous chapter's discussion of the Digby *Mary Magdaelene*, are thus introduced into this narrative of chivalric adventure. It is this genre's markers that thus foreshadow alternative endings to Arthur's kingdom.

But not quite yet. Although Launcelot had been chaste for a while, in Book XVIII he falls to his old ways. Not long after, the end is signalled again when in rescuing Guenevere from being burned as an adulteress Launcelot accidentally kills one of Gawain's brothers (XX. 8; vol. 2: 470–2). War is waged against Launcelot, an unsteady peace is made and Guenevere is returned to Arthur (XX. 15; vol.2: 486), but nothing remains as it was. In Book XXI we learn of Mordred's attempt to take England and Guenevere, the destruction of the knights, Mordred's killing of Arthur and Arthur of Mordred, and the return of Excalibur to the lake. Reflecting Galahad's influence, Guenevere removes herself to a nunnery, Launcelot and his compatriots become monks, Guenevere dies, as does Launcelot shortly thereafter, and Constantine becomes the next King of England.

While Merlin's vision singling out the one cause of Camelot's demise is true in one sense, he is also predisposed to select the one strand of the story he can see. As with any interpretation, his too is only one reading. Indeed, some of his prophecies are so ambiguous they could be pointing to other stories. In other words, not only do many strands lead to an ending, but a narrative's various sites can be framed differently to generate different stories. Re-writing may intend to follow the same narrative pattern, as Arthur tries to write the same story over and over again, but it can also mean finding other stories that connect the same, or different, sites. This, too, is part of the historian's dilemma of selecting data and linking them, for in spite of its authoritative presentation and eliciting of *semantically* inclined readers, a history is never final. Indeed, as Malory writes, oscillating constantly between *semantic* and *critical interpretation*, as well as between chivalric and spiritual worlds:

> Yet some men say in many parts of England that King Arthur is not dead, but had by the will of Our Lord Jesu into another place; and men say that he shall come again, and he shall win the holy cross. I will not say that it shall be so, but rather I will say, here in this world he changed his life. But many men say that there is written upon his tomb this verse: HIC IACET ARTHURUS, REX QUONDAM REXQUE FUTURUS [here lies Arthur, once and future King]. (XXI. 7; vol. 2: 519)

If Arthur doesn't return, we can be sure that stories, and histories, about him will.

Having problematized the writing of history in a narrative we tend to associate with fiction, but about which *literati* of this period were divided, I hope the rhetorical and semiotic issues of the remaining chronicles are more evident, and that we can feel somewhat confident as *critical interpreters* with regard to their structures. The *Morte* was written in about the middle of our period, in the fifteenth century, while Robert Mannyng of Brunne's *Chronicle* and John Barbour's *Bruce* were written in the fourteenth century, around the beginning of our period, and finally, Thomas More's *History of Richard III* was written in the sixteenth century, towards the end of our period.

Robert Mannyng of Brunne's *Chronicle*

Histories after the Norman Conquest tend more than earlier histories to contain or refer to documents (some of which are forgeries) and to use such evidence rhetorically with political patronage in mind. Interesting as it plays with and also against this perspective is Jean Froissart's *Chronicles*, which in four massive books covers England's national and international events of political interest during the period 1322–1400, from the viewpoints of a French writer with ties to the English court. Probably of more relevance here, however, is a narrative that is pretty deeply saturated in English culture of the time, Robert Mannyng of Brunne's *Chronicle*, which was completed in 1338 and survives in two complete manuscripts and a fragment.

The author, who had connections with the English Gilbertine order, was born in the latter half of the thirteenth century in Bourne, Lincolnshire, and besides the *Chronicle*, also wrote *Handlyng Synne*, begun in 1303. *The Chronicle* has a total of 36 982 lines with the verse of Part I crafted in octosyllabic couplets, and Part II composed in rhymed couplets, usually with five or six stresses. The narrative relies on Geoffrey of Monmouth's *Historia Regum Brittaniae* (History of the Kings of Britain) (1136), the *Historia Ecclesiastica Gentis Anglorum* (Ecclesiastical History of the English People) by the Venerable Bede (673–735), contemporary French and English romances, as well as on Ovid and Juvenal. But in the main, as the narrator himself indicates, Part I essentially translates into English from the French Wace's *Roman de Brut* (1155), and Part II translates from the Anglo-French verse *Chronicle* written by a contemporary, Pierre Langtoft. Mannyng describes his indebetedness as a sort of *translatio studii*:

> Als Geffrey in Latyn sayd,
> so Mayster Wace in Frankis layd.
> þe date of criste was þan þis lyue,
> a thousand ȝere fifty & fyue.
> Than com out of Brydlyngton,
> Pers of Langtoft, a chanon.
> Als Mayster Wace þe same he says,
> bot he rymed it oþer ways.
> He begynnes at Eneas:
> of alle þe Brute he tellis þe pas,
> & sþen* alle þe Inglis dedis;
> feyrere langage non ne redis.
> After þe Inglis kynges, he says þer pris
> þat alle in metir fulle wele lys.
> And I, Robert, fulle fayn wald bringe
> in Ynglis tonge þer faire saiynge.
> God gyf me grace wele to spede,
> þis ryme on Inglis forto rede.

[I. 183–200: As Geoffrey (of Monmouth) related it in Latin, so too Master Wace recorded it in French. The date was then after Christ, one thousand fifty-five (actually 1155). Then there was from Bridlington, Peter of Langtoft, a canon. He says the same as Master Wace, but he rhymed it differently. He begins with Aeneas: he tells all the episodes of Brut and then (*'sþen' seems to be an error for 'þen') all the English deeds; you can't read it in fairer language. After the

English kings, he tells of their worthiness and all that lies very well in
meter. And I, Robert, would like very much to translate into English
their fair tales. God give me grace to do it well, to read this rhyme into
English.]

Not only is this a *translatio studii* (transferral of culture) because it
conveys a list of writers, but it's also a *translation*, and one, it should
be added, that records the *translatio imperii* (transferral of empire)
from one kingdom to another.

What is also interesting is Mannyng's compliment to Langtoft,
which suggests that Anglo-Norman was considered the courtly
English of the day. Nonetheless, as Mannyng states earlier (I. 55–70),
he's writing for those whose primary, and perhaps only, language is
English:

> Als þai haf wryten & sayd
> haf I alle in myn Inglis layd
> in symple speche as I couth
> þat is lightest in mannes mouth.
> I mad noght for no disours,
> ne for no seggers, no harpours,
> bot for þe luf of symple men
> þat stange Inglis can not ken.

> [I. 71–8: As they have written and said, I have laid it in my English in
> as simple speech as I could, which is easiest on men's lips. I did not
> make it for entertainers, nor for reciters, nor for harpers (all profes-
> sionals who would recite poetry to audiences), but for the love of
> simple men, who do not know the foreign English.]

For such Model Readers as constitutes Mannyng's projected audience
(note that he addresses nobles in the first line), *The Chronicle*, as he
informs us, will tell the complete history of England:

> Lordynges þat be now here,
> if ʒe wille listene & lere
> alle þe story of Inglande
> als Robert Mannyng wryten it fand
> & on Inglysch has it schewed,
> not for þe lerid bot for þe lewed,
> ffor þo þat in þis land won
> þat þe Latyn no Frankys con,

ffor to haf solace & gamen
in felawschip when þai sitt samen.

[I. 1–10: Nobles that are now here, if you will listen and learn the whole story of England as Robert Mannyng found it written and translated it into English, not for the learned, but for the ignorant, for in this land there live those who know neither Latin nor French, (it's for them, so they can) have pleasure and entertainment in fellowship when they sit together.]

Although Mannyng doesn't begin his pleasurable story with Adam and Eve, he's not very far from them: he begins with Noah, moves to Aeneas, then to Brutus, and on to Cadwallader, 'þe last Bryton þat þis lande lees' (I. 30: 'the last Briton, who lost this land'). After the Britons come the English, who at that time are Saxons, led by Vortigern who is defeated by ancestors of the present race of Englishmen. After telling us what he is going to do for about 50 more lines, Mannyng then *critically* compares his two major sources, Wace and Langtoft, before going into his introductory sketch in detail.

Beginning in biblical times, the narrative moves to the Greeks and thereafter mingles biblical with Greek mythology. Importantly, Mannyng also tells of Troy's destruction (I. 439 ff), thereby echoing others who read the Trojan War as critical to the founding of Britain, a war which 'Dam Venus' (I. 515: 'Lady Venus') had much to do with. He details her conversation with Paris, which led to the prince's giving her the apple, or in this case, the 'balle'. Going on for hundreds of lines with the Trojan story, Mannyng then details the exemplary life of Brutus, the hero who founded Britain and whose out-of-wedlock parents are Aeneas' grandson, Sisillius, and the niece of Aeneas' second wife, Lavinia (who is not named). When the lovers' liaison is discovered, Sisillius' half-brother, who had become King, seeks counsel about their covert liaison, resulting in their exile.

In exile, Brutus' mother dies in childbirth. When Brutus is 15 he accidentally kills his father in a hunting accident. Desolate, Brutus exiles himself and arrives at Troy, whose citizens are vassals to Greece; there he meets the sons of Priam and Achilles. Through his noble qualities Brutus quickly becomes well-known and is asked to lead the Trojans, 7000 knights strong, in battle against the Greeks. In the manner of the *Star Wars* sequels and prequels, the Greeks and the Trojans battle once again. However, this time the slyness of the Greeks is evinced by Brutus, who creates his own 'Trojan Horse': he has a Greek prisoner function as the lure to the Greeks defending a pass. With the guards ambushed, Brutus leads his men into the Greek stronghold and defeats the enemy.

Distributing the booty among his men, Brutus then holds a counsel to determine what course of action they should take. They all agree to ask the Greek King and his brother for permission to leave and find another country and to request that the King's daughter, Ignogyn, become their Queen. Left without much choice, the Greek King agrees and gives them ships to transport them to parts unknown. On the third day of their voyage they land in Leogice, which seems like a pretty nice place to stay. However, they come upon an empty town with a temple dedicated to Diana, the goddess of the hunt. There, Brutus consults the goddess and is told, in a dream, to journey to a very fruitful, wonderful land:

> Ouer France toward þe west
> is an Ilde, on of þe best.
> Wele likand is þer wonyng
> & plenteuous of ilk a thyng,
> ffrute to bere, gode es þer londe...
> Albion is now þe name;
> þhorh þe salle it haf oþer fame:
> þer salle þou gyn a newe Troie,
> to alle þi kyn newe ioie,
> & þe kynde þat comes of þe,
> thorh alle þe werld wirsciped salle be...

> [I. 1379–90: Beyond France, toward the west is an island, one of the best. Very pleasing it is there to live and plentiful of each thing, the land is good for bearing fruit ... Albion is now its name; through you it shall have other fame; there you shall begin a New Troy, to all your race new joy, and all the people who will be descended from you, throughout all the world shall be worshipped ...]

After 500 lines and some adventures, they land in Albion, but 'Whan Brutus com, þat name was gon' (1852: 'When Brutus came, that name was gone'). We are told that the Trojans took Brutus' name for the land and themselves, and thus, they became Britons living in Britain (I. 1859–61). Their city becomes 'Trinouaunte', New Troy (I. 1905–6), which is what it is called until King Lud arrives, which induces the Saxons to call the town 'Luden', a name that is eventually transformed into 'London' (I. 1919). Elements of Brutus' tale echo stories we've treated in a variety of genres: the *translatio* topos, the violent circumstances of the hero's birth, the hero's clearly marked superiority, and the need for counsel. In a sense, histories of this period are continually re-writing these elements.

Mannyng's narrative continues, proceeding from king to king with stories that include King Lear's tragic tale (I. 2261–2584) along with that of Merlin, King Uther and King Arthur (I. 7841–13740). Unlike Malory's *Morte*, however, Mannyng also focuses on Merlin's early childhood. He begins by relating how King Vortigern attempts to build a castle that keeps collapsing. Vortigern is told that a wise child must be slain and his blood mixed with the mortar and stone. Merlin, 12 at the time, is the wise child, but when brought before the king he explains that the problem isn't architectural. Rather, deep in the ground two dragons, one red and one white, are at fault. So, the ground is excavated, the fearsome dragons appear, fly into the air, fight and breathe fire, until the white defeats the red (I. 7841–8090). Merlin's reputation is secured. Thus, Vortigern asks him to prophesy his future, and the boy uses the dragons to do so. Vortigern is the red dragon, and the Saxons will defeat him. Further, King Aurelius will be poisoned and his brother, Uther, will gain the crown, and then Arthur will reign (I. 8121–58). Events transpire as Merlin predicts, and he warns or advises each subsequent king.

As with Geoffrey of Monmouth's Latin narrative of English kings, the material concerning Arthur in Mannyng's *Chronicle* comprises the longest section. Indeed, the narrator himself comments on Arthur's popularity:

> In alle londes wrote men of Arthoure;
> his noble dedis of honoure,
> in France men wrote & ʒit write;
> here haf we of him bot lite.
> Tille Domesday men salle spelle
> of Arthure dedis, talk & telle.
>
> (I. 10415–20: In all lands, men wrote of Arthur; of his noble deeds and worthiness in France men wrote and still write; here we have only little about him. Until Doomsday men will narrate of Arthur's deeds, talk and tell.)

But Mannyng's version of Arthur's reign is more martial and less courtly than Malory's later *Morte*.

Thus, soon after his coronation Arthur fights the Saxons, along with others, including the Scots and the Irish. Having won, he gives the north to three of his warriors, one of whom was Lot, who marries Anne (not Margawse), and they become the parents of Gawain, the courteous (I. 10231–44). Then, Arthur marries Guenevere, a beautiful maiden, but they remain childless (I. 10245–58). After that, it's back to action, and battles ensue. When, much later, the Roman Emperor's messengers demand tribute from Arthur and his court, Arthur refuses and they engage in war. He entrusts his cousin, the evil Mordred, with the land and with Queen Guenevere, with whom he secretly has an affair (I. 11745–58). Arthur is victorious, but on his way to Rome in triumph messengers inform him of his sister's son's treachery (I. 13465–94). Arthur rushes back to Britain, and the two armies meet at Whitsand. Many die, among them Gawain, but Mordred escapes to Winchester with Arthur chasing after him and besieging the town. They fight, and many a man is lost. Mordred again escapes, this time to Cornwall, with those who had forsaken Arthur. Meanwhile, Guenevere flees to a nunnery in Wales and takes the veil. The final battle occurs, '& þer was slayn in þat stoure/ of þe rounde table þe floure' (I. 13701–2: And there was slain in that battle the flower of the round table).

In addition to Arthur's story, Mannyng also tells of the arrival of important churchmen, like St Bede, St Gregory, and St Augustine (not of Hippo, but a monk who arrived in England from Rome in 597) (I. 14251–740), before beginning with Cadwallader's death in Part II. From here on, Mannyng mingles religious with political stories, while he focuses on England's relations with Ireland, Wales and Scotland, as well as with France and Flanders. For example, he relates details about Henry II's reign (1154–89), including his marriage with Eleanor of Aquitaine (II. 3130–1) and his conflicts with Thomas Becket, Archbishop of Canterbury (II. 3148–209), leading to the infamous slaying of the churchman in the cathedral:

> [þe kyng] said bot tille a knyght þat Thomas him misbede,
> & if he had had men as he wend of renoun,
> þei suld haf venged him of suilk a clergioun.
> Foure kyngtes it herd withouten any more;
> to Canterbiri þei ferd & slouh Thomas right þore.

II. 3205–9: The King said when will a knight harm that Thomas, and if he had had men, as he thought, of excellence, they should have avenged him of such a clergyman. Four knights heard it and without further ado, they went to Canterbury and slew Thomas right there.]

Henry, of course, does penance for his deed (II. 3467–71). Mannyng also relates of Richard the Lionhearted's victory at Acres, along with a passage describing how the English King received a miraculous message wrapped about an arrow and sent by the Holy Ghost, in which all the Saracen plans were exposed (II. 4425–31). Perhaps, St George was at play here too.

The last 3000 lines and more of *The Chronicle* focus on King Edward I (1272–1307), who is introduced while still a prince advising his father (II. 5229–30), King Henry III (1216–72). Included in this account are Edward's battles with the Scottish, clearly conveyed from the English perspective, but with some respect for the enemy. For example, William Wallace is finally caught in 1305, and although he is marked negatively, 'þat maister was of theues' (II. 8039: 'who was master of thieves'), Mannyng also describes his capture as a betrayal by Jack Short. Likewise, his execution at London, which Mannyng may actually have witnessed, is detailed, pretty much as the recent film *Brave Heart* depicted, and reports the event with relative objectivity. In other words, Mannyng does not insist on Wallace's dastardly deeds, nor does he explicitly characterize the punishment as fitting. Rather, he draws somber equations that explain why Wallace was executed the way he was, but leaves these *signs* unmarked with *connotations*:

> þe first dome he fanged, for treson was he drawen,
> for robbrie was he hanged, & for he had men slawen;
> & for he had brent abbeis & men of religion,
> eft fro þe galweis, quick þei lete him doun
> & bouweld him alle hote & brent þam in þe fire.
> His hede þan of smote, suilk was William hire …

> [II. 8051–56: The first punishment he got, for treason he was drawn; for robbery he was hung and for the men he had killed; and since he had burned abbies and men of religion, again from the gallows alive they released him and disembowelled him and burned them in the fire. They then cut off his head, such was William's wages …]

The *Chronicle* goes on to tell how since William 'mayntend þe werre at his myght' (II. 8057:'maintained the war with all his might'), he was quartered, and his body parts sent to various towns as warnings. At this point, the narrative turns to the next Scottish enemy, 'Of William haf ȝe herd how his endyng was,/ now of Kyng Roberd to telle ȝow his trespas' (II. 8069–70: 'Of William have you heard how his ending was, now you will be told of King Robert's trespass').

Mannyng was at Cambridge in 1306, at a feast also attended by Robert and Thomas Bruce (II. 8225–34), where Robert ' ... sauh alle þe gest þat wrote & mad þis ryme' (II. 8234: 'saw the whole chronicle that wrote and made this rhyme'). After briefly telling of the Scottish leaders' activities, he relates how King Edward I's men capture the Bruces on Ash Wednesday as they are leaving mass and take them to be executed. This is the last incident narrated before Mannyng begins to sum up and end his chronicle by focusing on Edward's burial and referring to Edward II's vow to destroy the grandson of the Bruce (II. 8327) ... more on this story below.

Mannyng's *Chronicle* is structured linearly and elicits, for the most part, *semantic* readers, who recognize in the tales of Brutus, Merlin and Arthur 'historical' frameworks that essentially convey the glory of nations. While presenting a number of tales which we would label fictional, Mannyng situates them within an authoritative chronology. However, with the array of kings and armies who have ruled, conquered and expanded England, and especially with the segments on Brutus and Arthur, *semantic* readers may very well be moved to exercise *critical interpretation* as well. Indeed, the multifarious stories underscore at least this lesson: failures and victories don't determine the worth of the English nation. It's the chivalric ethos.

If this is true for the better part of the history, then the closing section on Edward's reign actually raises questions and suggests other stories, maybe to be written by other historians. On the most obvious level, will Edward II be able to keep his vow? But also, Mannyng's selection and framing of events – for example, to depict treachery in Wallace's capture or to emphasize the Bruces' capture on Ash Wednesday while coming from mass – belong, rhetorically, to a different narrative, one which may see reason for Scottish insurgence.

John Barbour's *Bruce*

Edward I (1272–1307) annexed Wales in 1284, and made it the property of the heir to the English throne (1301). As Mannyng relates, Edward also tried to dominate Scotland, while waging war against the French as well. The French and the Scottish became allies, and the English sought the support of the Flemish. This particular set of hostilities against the Scottish began when Edward was asked to help determine who was to become Scotland's next ruler, since in 1286 Alexander III died, and then in 1290 his seven-year-old heiress, Margaret, died as well. Rather than supporting Robert Bruce, Edward declared in 1292 for John Balliol, whom he subsequently treated as his vassal. For a while Balliol consented to this redefinition of terms, but then, following the advice of a number of his lords, he allied himself with the French King Philip IV (1285–1314). Between 1296 and 1307, nine English armies advanced on Scottish territory only to meet the fierce resistance led by William Wallace and Andrew Moray.

About half a year after Wallace was heinously killed in 1305, Robert Bruce, grandson of the 1290 claimant, rose against Edward in February 1306. Edward I died in July 1307, Edward II was apparently incompetent, and this Bruce began destroying English-held castles. In 1314, Robert the Bruce defeated the English at Bannockburn, near Stirling, even though the odds were two to one in Edward's favor. More Scottish raids ensued, the French began to renew their battles against the English, and in 1327 Edward II was deposed by his own Queen the French Princess Isabella and her lover Roger Mortimer. So much for his promise to destroy the Bruce, as recorded at the end of Mannyng's chronicle. In 1328 the Treaty of Northampton recognized Bruce as King of an independent Scotland. In 1329, Pope John XXII granted the Scottish kings full rights of coronation and anointing. In 1329, King Robert died.

Less than 50 years after the death of Robert Bruce (1274–1329), *The Bruce* (1376) focuses on the battle to establish an independent Scottish state. Written in what some call northern English and others call early Scots, the long narrative poem comprises 20 books, containing about 13 500 lines of octosyllabic couplets, and covering events from 1286 through 1332.

The Bruce's author, John Barbour (b. *c.* 1320), was the archdeacon of Aberdeen from August 1357 until his death on 13 March 1395 and served under David II (1329–71) as well as under Robert II (1371–90).

Even after he had become archdeacon, Barbour continued to study at Oxford and Paris, which sheds some light on the erudition evident in his poem. For example, Barbour often alludes to classical and biblical literature to draw parallels between Scottish heroism and that of the ancients, including allusions to Troy, the biblical story of the Maccabees, the romances of Alexander and of Thebes, the death of Julius Caesar, and the tales of King Arthur. The history survives in two manuscripts (one from 1487 and the other from 1489), along with five principal editions (the earliest printed in about 1570–1).

The Bruce was written at a politically instable time both within and without the kingdom, during the reign of David II who was held hostage in England and for whose return and in lieu of missed ransom payments the Scottish agreed to English succession of the Scottish throne. Writing of the leader who led the battle for independence in times like these, Barbour seeks out an audience that more or less demonstrates a *semantic* proclivity. He begins his narrative with a reference to the rhetorical principle of *docere et delectare*, teaching while pleasing:

> Storys to rede ar delitabill,
> Suppos that thai be nocht bot fabill;
> Than suld storys that suthfast wer,
> And thai war said on gud maner,
> Hawe doubill plesance in heryng.

> (I.1–5: Reading stories is a delight even if they are nothing but tall tales; stories that are truthful and are eloquently told are doubly pleasing to listen to.)

But he also reminds his readers of the semiotic function – in the Augustinian sense – that stories have to represent a greater truth, especially old stories:

> For aulde storys that men redys,
> Representis to thaim the dedys
> Of stalwart folk that lywyt ar,
> Rycht as thai than in presence war.

> (I. 17–20: For old stories that men read represent to them the deeds of brave people who lived earlier, right as they then were in life.)

Such representative lives, Barbour tells us, were those of 'king Robert off Scotland' (I. 27) and 'gud Schyr Iames off douglas' (I. 29). Although he plans to tell these histories, Barbour himself calls his narrative a romance (I. 443–4).

Beginning with Alexander III's death in 1286, Barbour sketches the struggle to determine who the new King of the Scots will be. Edward I offers the crown to Bruce if he will pay homage to the English king. Bruce refuses, and Balliol is made regent. According to some modern historians, though, Balliol had the better claim to the throne, and similarly discordant, in 1296 and in 1302, Robert I actually joined forces with Edward I. But that's another story. Barbour's story is the attempted oppression by the English of the Scots, as signalled by the introduction's closing lines on freedom (I. 225–74):

> A! fredome is A noble thing! ...
> Fredome all solace to man giffis:
> He levys at es that frely levys! ...
> And suld think fredome mar to prys
> Than all the gold in warld that Is ...

> (I. 225–40: Ah! Freedom is a noble thing! Freedom gives complete solace to a man. He lives at ease who lives freely. And one should think to prize freedom more than all the gold that is in the world.)

The narrative goes on to describe the struggle for freedom under Bruce and his trusted friends, among them James Douglas, and in doing so conflates the first Bruce and his grandson. Douglas is presented to Edward I and claims his father's lands. Bruce and Comyn discuss the state of affairs, and the latter offers Bruce the kingdom in exchange for Bruce's lands. Bruce agrees, not realizing that he will be betrayed, and contracts are signed.

Juxtaposed, then, to some general words on treason, Barbour's narrator now refers to the *translatio studii et imperii*, leading to Arthur's death:

> Wes nocht all troy with tresoune tane,
> Quhen x ʒeris of the wer wes gane?
> Then slayn wes mone thowsand
> Off thaim with-owt, throw strenth of hand,
> As Dares in his buk he wrate,
> And Dytis, that knew all thar state.

Thai mycht nocht haiff beyn tane throw mycht,
Bot tresoun tuk thaim throw hyr slycht.
And Alexander the conqueroure,
That conqueryt Babilonys tour,
And all this warld off lenth and breid,
In xij yher, throw his doughty deid,
Wes syne destroyit throw pwsoune,
In his awyne hows, throw gret tresoune.
Bot, or he deit, his land delt he:
To se his dede wes gret pite.
Iulius Cesar als, that wan
Bretane and fraunce, as dowchty man,
Affryk, arrabe, egipt, Surry,
And all evrope halyly;
And for his worschip & valour
Off Rome wes fryst maid Emperour;
Syne in hys capitole wes he,
Throw thaim of his consaill priue,
Slayne with punsoune rycht to the ded.
And quhen he saw thar wes na rede,
Hys Eyn with his hand closit he,
For to dey with mar honeste.
Als Arthur, that throw chevalry
Maid Bretane maistres & lady
Off xij kinrykis that he wan;
And alsua, as A noble man,
He wan throw bataill fraunce all fre;
And lucius yber wencusyt he,
That then of Rome wes emperour:
But ʒeit, for all his gret valour,
Modreyt his Systir Son him slew,
And gud men als, ma then Inew,
Throw tresoune and throw wikkitnes,
The broite beris tharoff wytnes.

(I. 521–60: Wasn't all Troy taken by treason, after ten years of the war were over? Then there were slain more than a thousand of them, through armed combat, as Dares wrote in his book, and Dictys, who knew all their condition. They might not have been overcome by might, except that treason took them through its slyness. And Alexander the conqueror, who conquered Babylon's tower, and all this world long and wide, in 12 years, through his mighty deeds, was then destroyed through poison in his own house, through great treason. But, before he died, he distributed his land. To see his death was great pity. Julius Caesar also, who had conquered Britain and France, as a brave man, Africa, Arabia, Egypt, Syria, and all of Europe wholly; and for his worthiness and valor was made the first Emperor of Rome. Then he was in his capitol, and through those of his private counsel, he was slain treacherously right to his death. And when he saw there was no use, he closed his eyes with his hand in order to die with more honesty. Also Arthur, who through chivalry made Britons masters and ladies of 12 kingdoms that he won, and also, as a noble man, he won through battle all France; and Lucius Iberius he conquered, who was then Emperor of Rome: But yet, for all his great valor, Mordred, his sister's son slew him, and good men as well, more than enough, through treason and through wickedness. *The Brut* bears witness of this.)

I've cited these lines in their entirety, because they show how Barbour modifies the *translatio studii et imperii* topos to emphasize evil and its continuance, for indeed, as we are told, Comyn will betray Bruce to Edward.

But Bruce escapes, confronts Comyn and kills him (apparently in a church, which Barbour doesn't mention). Douglas supports the Scottish leader, and the two swear friendship. Bruce is crowned King of Scotland, and preparations are made for the Battle of Methven in which Bruce is defeated. A reference to the women at the siege of Thebes precedes Barbour's portrayal of Douglas' protection of the Scottish women. Such references to the chivalric behavior of the Scottish forces towards women punctuate the narrative, thereby subliminally associating the Scots with Arthurian-like greatness, not just for their own, but for all the oppressed. For example, Bruce even stops his army in Limerick, although they are advancing at the time against the Irish, to pitch a tent for a poor washerwoman in labor (XVI. 279 ff).

Battles continue, betrayals of the Scots abound, and Edward dies while on the way to attack Bruce, but not before he sentences prisoners of war to death. Constantly on the defensive, Bruce has numerous narrow escapes. He experiences victory with his 600 men against 3000 of the English at the battle of Loudon hill. Barbour also details the Battle of Bannockburn fought on Monday, 24 June 1314, during which English archers seem to be able to determine the outcome in their favor, until Bruce stirs his men to glory. The English are roundly defeated, and Sir Philip Mowbray surrenders Stirling castle to the Scottish leader. Focusing on the condensed Bruce's series of battles with three English Edwards, finally, Edward III makes peace with King Robert, whose son is betrothed to Joan of the Tower, King Edward's sister. The English give up all claim to Scotland for 20 000 pounds. King Robert falls ill, David and Joan are married and crowned King and Queen, and the Bruce dies, to the lament of all his people.

Of particular interest here, an unusal *translatio* also marks the ending of the narrative – the type of *translatio* or transferral of remains that is associated with saints' lives. That is, Douglas leaves with Bruce's heart for the Holy Land. But embroiled in a battle against the Saracens along the way, Douglas keeps throwing the encased heart in front of him, fighting his way to it, and starting over again. He is nonetheless killed in the attempt to rescue Sir William Sinclair. Both his body and Bruce's heart are recovered, the former buried in Douglas church and the latter at Melross. Finally, Sir Thomas Murray, who had been appointed regent, is poisoned, and thus Barbour ends with the deaths of these leaders.

In a sense, Barbour's *Bruce* provides a continuation of Mannyng's *Chronicle*, although from a different perspective. Indeed, the two instances of *translatio* referred to here articulate a stridently different set of perspectives. Having no investment in the Brut who founded Britain, Barbour explores more widely through classical literature and history – thereby, for example, being able to praise Caesar – and extracts a different lesson from the *translatio* topos than writers revelling in Britain's glory might. Likewise, Barbour's description of Douglas' battle to find Bruce's heart an appropriate resting place modifies the less martial associations with *translatio* that are propagated to designate God's chosen. Barbour's perspectives on *translatio* thus not only tell different stories than those written by English historians, they also demonstrate that alternate histories *can be written*. The message to Barbour's contemporaries seems clear.

Thomas More's *The History of King Richard III*

Probably most of us think of Thomas More (*c.* 1477–1535) as the author of the Latin treatise on an ideal government, *Utopia*, and as a statesman who refused to bend to Henry VIII's wishes, for which defiance he was executed. But, as mentioned earlier, he was also a colleague of Erasmus, a scholar, a champion and focal point of the new humanism, a defender of the Catholic faith, and a highly witty and eloquent detractor of tyranny. He is even depicted in a play entitled *The Book of Sir Thomas More*, written anonymously around 1590, which also portrays him as giving theatrical advice to players who are commissioned to perform *The Marriage of Wit and Wisdom*.

More's *History of King Richard III* was praised by Ascham as a superior pamphlet (mentioned in Chapter 2) and survives in both English and Latin versions. Neither of the versions is complete, focusing on events for the most part before Richard became king (1483–5). Although neither was published until after More's death, at least the English version was known in the 1530s. Indeed, modified parts of the narrative appear in chronicles, such as in Hall's *Union of the Two Noble and Illustre Families of Lancaster and York*, and may have served as sources for Shakespeare's history play about the Yorkist monarch.

Although some of the facts reported in *The History of King Richard III* are inaccurate, More is certainly consistent in eliciting the sympathies of a *semantic* reader against Richard who, from his perspective, is unworthy to rule. Perhaps working on his narrative between 1514 and 1518 (although his nephew William Rastell declared it was written about 1513), More pulls no punches in portraying the evils of tyranny. Yet, he begins as one might expect a historian to begin, in the *origins* that led to the situation being described:

> King Edward, of that name the Fourth, after that he had lived fifty and three years, seven months, and six days, and thereof reigned two and twenty years, one month, and eight days, died at Westminster the ninth day of April, the year of our redemption, a thousand four hundred four score and three, leaving much fair issue, that is to wit, Edward the Prince, a thirteen year of age; Richard Duke of York, two year younger; Elizabeth, whose fortune and grace was after to be queen, wife unto King Henry the Seventh, and mother unto the Eighth; Cecily, not so fortunate as fair; Bridget, which representing the virtue of her whose name she bare, professed and observed a religious life in Dartford, a house of close nuns; Anne, that was after honorably married unto Thomas, then Lord Howard and after Earl of Surrey. And Katherine which long time tossed in either fortune, sometime in wealth, oft in adversity, at the last, if this be the last, for yet she liveth, is by the benignity of her nephew, King Henry the Eighth, in very prosperous estate and worthy her birth and virtue. (3–4)

Beginning in factual detail (some of it inaccurate), More evokes the sense that what will follow will be objective, true and inevitable. In this opening passage, for example, he begins with Edward IV's death and ends with his last surviving child, whose well-being is secured by the current king, thereby creating a contrast with the subject of this narrative and suggesting at the same time that the rightful king is now on the throne.

Readers in More's literary system did encounter depictions of Richard as evil, and this initial framework enables them to focus on the context that, purportedly, Richard almost completely destroyed. Yet, the sense of outcome-informed objectivity continues, as More describes how well-loved Edward was, even though, 'he was of youth greatly given to fleshly wantonness' (5). He goes on to describe the struggles between the Houses of York and Lancaster, before he finally comes to the subject of his treatise:

> Richard, the third son ... was in wit and courage equal with either of them, in body and prowess far under them both: little of stature, ill-featured of limbs, crook-backed, his left shoulder much higher than his right, hard favored of visage, and such as in states called warly [warlike], in other men otherwise. (8)

Again, weighing the positive with the negative, More seems objective. He goes on to describe Richard as better at war than at peace. However, although he was generous,

> He was close and secret, a deep dissumuler [dissembler], lowly of countenance, arrogant of heart, outwardly coumpinable [friendly] where he inwardly hated, not letting [hesitating] to kiss whom he thought to kill; dispiteous and cruel, not for evil will alway, but ofter for ambition, and either for the surety or increase of his estate. (9)

The language here is more pointed and prepares readers for the report that Richard killed Henry VI with his own hands and contributed in some form to the murder of his own brother, Clarence. Only after some detail about these deeds does More go on to write, 'But of all this point is there no certainty ... ' (*ibid.*).

In the course of the narrative, Model Readers are asked to suspend their *critical* propensities, as More establishes the framework by means of moral judgments. For example, he admonishes against ambition in a sovereign, since the vice is a 'pestilent serpent' (13). This moral framework, when set against apparently factual detail, allows More to present Richard's story in a literary manner and focused on his treacherous deeds.

Thus, we learn among other things of how Richard III, then the Duke of Gloucester, secretly plots the destruction of Sir Anthony Woodville, Lord Rivers, the guardian to the new King, Edward V. The Duke of Buckingham and Lord Hastings prove to be willing allies in Richard's plans to gain more power, particularly when Richard, as protector to the young king, proves to be less than pleased that the king's mother took sanctuary with her other son and daughters. Here, More slows down the pace of the narrative to devote quite a bit of space to the different emissaries, their speeches, the Queen's responses and the emotions involved, before Richard's allies finally convince the Queen to leave her second son to the protector, even against her better judgment.

It's in the direct quotes of the 'players' that More most subtly elicits the *semantic* reader, even though the *critical* reader must know that if there were actual witnesses to these meetings who recorded the dialogues, they probably didn't have such perfect memories. Nonetheless, in arguing against the institution of sanctuary, for example, the Duke of Buckingham charges the Queen with 'Womanish fear, nay, womanish frowardness ... ' (29), before he goes on to argue that sanctuary is the refuge of rogues and, in fact, not legally necessary since it's unlawful to harm anyone anywhere. The flexing of rhetorical muscle here is obvious and powerful. But More also devotes several pages to the Queen's response, which is likewise not without rhetorical finesse. Not willing to engage the Duke in an argument of legal necessity, the Queen bases her denial, first, on the needs of a mother to be near her children and, second, on precedent, pointing to how she had taken sanctuary earlier when Edward IV was forced to flee the country. Worn down by their persistence, however, Elizabeth finally delivers her younger son, asking them to be faithful to their word. We learn shortly thereafter, clearly from the historian's perspective of having found the true intention:

> When the protector had both the children in his hands, he opened himself more boldly ... when he had imprisoned the queen's kins-folks and gotten both her sons into his own hands, then he opened the rest of his purpose with less fear to them whom he thought meet for the matter ... (42–3)

We also learn that Richard believed he could not avoid 'this wicked enterprise' (43) and so stuck to his course.

The drama of these pages, especially to those readers who already know the story (and More's audiences would have known), lies in the agony suffered by Elizabeth and the relentless use of language, legal terminology, and veiled threats against her. As just indicated, it's clear that these actual words and the feelings imputed to the various characters cannot be verified. Rather, they articulate the historian's imaginative leap, of the kind made by Merlin, which enables More to connect visible links and shape silences into a coherent narrative.

Critically, as this passage exemplifies, More's vision of Richard's villany is centered not in aggressive martial campaigns, not even in the loose alliances that Richard made and broke, but in the manipulation of appearances, in the *rhetorical* awareness of the need for a king to be accepted by his audiences and to generate *signs* of imperial worthiness. This is clear in the wearing down of Elizabeth, which proves successful, and it is also clear in a later scene depicting Richard trying to appeal to the people. Here, More depicts Richard as someone staging and directing the play, 'Here is our chosen King' – one rehearsed by writers of histories and fiction over and over again in this literary system.

While Edward's children were in his custody, Richard first plotted to accede to the throne by claiming they were bastards, a typical literary theme for *literati* of the time:

> ... it was by the protector and his council concluded that this Doctor Shaa should in a sermon at Paul's Cross signify to the people that neither King Edward himself nor the Duke of Clarence were lawfully begotten ... According to this device, Doctor Shaa, the Sunday after, at Paul's Cross in a great audience (as alway assembled great number to his preaching), he took for his tyme [theme] ... 'bastard slips shall never take deep root' ... And when he had laid for the proof and confirmation of this sentence certain examples taken out of the Old Testament and other ancient histories, then began he to descend into the praise of the Lord Richard, late Duke of York, calling him father to the lord protector, and declared the title of his heirs unto the crown, to whom it was, after the death of King Henry the Sixth, entailed by authority of parliament ... Now was it before devised that in the speaking of these words the protector should have comen in among the people ... to the end that those words, meeting with his presence, might have been taken among the hearers as though the Holy Ghost

had put them in the preacher's mouth and should have moved the people even there to cry, 'King Richard! King Richard!' – that it might have been after said that he was specially chosen by God and in manner by miracle. (67–9)

The staging of this event counts on Doctor Shaa functioning as a spin doctor who can whip crowds into a frenzy.

However, all the careful attention to the *dramatic text* and to the staging of the *performance text* didn't work, because the actors had no sense of timing (a lesson also conveyed by Roister Doister). As More theorizes, either Richard was late or Doctor Shaa was overly eager. Whatever the cause, the punchline came too soon, so that when Richard did appear the public found this a 'shameful sermon' and greeted the protector in stony silence (69). Buckingham was given the task of spinning the failure into a success a few days later, and so in London's Guildhall he gave a long speech intended to stir the crowd into welcoming their new king:

> When the duke had said, and looked that the people, whom he hoped that the mayor had framed [disposed] before, should after this proposition made have cried 'King Richard! King Richard!' – all was hushed and mute and not one word answered thereunto. (76)

According to More, the Duke actually repeated his speech – the absolute error that should never, ever be committed of any *performance text* – but still nobody cheered. Now the recorder was made to repeat the speech, apparently since the Duke felt his inability to reach the people didn't have to do with the message. The recorder did so with some modification and still nobody stirred. A fourth attempt consisted of directly asking the people whether they would accept the prince as their king, which, however, led to whispering. Finally, at the back of the audience, some of the Duke's servants started yelling the long awaited for 'King Richard! King Richard!' (78). On the next day, the Duke and the mayor 'reported' the people's good will, and 'These words much moved the protector ... ' (81).

More never does get to the murder of the princes with this narrative, but it is clear that for him, Richard's evil actions are related to how he attempts to manipulate reports, language, and appearances to effect his will. Presenting these two instances, in one of which Richard succeeds and in the other of which he fails, More actually stimulates his readers' *critical* sensibilities, even while apparently eliciting a *semantic* readership. On the obvious level, arranging his material according to his own situated interpretation, More aims at getting at Richard's true stature and intentions: twisting language in a twisted body, Richard cannot understand the complexities involved in ruling wisely.

But if readers absorb how important reports, language and appearances are to Richard's malevolent designs, then they will become very aware of presentation. Indeed, for Richard, all is focused on the manipulation of the surface, and his reading of the surface is *critically* geared to traditional scenarios such as the Queen's taking of sanctuary or the people's frenzied support of a king. That is, Richard's cynicism leads him to believe that, like himself, people always have ulterior motives. Thus, he can stage the scenario that will checkmate the Queen, because she *won't* reveal what she believes to be true, that Richard will betray her children. She *does* act with ulterior motives. But when the people *refuse to hide* their distaste behind a traditional and formal surface, Richard's directing and playscripting abilities are at an end. In this manner, More's narrative makes use of the dynamics of theater and drama to visualize his *critical interpretation* of Richard's rise to power, since that rise was itself, in More's reading and our terms, rhetorically and semiotically staged.

*   *   *

The amalgam of history and fiction found in the period's historical narratives may seem more fiction than history to today's readers. But just think about how our daily news broadcasts jam data into pre-fab narratives, designed to tell the same story over and over again: the rich and powerful lead corrupt and tragic lives; the good defenders of peace must defeat the evil aggressors; and those who die young are saints. Breaking out of the hermeneutic circle, if at all possible, can probably only occur if *literati* generate different stories. But that's the subject of the next chapter.

Notes

1. Nowadays, many historians still view historiography, the study of the writing of history, with some suspicion, preferring 'to do history' rather

than to tinker with its presentation. Nonetheless, Louis Mink (Mink 1987) and his student, Hayden White (White 1973) provide astute analyses of how history is dependent upon rhetorical structures to convey its images of truth. Also see Timothy Bahti's study, which introduces philosophical discourse and surveys how history came to be a university discipline (Bahti 1992).

2. If you're interested in reading further, philosophers to consult are Friedrich Schleiermacher (1768–1834), Martin Heidegger (1889–1976), and Hans-Georg Gadamer (1900–). It's probably better, however, to consult first a history of philosophy to gain an overview, hermeneutically encircling as that may be.

5 Narrative and Lyric Poetry

It may be true that we cannot step outside our hermeneutic circles. Who knows. But we can certainly become *aware* of hermeneutic circularity when we encounter a striking image or touchstone, one which telegraphically conveys something we've been mulling over and which suddenly, through the touchstone, seems crystal clear. Like a pebble thrown into a still pond generating ever more circles, such a touchstone can encompass ever larger frames of reference – all in the same shape, more or less, but covering ever more territory. But then just perhaps in the covering of more territory, other touchstones will create other circles. Their fields of *interpretants*, to use Peirce's term, may criss-cross into a plethora of arcs, shapes, images that could, through the resulting patterns of reflection and refraction, give us a deeper, different, understanding of our pond. If we take the time to examine our own touchstones, perhaps it's possible at least to see that there are other perspectives, maybe even enter them for a while, and finally to be aware that there are still others. In any case, it seems important to recognize these touchstones as such – even epiphanies need refashioning.

Touchstones and hypersigns

One of my touchstones materialized as I was doing research for my PhD thesis in Münster, Germany. The day after we arrived, we walked about the town, and I properly took note of medieval and early modern structures, dutifully analyzing and mentally categorizing them according to what I had read and the illustrations I had seen. A couple of days later, I went back to the cathedral to take notes and clarify some details. I was overwhelmed. Hundreds of people were hawking their brightly colored wares and huge amounts of aromatic foods at temporary stands, and multitudes more were bargaining for and buying them.

Somewhat perplexed, I made a half-hearted attempt to reference the panoply of colors, sounds and smells exploding right before my eyes and snatched at a fleeting memory of the New Testament story depicting Christ's most aggressive action, the scourging of those who sold their wares before the temple. Perhaps this scene might be read as a sign of difference: the hold of religion on society is simply not as strong in the twentieth century as it was during the period studied here. But then it struck me that even though a political system marries church and state and the day-to-day operations of a society may very well be framed by religious policy (Catholic or Anglican) – high feast days frame the calendar; guilds put on plays with religious themes and honor patron saints; church attendance becomes a test of loyalty to a state; marriage, birth and peccadilloes or greater faults are marked by religious ritual – *even so*, religious institutions could not have attained such material power without some further, material, marriage of the religious with the secular. And indeed, as I later learned, markets held in front of religious institutions were sanctioned in the late medieval period and, moreover, *signified* that the community had acquired the rights and privileges of a town.

Essentially, a touchstone is a special kind of sign, one whose infinitely receding and multiply associative *interpretants* a reader endows with inordinate value. When I had first walked through Münster noting buildings of interest, I chose to select among all the signs the city had to offer those that *stood for* my interests. The cathedral, city wall, churches and numerous artifacts – although actual concrete objects – are also signs in this sense. For their original audiences they were signs as well; they *stood for*, among other things, worship, protection and privilege. Today's audiences may respond in a similar way, but further interpret these objects as signs belonging to the distant past. Moreover, for me, the crowds of people milling around in front of the cathedral on my second go-around also became what Maria Corti calls a *hypersign* – a sign which depends upon, while breaking away from, the texts that make up the literary system (Corti 1978, 131–7). As such, the *hypersign* describes those elements of signs that allow for *multiaccentuality*, to use Vološinov's term.

When I half-heartedly read the colorful scene against the New Testament, I was drawing on a number of the literary system's religious traditions. Thus, I was relying on a biblical passage to interpret, dividing the scene into the secular and the spiritual, and insisting on the dominance of the cathedral not only architecturally but also socially. At the same time, I was ignoring the complexity of the *hyper-sign*, allowing one side – the religious – to dominate over the other – the secular, and thus interpreting the secular in opposition to the religious. This form of reading is more or less linear and attempts to focus on one side of the dichotomy rather than on a fruitful marriage of the elements that comprise it. It's the form of reading that is encouraged by a quick glimpse at Uccello's *Battle of San Romano* and ignores its status as a hypersign – it's that comfortable settling into a simple causality which ultimately proves constrictive.

Resuscitating the components of a dichotomy can prove as revealing as the criss-crossing of arcs belonging to the different circles spreading out over our pond. What I want to emphasize here is that although the infinite chain of a sign's *interpretants* may have accumulated chronologically, over time their effect on readers – if stimulated by the rhetorical sophistication of a text – may very well be a *simultaneously experienced* field of signs with different perspectives, locking into different, recognizable arcs and hence reflecting while refracting what we thought we knew. Such poetry is what I wish to examine in this chapter. But first, some preliminaries.

Lyric poetry

The colors, sounds and smells of the marketplace in Münster allowed me to envision a more lively past, one that complexly textures the contexts that produced other artifacts and narratives of this period, such as its poetry, a literary type of text which Corti categorizes as a *hypersign* as well. Aimed at conveying meaning beyond its words' literal level, poetry counts on figurative language and shared contexts to express messages – frequently, well-known messages. In other words, communication in poetry is to take place below its often enigmatic surface.

Yet, ironically, even though this emphasis on underlying meaning proves to be the 'meeting place' between poet and reader, the poet must focus her or his attention to the surface, to crafting language in such a manner that it appeals to readers and lures them to search beyond the apparent message. In other words, a poet must expend energy on shaping language to accommodate the vision that impelled her or him to write.

This particular approach to poetry may seem odd to us – we tend to eschew words like 'craft' and 'artisanry', associating them with tedious, learned and almost automatic activity. Instead, we are more apt to think of 'The Poet' as an inspired genius, whose art effortlessly flows into the exact, right and only words possible – the poet is the visionary, the bard, the chosen one. It may be a surprise that this image of the visionary poet has existed in some form for quite some time. Originally, a Roman writer, Ennius (239–169 BCE), used the Greek term *vates*, which means 'prophet' or 'seer' in a derogatory context to refer to his predecessors. But during the Augustan era (43 BCE–69 CE), the term was used positively to denote the poet as master of truth. Nonetheless, at the same time, this image of the poet was also accompanied by the idea that she or he must master the craft and that art benefits from artisanry.

Whether crafting long narratives or short lyric pieces, poets shape language that not only connotes differently from prose, it can also open up different perspectives. Such poetry allows us the time to slow down and inspect meaning. When doing so, poets spark those different – and in this sense, new – stories that our hermeneutically encircled consciousnesses try hard not to let us see. This is the special aspect of the literary art – to articulate a vision, a reading, in such a way that it seems strikingly and suddenly illuminating, regardless of how quickly or how painstakingly the poet crafted the vision.

Usually, when we speak of poetry in this vein, we mean lyric poetry, one of the absolute staples of the literary system, which briefly conveys highly charged, emotional communication. When Roman Jakobson articulated his six-point communication model (mentioned in the Introduction), he had done so to be able to discuss poetic communication, which transforms the model into the following (Innis 1985, 154):

REFERENTIAL (context)

POETIC (message)

EMOTIVE (addresser)...................................CONATIVE (addressee)

PHATIC (contact)

METALINGUAL (code)

Hence, poetic communication is focused on the message *per se*, but different genres can emphasize other functions. Thus, epic poetry focuses contextually on the third person and is strongly *referential*;

supplicatory or exhortative poetry can focus on the second person, the addressee, and in such cases is primarily *conative*; and lyric poetry centers in the first person, the addresser, and hence is strongly *emotive*. As we have seen, metaliterary communication may emphasize either the contact, and hence be primarily *phatic* (the love letter scene in *Ralph Roister Doister*, for example) or it may focus on the code, thereby foregrounding what Jakobson calls the *metalingual* (Lady Bercilak's toying with Gawain about his not adhering to expectations generated by the art of love). Lyric poetry does tend to depict the emotional state of the poet-narrator, but in this period, it very frequently does so in the persona of the lover-poet, meditating on or complaining of his beloved, hence highlighting *phatic* and *metalingual* functions as well.

Actually, love poetry is an ideal arena for the criss-crossing of arcs. Its conventions are so well-known that they can be implied with a mere word, a phrase, in the right context. Moreover, love poetry is a quintessentially rhetorical medium. First, all readers everywhere have some purchase on the subject, making communication potentially fairly straightforward. A lover, conventionally portrayed as male, begs his beloved, conventionally portrayed as female, for her favor.[1] Since the message is relatively clear, poets and readers can focus on the 'how'. Thus, the lover-poet courts her with a variety of persuasive schemes: she doesn't know he's alive, he's writing to immortalize her, even a mere look from her in his direction would transport him instantaneously to paradise. An inherent part of this scenario, moreover, is *metaliterary*, since the poet draws attention to his courting, to his persuasive schemes. Less obviously, the addresser–addressee relation *seems* to be directed from individual lover to individual beloved, but 'behind' that relation is a poet addressing a community of readers. It is this fact that is particularly interesting for our semiotic and rhetorical analysis of poetry.

During the period under study here, such poetry is strongly influenced by Ovidian conventions. Thus, the lover-poet is often sleepless, or love-sick. He complains that she doesn't know he exists, although he is trying to improve himself in order to win her love. In more bitter modes, he warns her that he has the power to enhance or malign her reputation through his poetic art. More often, though, he wishes to be near her, for her to observe his tear-stained poems and letters, for the time to fly until he's with her again and to screech to a halt when in her presence.

Of course, not all *literati* of the period are as equally enamored of Ovid or Ovidian conventions. For example, John Lydgate, a Monk of Bury (*c.* 1370–*c.* 1449), wrote the *Troy Book* (with over 30 000 lines) from about 1412 to 1420 and claims in his 384-line prologue that Homer lied, and Vergil and Ovid aren't to be trusted, uttering a special warning against Ovid:

> Ovide also poetycally hath closyd
> Falshede with trouthe, þat makeþ men ennosed
> To whiche parte þat þei schal hem holde –
> His mysty speche so hard is to vnfolde,
> That it entriketh rederis that it se.

[Prologue, 299–303: Ovid has also poetically combined falsehood with truth, making people perplexed as to which part they should hold to – his misty speech is so hard to unfold, that it beguiles readers who see it.]

Lydgate's reaction seems at least to confirm how widely popular Ovid is.

In Rome's Augustan period, the conventions of the lover-poet are embedded in brief lyrical poems, composed as vignettes in a narrative that portrays the lovers' relationship from its inception and through its ups and downs (Luck 1969; Lyne 1980). Some readers have been convinced that the women the poets address in these lyrics are the poets' actual lovers. Lyric emotions are, after all, both very conventional and highly individual. Just think how easily we tend to agree on what is or is not romantic (no matter what we feel about it), and yet, how moved we are by a romantic gesture from 'someone who counts'. Such lyric sequences influence poetry in the period under study here. Indeed, especially early modern lyric poetry in England is shaped by the Ovidian-influenced love sonnets penned by Francesco Petrarca (1304–74), so much so that nowadays sonnets of the period are categorized as either Shakespearean or Petrarcan, depending on the rhyme scheme and structure.

One author of such lyric sonnets is the ambassador and political figure, Sir Thomas Wyatt (*c.* 1503–42), who was mentioned in Chapter 2 as Ascham's authority for the idea that unkindness propagates the world's ills. A humanist author of a variety of classically influenced writings, Wyatt's approximately 90 lyric poems demonstrate the influence of the Italian scholar and poet Petrarca, mentioned in the

Introduction as the inventor of the term *medium aevum*. For example, the following sonnet is a loose translation of Petrarca's *Rime* 258:

> The lively sparks that issue from those eyes
> Against the which ne vaileth no defence
> Have pressed mine heart and done it none offence
> With quaking pleasure more than once or twice.
> Was never man could anything devise
> The sunbeams to turn with so great vehemence
> To daze man's sight, as by their bright presence
> Dazed am I, much like unto the guise
> Of one ystricken with dint of lightning,
> Blinded with the stroke, erring here and there.
> So call I for help, I not when ne where.   *know not when nor*
> The pain of my fall patiently bearing.
> For after the blaze, as is no wonder,
> Of deadly 'Nay' hear I the fearful thunder. (84)

Fitting the criteria of lyric poetry mentioned above, this sonnet depicts the lover-poet as helpless when gazing into his beloved's eyes and stunned by her refusal of his suit. The controlling conceit is light imagery, which accords well with the period's theories about love, said to pierce through to the heart by means of the eyes. In the beginning octet, her eyes are sparks and sunbeams, which do not hurt the lover-poet, but which daze him. In the closing sestet, the light imagery rumbles into a thunderstorm, whereby his beloved's eyes are analagous to lightning that render the wandering lover-poet helpless and vulnerable when he hears the thunder of her refusal.

Thus, light and imperious power are associated with her, while helpless confusion is associated with him, perhaps reflecting actual emotions, perhaps written to elicit a response of 'poor baby'. In this use of a metaphor – her eyes are shining lights – the sonnet shifts perspectives on the metaphor to tell the story of the poor rejected lover up against the lady of *daunger* (something like 'haughty pride'), the *belle dame sans merci* (the beautiful lady without mercy). Since both types are so well-known, however, the poet can focus on the elaboration of the conceit. Indeed, translating and modifying Petrarca while writing of love, Wyatt and other sonneteers in this period use the sonnet form to demonstrate their eloquent style, thereby extending conceits and turning perspectives on the edge of a metaphor.

But such use of conventions is not without its alternate, sometimes ironic voices, a tendency attributable to the inherently metaliterary strands of love's poetry. For example, about half a century later, in 1573, a volume of poetry was published which was found offensive and seized by Her Majesty's High Commissioners. It was replaced two years later with another volume, which was also seized, and indeed it was not all that different from the first. Its divisions were three: Flowers, Hearbes and Weedes (Weiss 1992). It is generally accepted that the anthology of poems, *A Hundreth Sundrie Flowres*, was written largely, if not entirely, by George Gascoigne, who after the second confiscation apparently gave up writing lyric verse altogether and turned to didactic genres, translation and non-fiction. What was so offensive, it seems, is the same problem that hounds love's lyric poetry in almost any period – the *semantically*-lodged accusation that the characters and passions depicted are real, and hence the poetry is indiscreet. For the record, Gascoigne dismissed this claim as absurd.

Perhaps most interesting, and controversial, is the narrative referred to as 'The Adventures of Master F.I.', re-written in the second version as 'The Pleasant Fable of *Fernando Jeronimi and Leonora da Valasco*, translated out of the Italian riding tales of Bartello', and found in the section called Weedes. The narrative relates of F.J.'s dubious success (rape) with (of) his less than faithful beloved (in the first version, from the northern parts of the realm; in the second, in Italy). The story is framed by prose passages wherein the narrator, G.T., addresses questions and comments on the communication between the lovers, like the following, written by F.J. to Mistress Elinor:

> Such is then the extremite of my passions, the whiche I could never have bene content to committe unto this teltale paper, were it not that I am destitute of all other helpe ... And lette this poore paper (besprent with salte teares, and blowen over with skalding sighes) bee saved of you as a safegarde for your sampler, or a bottome to winde your sowing silke ... (384)

Here, the lover-poet imagines his beloved in an ideal world, saving his tear-stained letter. In drawing *ostensive* attention to the letter, Gascoigne also draws attention to its creation. Moreover, since *in the world of the narrative* the letter is an individual object, the words seem intended for one specific individual. However, it is also an (imaginary) individual object that is (re-) printed in *A Hundreth Sundrie Flowres* as well. And it also articulates one of the age-old conventions in love's literary system. For example, in the fourteenth century romance *Troilus and Criseyde* (discussed below), Chaucer has Pandarus instruct his charge on how to write a love letter to Criseyde:

> Towchyng thi lettre, thou art wys ynough.
> I woot thow nylt it dygneliche endite,
> As make it with thise argumentes tough;
> Ne scryvenyssh or craftyly thow it write;
> Biblotte it with thi teris ek a lite ...

> (II. 1023–7: about your letter, you are wise enough. I trust you won't compose it in sophisticated manner, with difficult arguments; don't be bookish or overly ornate; also blot it with your tears a little ...)

And Troilus complies:

> This counseil liked wel to Troilus ...
> And sette hym down, and wrot ...
> And with his salte teris gan he bathe
> The ruby in his signet, and it sette
> Upon the wex deliverliche and rathe.

> (II. 1044–88: Troilus liked this advice ... and set himself down and wrote ... and with his salt tears, he bathed the ruby signet-ring, and set it on the wax immediately and quickly.)

Is he earnest, or is courting a game? Likewise, F.J.'s poetic efforts make it appear as if he 'really has it bad':

> Love, hope, and death, do stirre in me such strife,
> As never man but I led such a life.
> First burning love doth wound my hart to death,
> And when death comes at call of inward griefe,
> Colde lingering hope, doth feede my fainting breath
> Against my will, and yeeldes my wound reliefe:
> So that I live, but yet my life is such,
> As death would never greve me halfe so much.
> No comfort then but only this I tast,
> To salve such sore, such hope will never want,

And with such hope, such life will ever last,
And with such life, such sorrowes are not skant.
Oh straunge desire, O life with torments tost
Through too much hope, mine onely hope is lost.
                                        Even He. F. J.   (394)

Conventionally complaining of love's bondage, which keeps the lover in hope and desire, the narrator here plays with the tensions that keep the lover torn between the wish for death and the hope for life. As he distributes his hope, love and desire through the poem's lines, he creates the sense that he's sighing over his state in soliloquoy. This is another convention that helps make the poem seem highly individualized. However, right after this we learn from the framework: 'This Sonet was highly commended, and in my judgement it deserveth no lesse'. Whatever its origins, the poem is in the public domain *even in the world of the narrative.*

With these kinds of cues, G.T. – the narrator-reader, so to speak – creates an intimate relation with *A Hundreth Sundrie Flowres*'s readers, drawing them into that quasi-*critical* plane where they are equals (Hughes 1997; Rowe 1981). Both sets of readers view the lover's pains, as if the love story were being acted out on stage. And thus, the poem *is* there *ostensively* for our observation, as highlighted by the framing comments. In other words, Gascoigne creates at least two worlds – besides the world of the lovers, there's the world of the *literati*. And in doing so, the irony of love's literary system – where individual passion is expressed in universal conventions – becomes apparent. Although the collection obviously garnered *semantic interpretation* from some of Gascoigne's readers (notably the censors), inserting the prose framework with its narrator-readers has the potential of reinstating the dialectic that might encourage *critical readers* to perceive the highly rhetoricized nature of courting.

The rhetorical framework of courting is more obviously foregrounded in ironic treatises such as Ovid's *Ars amandi* (Art of love) or its twelfth-century *translatio*: Andreas Capellanus' Latin *De Amore* (On Love). Similar to the *Ars*, Capellanus' treatise begins by presenting how a lover is to win love; proceeds to explain how he is to sustain it; and then divulges how to extract oneself from a relationship. Andrew the Chaplain also includes, in the first section, a lengthy passage depicting various couples engaged in the art of flirtation as models in this 'how-to' treatise. The pairs are brought on stage according to their stations in life. For example, in dialogues, a knight is depicted suing for the love of a Lady from the higher nobility, then from the same class, and finally from the lower nobility. The most cynical scenario suggests that a peasant woman may be raped, not requiring dialogue. *De honeste amandi* also depicts courts of love presided over by Eleanor of Aquitaine and her daughter, Marie of Champagne. Cases brought to these judges include such specimens as: if a woman has two lovers who are in all ways equal, whom should she choose? The judge decides, thereby settling ambiguity, but frequently in an unsettling manner, and at times contradicting one of the laws declared by the court as authoritative, without addressing the contradiction.

Although most scholars would agree that both Ovid's treatises on love and Capellanus' *De Amore* are intended to be read ironically (Ginsberg 1988–89; Monson 1988), still the problem remains that some of these treatises' readers would like to remain in the *semantic* realm. The world depicted *is* the world of love, so the argument might go. Yet, although sharing much with 'our world,' *literary* love is at times different from the 'real thing'. Literary love provides a stage for lovers to wile away the hours in agony and sighing for a glimpse of their beloveds. I use the term 'stage' because, essentially, the lover-poet hopes and envisions himself as being read by his most desired reader, his beloved, and hence puts on his best persona to persuade her of his worth – all this in the world of the poem, which is also to be viewed by a third party: the *other* readers, us.

Ovidian lovers

Between the time Cicero composed his treatises on rhetoric and Quintilian amplifed on rhetorical knowledge of the time, Ovid wrote highly polished, rhetorically sophisticated Latin verse. While recognizing that in the literary system of his day, epic was the star-maker, Ovid opted to write of love, even in his most well-known poem, the *Metamorphoses*, which exhibits characteristics of the epic genre, but which nonetheless focuses on love in all its manifestations. That is, the *Metamorphoses* arranges a collection of love stories on a faintly visible diachronic frame, stretching from the inception of the world to Ovid's own day – in other words, a history that focuses on the marginalized. As such, the *Metamorphoses* not only exhibits characteristics of the hypersign, but does so in an antithetical context; it functions as an *antithetical hypersign*, making the dialectic between various frameworks highly visible.

In addition to one of Ovid's tales from the *Metamorphoses*, the poetry that will be discussed in the remaining part of this chapter presents lyric love in the manner practiced by Wyatt and Gascoigne, but in narrative form. While Ovid may not be a direct influence, the poetry partakes of Ovidian conventions. For *literati* of our period, Ovid is *the* authoritative source for lyric love.

Among his many tales, I've chosen to look at the story of Pyramus and Thisbe, a tale of 113 lines (IV. 55–167) relating how parental disapproval incites two young lovers to elope. Having arranged to meet in the woods, Thisbe unfortunately arrives first, sees a lioness bloodied from a meal, and flees for protection. But the heroine also drops her veil, which the animal paws, and which Pyramus shortly thereafter finds. Misreading the signs, the hero kills himself in despair. Thisbe returns, sees curiously darkened berries, finds Pyramus, and comprehends what has occurred. Unable to restrain her grief, she kills herself. Finally, the lovers' parents repent and bury their ashes in one urn, while the berries perennially display their new color, stained from the lovers' blood.

In addition to the unrestrainable passion exhibited by the two lovers, this very short tale portrays the lovers as *literati* in a special system, in love's literary system. In the beginning, for example, we learn that the two lovers desperately seek a chance to communicate with each other in some way, any way. Finally, they find a crack in the wall dividing their houses and use it to express their love. Ovid draws attention to the act in the following manner:

> fissus erat tenui rima, quam duxerat olim,
> cum fieret, paries domui communis utrique.
> id vitium nulli per saecula longa notatum –
> quid non sentit amor? – primi vidistis amantes
> et vocis fecistis iter ...

> (IV. 65–9, Miller-Goold translation: There was a slender chink in the party-wall of the two houses, which it had at some former time received when it was building. This chink, which no one had ever discovered through all these years – but what does love not see? – you lovers first discovered and made it the channel of speech ...)

At the basis of literary love is the lovers' urge to communicate, one with the other, alone, in a world of their own. Thus, lovers speak a different language. Before they found the crack in the wall, for example, they spoke with nods and signs, 'nutu signisque loquuntur' (IV. 63), which they alone understood.

Demonstrating their ability to communicate in difficult circumstances, Ovid suggests that it is their heightened awareness that causes them to misread as well. Thus, Thisbe reads the lioness (IV. 96–101) in terms of its conventional fierceness, missing the signs of its satiety (IV. 97–8) and drawing the animal into her tale only as a potential hinderance to the lovers' meeting. And her misreading has a snowball effect: Pyramus misreads the resulting synecdoche, the blood on her veil (IV. 107–9). Although from one perspective the lovers' misreadings are eminently avoidable, careless errors typical of those committed by passionate youth, on another level their readings make sense. Readers not already familiar with the tale, for example, might very well read as Thisbe did. It's not difficult to imagine fixing one's attention on an animal's potential rapacity, convinced that its sudden appearance has direct consequences for the observer. Ovid even encourages us to misread and miss vital clues too. Thus, although Thisbe's veil plays such a crucial role in this tragedy, it is her quiet, surreptitious and intense exit from home to the lovers' *rendez-vous* that attracts attention. In fact, the veil is only intimated in that she 'fallitque suos adopertaque vultum' (IV. 94: tricked her [family] and hid her face).

Although Thisbe tragically misreads the lioness, she nonetheless is an insightful reader and an avid storyteller as well, as literary lovers tend to be. Thus, as mentioned earlier, when she sees her lover, takes in Pyramus' final gaze, and recognizes her own veil, she pulls the pieces together and comprehends the whole story in an instant (IV. 147–9). But even just a bit earlier, her status as one of love's *literati* becomes apparent, as she returns to the mulberry tree – 'oculis animoque requirit' (IV. 129, Miller-Goold translation: 'seek[ing him] both with eyes and soul'), she eagerly considers how she will *tell* Pyramus *her adventurous tale*, 'quantaque vitarit narrare pericula gestit' (IV. 130, Miller-Goold translation: 'eager to tell him how great perils she has escaped').

Lovers, then, in love's literary system are also *literati* in the greater literary system, creating worlds within worlds and functioning in multiple roles: they are characters in a 'play', they are authors of the 'play', and they are readers of each other as well. And as such, they are also mirrors of the *text* that presents them to the *text*'s readers.

One of Ovid's readers in the early fourteenth century was the anonymous author of the *Ovide moralisé*, who translated tales from the *Metamorphoses* into French octosyllabic couplets, not only providing evidence of the Roman poet's influence, but also of how the tales were received by at least this author, for after each tale, the author moralizes it for Christian consumption. For example, the tale corresponding to Pyramus and Thisbe is mainly different in that it amplifies the lovers' emotions. Thus, the tale emphasizes the effects the god of love has on the two lovers, and Piramus is described in one place as, 'Plains de souspir et plains de plour,/ Plains de penser et plains de cure' (376–7: 'Full of sighs and full of tears, full of thoughts and full of worries'). Likewise, for almost a hundred lines, Thisbe complains of her inability to embrace her lover, faints three times from desire, and prays to the god of love for advice (451–536). The poem continues in its expansionist mode as Piramus foreshadows his own death (638–9, 733–7). When he kills himself, he dies kissing her veil (1008–15), and Thisbe's plaint goes on for 59 lines (1061–119) addressing the sword, the tree, the moon, the fountain and the woods.

Then, quite unexpectedly to a reader of the original, Pyramus sees her and, barely able to speak, asks if she is still alive before he dies. It is then that Thisbe kills herself (1138–41). Even more of a surprise, in moralizing the tale, the author interprets the lovers' story as illustrative of how God, for love of humankind, was incarnated into a human body and suffered in order to rescue souls from the evil in the world (1170–1267). The lion eats up sinning souls, and the mulberry bush is free-associated with the cross on which Christ's blood was shed for humankind. The author continues to tell of Christ's great sacrifice and the glory of martyrs. It's clear that while the tale differs from the original mainly in rhetorical flourish, the interpretation, one which Eco might very well label as an example of major *hermeneutic drift*, shifts perspectives on the tale completely and in doing so focuses on a set of theological analogues rather than the *metaliterary* dimension more obviously a part of Ovid's tale.

Also useful as brief comparison is another tale from the fourteenth century, one by Giovanni Boccaccio from his collection of 100 tales, most of which are also amorous, entitled the *Decameron* (1353). Boccaccio's tales are organized around the flight of ten Florentine nobles, the *brigata*, into the countryside to escape the plague devastating Tuscany. On each of ten days, one of them rules as the king or queen and decides upon a theme, which is to be illustrated by each of the others in a tale. At the end of the ten days, however, they return to Florence not wholly convinced that their brief respite in the countryside did them any good.

The tale of interest here recounts the love between Guiscardo and Ghismunda. Rather than an imitation or translation, it shows Ovidian influence. Fiammetta tells this tale as the first on the fourth day, on which Filostrato is king. Guiscardo and Ghismunda must keep their love secret because his social rank is inferior to hers. To complicate matters, her father, Prince Tancredi of Salerno, dotes on his daughter and wishes to keep her with him at all times. When, by accident, he discovers the two in bed, he has Guiscardo imprisoned. He confronts his daughter and tells her he has killed her lover to learn her true feelings. Ghismunda deplores his action, argues for the primacy of love over reason, true nobility over inherited nobility, and youth's passions over old age's ennervated and routine lifestyle. Not pleased with her devotion to Guiscardo, let alone convinced by her arguments, Tancredi then has him 'really' killed. The heart is secretly delivered to Ghismunda in a vessel, over which she weeps before pouring an apothecary's poison onto it. The heart dissolves, and she drinks the potion before informing Tancredi he has failed in his attempt to separate the two, for she has become her lover's tomb. Upon her death, Tancredi has the two buried in one grave.

Echoes of Ovid's Pyramus and Thisbe are reversed and modified in Boccaccio's tale. For example, unlike Thisbe, Ghismunda is foregrounded as highly rational, although both heroines express the wish to be buried with their lovers before killing themselves for love. Likewise, resembling Ovid's tale, this one too is fueled by parental disapproval, but there is a focused and named parent involved in Boccaccio's tale, along with the additional concrete rationale of socioeconomic class playing a role.

Ovid's influence via Boccaccio continues in our period as well, since Boccaccio's tale is translated and elaborated into at least two fifteenth-century versions, one by an anonymous poet and the other by Gilbert Banester (c. 1420–87), the latter of which amplifies the emotional aspects of the tale. Indeed, the Latin translation is one of the tales of the period most often published since the invention of the printing press, with 24 editions appearing between 1470 and 1500. In the early sixteenth century, William Walter translated it from the Latin into English, and in 1562, Edward Lewicke composed another version of the tale, based on a version found in Sir Thomas Elyot's *Boke Named the Gouernour*, which was discussed in Chapter 2.

In focusing on the emotional, however, translations of Boccaccio's tale ignore some of the subtleties in Boccaccio's telling, just as the *Ovide moralisé*'s telling of Pyramus and Thisbe missed out on the *metaliterary*. Just one example here. In Boccaccio's tale we learn that after hearing Fiammetta's story, Filostrato, described as 'il re con rigido viso' (the king with the rigid face), has no sympathy:

> Poco prezzo mi parrebbe la vita mia a dover dare per la metà diletto di quello che con Guiscardo ebbe Ghismunda, né se ne dee di voi maravigliare alcuna, con ciò sia cosa che io, vivendo, ogni ora mille morti sento, né per tutte quelle una sola particella di diletto m'è data.

> [IV. 2. 2–3; 488: A small price, it would seem to me, to give my life for half the bliss Ghismunda had with Guiscardo. Nor should any of you ladies be surprised with this, considering that in living, I feel a thousand deaths every hour and for all that I am not allowed a single particle of delight.]

As might be surmised from later translations of the tale, most readers would probably agree that Fiammetta's story appropriately illustrates the day's theme. Nonetheless, Filostrato reads it as blissful. He judges the fictional lovers' union – which ends in death – to be a paradise when compared to the living hell he suffers. In other words, Filostrato actually creates another tale, a reading of Guiscardo and Ghismunda that differs from the narrator's in more than simple word and style choices. His tale, ironically, is a very individually positioned articulation of the tried and true convention expressed earlier in Ovid's tale, and later in F.J.'s poem: the lover-poet who would readily die for love, if it meant being with the beloved. As Filostrato's reading *metaliterarily* suggests, that one reads at all *means* one creates.

*   *   *

Wyatt and Gascoigne's poetry demonstrate the tendency to write elaborate verses in sonnet form that prevail especially in the latter part of the period under study here. Influenced by Petrarcan and Ovidian conventions, they also point to the inherently rhetorical, *metaliterary* structures and language of literary love. For Ovid's tales present passion in precisely this manner, as seen in Pyramus and Thisbe's story which is not only translated, as the *Ovid moralisé* exemplifies, but which is also influential, as Boccaccio's tale of Ghismunda and Guiscardo demonstrates.

Below I briefly discuss three narratives: one from slightly before the period discussed here, *Sir Orfeo*; one at the beginning, Chaucer's *Troilus and Criseyde*; and one from slightly beyond, Shakespeare's *A Midsummer Night's Dream*. I discuss these three narratives separately, because they offer quite different perspectives on literary love, yet are recognizably Ovidian. *Sir Orfeo* portrays passionate married love; *Troilus and Criseyde* portrays what at first appears to be the literary love couple *sine qua non*; and *A Midsummer Night's Dream* portrays illiterate literary love. All three, then, communicate myriad different strands that lock into different arcs as they tell their stories in a highly conventionalized, highly rhetorical sub-system – love's literary system – in which communication is so heightened, a poet *could* convey meanings only through nods and signs.

Sir Orfeo

Ovid's depiction of tragic love intensifies passion while concomitantly emphasizing communication, and by implication the rhetorical nature of literary love – not only in terms of lovers who read each other as texts, but also in terms of the creating of love poetry to win the beloved as well as the *self-reflexive* acting out of love stories as other lovers had done before. The Middle English *Sir Orfeo*, on the other hand, portrays passionate love that itself works antithetically to literary love's system.

The anonymous *Sir Orfeo* is extant in three manuscripts, the Auchinlik manuscript, Harley 3810, and Ashmole 61 (Bodleian 6922). Here, I will be focusing on the narrative as presented in the first of these manuscripts, which stems from about 1330 and was probably produced in London.

Sir Orfeo is a verse narrative of 604 lines, whose hero, King Orfeo, is passionately in love with his wife, Heurodis. The narrative begins with a prologue that introduces the tale; then focuses on the king's love of harping – 'He lerned so, þer no-þing was/ A better harpour in no plas' (31–2: 'He mastered [it] so, that there was no better harper anywhere') – and then relates of the couple's nobility and virtue. Interesting,

Orfeo's lineage is described as follows:

> His fader was comen of King Pluto,
> & his moder of King Juno,
> þat sum-time were as godes y-hold
> For auentours þat þai dede & told.

[43–6: His father descended from King Pluto and his mother from the regent Juno, who were once thought to be gods for the adventures that they did and (were) told (of them).]

Besides the disconcerting introduction of the Queen of the Roman gods as a King, the use of classical mythology here may seem surprising, until we realize that this narrative relates a tale about Orpheus and his wife, Eurydice.

In the *Metamorphoses* (X. 3–XI. 66), Ovid begins the story of their upcoming marriage. However, their ceremony is threatened by a bad omen: the wedding torch sputters. Not long thereafter, Eurydice is bitten in the ankle by a snake. Her spirit descends to Hades, to where all the classical era's dead go. Having mourned her on earth and finding no respite, Orpheus decides to make the perilous journey to seek out the Ruler of the Underworld, Pluto (adding yet another element of surprise for the reader of the Prologue to *Sir Orfeo*). The distraught lover pleads with the god and his wife, Persephone, with such enchantingly beautiful song that the rulers allow Eurydice to return to the mortal realm, on one condition: Orpheus must not look back at his wife until they have reached earth. Happily the two leave, but shortly before arriving at their destination Orpheus cannot refrain from looking back, only to see his wife's spirit fading away as she is returned to the Underworld. Thereafter, as Ovid portrays in a long section, the singer's mournful songs attract trees and stones; he sleeps with boys; we are treated to quite a few of his love tales; and he enrages the harpy-like women of Cicones, who tear him apart. His body parts are strewn about, and his head and lyre float down the river emitting mournful tones. Yet, his spirit descends to Hades, and he is again with his Eurydice, hardly able to believe his luck.

Although there were other authoritative versions available to the poet, notably those of Vergil and Boethius, *Sir Orfeo* still proceeds very differently from any of them as well as from known medieval versions. After the prologue, we learn that one beautiful May day, Heurodis rides out to their orchard along with two ladies. She soon falls asleep under an *ympe-tre* (a grafted tree, an orchard tree). Panicked upon waking, she tears at her skin, her hair, and her clothing and is unable to speak:

> Ac, as sone as sche gan awake,
> Sche crid, & loβli bere gan make:
> Sche froted hir honden & hir fet,
> & crached hir visage – it bled wete;
> Hir riche robe hye al to-rett,
> & was reueyd out of hir witt.

> (77–82: But, after she had awaken, she cried, and horribly had screamed: she rubbed her hands and her feet, and scratched her face – it bled wet; her rich dress she tore all to pieces, and she was driven out of her wits.)

The two ladies go for help and return with 60 knights and ladies who bring her back to the castle. Sir Orfeo begs his wife to tell him what frightens her. She replies she must leave, to which her husband responds:

> 'Allas!' quaβ he, 'For-lorn icham!
> Whider wiltow go, & to wham?
> Whider βou gost ichil wiβ βe,
> & whider y go βon schalt wiβ me.'

> (127–30: 'Alas!' said he, 'I'm lost! Where do you wish to go, and to whom? Wherever you will go, I will go with you, and wherever I go, you shall go with me.')

Heurodis then tells her husband that while she was asleep two knights came to her, telling her she must come to speak with their king, which she refused to do. They thus rode away and returned with their king, accompanied with a hundred knights and a hundred ladies. She continues:

> &, as son as he to me cam,
> Wold ich nold ich, he me nam,
> & made me wiβ him ride
> Opon a palfray bi his side;
> & brouȝt me to his palays …

(153–7: And as soon as he came to me, whether I wanted to or no, he took me, and made me ride with him on a palfrey by his side; and he brought me to his palace ...)

The foreign King then returns Heurodis to the orchard and tells her that she must be at the *ympe-tre* the next day, to be taken from her kingdom forever. If she refuses, he will make it worse for her wherever she may be.

Orfeo prepares himself against this threat by accompanying Heurodis the next day with an army of a thousand knights, who pledge they would rather lose their lives before they allow their Queen to be taken from them. They ride out in full force to the *ympe-tre* and arrange themselves around her. But before anyone can do anything, she is whisked away by the fairy folk.

Beside himself with anguish, Orfeo decides to leave his kingdom in the hands of his steward. He trades his royal garments for those of a pauper and takes only his harp along with him on his search. He travels the countryside for years, looking for his beloved Heurodis, and in the process suffers many travails as he grows more and more tired, haggard and unkempt. Through it all, however, he finds moments to play his harp and plays so beautifully that wild beasts approach to listen to him.

Sometimes, during his years of journeying, often on hot mornings, Sir Orfeo would see the fairy king hunting or his knights and ladies dancing. Then one day, he spies 60 ladies hawking and sees among them his beloved Heurodis. Stunned, neither can speak. The ladies spy Orfeo and depart, with him following close behind. They enter a rock which opens up on the other side to an astonishing castle so large that it sustains a hundred towers. Within the castle, he sees many strange sights.

þan he gan bihold about al
& seiȝe liggeand wiþ-in þe wal
Of folk þat were þider y-brouȝt,
& þouȝt dede, & nare nouȝt.

(387–90: Then he began to look all around and saw lying inside the wall people who were brought there and thought to be dead, although they were not.)

Some people walk about with no heads, some with no arms, and then Orfeo sees his own wife asleep under an *ympe-tre*.

Orfeo proceeds to the King's hall and, without revealing who he is or his goal, he asks whether he might play for him. The King expresses surprise, since the impoverished harper is the only person who has ever come to the hall without having first been summoned. But he assents, Orfeo plays, and all come to listen to his wondrous music. The King grants him anything he wishes, and Orfeo asks for the lady under the *ympe-tre*, a request the King of Fairies at first tries to deny – such a poor beggar doesn't deserve a beautiful and courtly queen. Nonetheless, he cannot refuse Orfeo without breaking his word, so the two leave with the King's blessing, and unlike the classical version, without any conditions.

Orfeo and Heurodis return to their city, Winchester, but they lodge with a poor man on a hill just outside the town walls first. Ignorant of who they are, the peasant tells them their own story to inform them of recent events in the kingdom. Orfeo decides to leave Heurodis with him, while he goes into the town to test his steward's loyalty. Fortunately, the steward proves generous and loyal. Then, the steward notes Orfeo's harp and asks where he obtained it. Orfeo fabricates a story implying his own death by wild animals. The steward is in despair, until Orfeo reveals himself and tells his story. The steward and the town are overjoyed, they send for Heurodis, and all live happily ever after.

The differences between the Ovidian and Middle English versions are substantial, as you can tell from these summaries. More importantly here, *Sir Orfeo* brings together many different strands important to the period under study here and functions, at the same time, as an *antithetical hypersign*. For example, both Orpheus and Orfeo master the playing of the harp to such a degree that nature's laws are suspended. Trees and animals succumb to their mastery, suggesting a reverence for the art of the poet. Moreover, both Orpheus and Orfeo travel to an otherworldly place in order to rescue Eurydice and Heurodis, and they achieve their task through the stunning beauty of their music, not through feats of arms, as Hector of Troy or one of Arthur's knights might do.

Yet, at the same time, Orfeo is no simple harper, he is also a king, ruler of imperial Winchester, who is loved by his people, as emblematized in the steward to whom he entrusts the management of his kingdom. Likewise, the Middle English narrative begins in May, with gracious ladies and knights punctuating the stream of events with their dancing and hunting. The narrative even betrays a vague suggestion of the Old Testament Ruth's faithfulness, when Orfeo pledges to accompany his wife wherever she goes. Moreover, in contrast to Ovid's gods, the King of Fairies adheres to a code of honor that binds him to his word as well as to a courtly pattern of behavior – a pauper does not aspire to a liaison with a noblewoman. In addition, the *ympe-tre* that exists in both worlds and the fairy world itself evoke Celtic analogues, as does the exceptional status granted the harper, who can enter any court on the strength of his talent.

Insofar as *Sir Orfeo* gathers together so many differing strands of this literary system that form parts of arcs, it serves as a touchstone for this period's conventions, a *hypersign*. Moreover, presenting the passion of lyric love through one of Ovid's tales, *Sir Orfeo* nonetheless modifies Ovidian conventions in a context that is traditionally antithetical to love's literary system – the lovers are husband and wife who experience a happy ending and love and live in a public, not a private, world – they are regents, and their story is so well-known *from that perspective*, that even a peasant can relate it. In other words, *Sir Orfeo* is not only a story about lost love re-gained, it's a story about loyalties within a feudal system, as well as a story about a harper's special sensibilities. Knowing what is important in life, the harper passionately acts upon this knowledge as well as communicating it to others – this makes him, in *Sir Orfeo*'s world, a ruler worthy of being loved.

Chaucer's *Troilus and Criseyde*

Geoffrey Chaucer's *Troilus and Criseyde* is written in the seven-line stanzaic form known as *rime royal* (a form attributed to the fourteenth-century poet and statesman) and covers five books, averaging about 1600 lines apiece. Its three main characters – Troilus, Criseyde and their go-between Pandarus (also Criseyde's uncle) – are mediated to readers from ancient Troy before the Greek forces decimate the town. The bookish narrator who functions as our bumbling guide, however, is no omniscient, timeless type; he is a self-conscious denizen of fourteenth-century England, who wishes, nonetheless, to dwell in the past.

The story relates how the love-scorning, battle-eager warrior,

Prince Troilus, turns completely around to become an ideal lyric lover (he even 'composes' one of Petrarca's sonnets in the process of falling in love – 'S'amor non è' – I. 400–420) once he sees the widowed and abandoned Criseyde, whose rarely featured father, the prophet Calchas has just deserted Troy to offer his visionary services to the future victors. Through the energetic and sometimes bawdy scheming of Pandarus, which forms the focus of the first two books, the two finally meet and eventually consummate their love in Book III. The final two books depict the action initiated by Calchas' demand that Criseyde be exchanged for the captured Trojan Prince Antenor, which leads to Criseyde's eventual treachery to Troilus in her new-found love for Diomede, a noble Greek warrior.

Returning to Troy before its destruction opens up the possibility of gathering other stories told in the city before it gets flattened into a topos used to preface other narratives. There certainly are a plethora of *translationes* in Chaucer's romance. Thus, in Book V, Criseyde is *transferred* to the Greek camp, Cassandra reels off a *translatio studii et imperii* from the Theban point of view, Troilus is *translated* into the eighth sphere upon his death, and, as cited in Chapter 1, the narrator lists poets beginning with Vergil and ending with his own contemporaries, Gower and Strode. Chaucer's narrator also refers directly to referents of the topos, but he does so to emphasize his intent *not* to follow the traditional path:

> And if I hadde ytaken for to write
> The armes of this ilke worthi man,
> Than wolde ich of his batailles endite;
> But for that I to writen first bigan
> Of his love, I have seyd as I kan –
> His worthi dedes, whoso list hem heere,
> Rede Dares, he kan telle hem alle ifeere –

> [V. 1765–71: And if I had undertaken to write of the arms of this same worthy man (a play on Vergil's opening line of the *Aeneid*), then I would relate his battles, but since I first began to write of his love, I have said as I am able – for his worthy deeds, whoever wishes to hear them, read Dares, he can tell them all together –]

And even when the Trojan War does seep into the poem's foreground, it is subordinated to love or peace as when, for example, Criseyde speculates on the progress of peace talks (IV. 1345–58), or when

Troilus uses the battleground to demonstrate his valor in hopes of winning Criseyde's love (I. 477–81).

For Chaucer's narrator, the interesting story to take from Troy is a love story, or, more specifically, he is smitten by the story of a character, the lovely Criseyde (Donaldson 1970, 65–83). As a reader, he can dwell on the pages that most move him. But since he has undertaken the task to communicate, to convey her tale (as lover-poets do), the narrator must eventually come to terms with Criseyde's betrayal of Troilus, which he is most unwilling to do. Indeed, the above summary given of *Troilus and Criseyde* is accurate in its outline, but all wrong in its emphases. The five-book poem foregrounds the lovers, and especially Criseyde, over all else.

Perhaps the narrator sees himself mirrored in the well-read Criseyde, for this is a poem that loudly proclaims its engagement with *auctores* (Wetherbee 1984). Not only is she highly literary, she too tries to ignore the war as well as the type of passion that engendered it – an *antithetical hypersign* if there ever was one. For example, Criseyde encourages Troilus to act with forethought, inspiring his love to be expressed through traditional literary forms: love letters, love-inspired poetry, and reputation-inspired love. Likewise, upon encountering her for the first time in a private space, in Book II, readers see her enjoying a passage from the *Romance of Thebes*. When Pandarus suggests that she give up her widow's trappings, Criseyde objects that she should actually 'in a cave ... bidde and rede on holy seyntes lyves' (II. 117–18: in a cave ... pray and read holy saints' lives). Finally, Criseyde requests that Pandarus tell her how he learned about Troilus' love (499–501) and responds to his tale as a sophisticated reader rather than as a potential lover, 'Kan he *wel* speke of love?' (II. 503, my italics: 'Can he speak of love *well*?'), as she does again later to Troilus' first, Pandarus-directed love letter (alluded to above): she 'Avysed word by word in every lyne,/ And fond no lak, she thoughte he koude good' (II. 1177–8: 'deliberated word by word in every line and found no fault, she thought he could [write] well').

Criseyde's readerly qualities make her a mirror of readers in general and of particularly *literary* literary lovers, as well as a refraction of the narrator. She is *The* Beloved – 'in flesh and blood' – the one to whom all literary lovers have been wailing and for whom they've been writing their supplicatory verses. The narrator is one of her most devoted readers, oscillating constantly between *semantic* and *critical* reading. For, not willing to move beyond the lyric, he, like other lover-poets, dwells in the same place reading the same lines over and over again. Underscoring this passion, Chaucer has the narrator slow down the story's pace in Book III to dwell in the memory of Criseyde's embraces and looks and minimize the distinction between narrator-reader and lover-poet. Indeed, Book III, in which the lovers meet and consummate their love, is the most lyrical book of the poem. Yet, although the lyric promises an eternity of bliss, both love and writing must succumb to the dynamics of time.

To emphasize the narrator's struggle with the forward movement of time, Chaucer distributes time within the otherwise narratively symmetrical books unevenly. For example, although Book I is set in April and Book II is set in May, it is unclear in which spring during the Greeks' ten-year siege of Troy the love story begins and how long the lovers are together. Likewise, the narrator's focus on intense lyrical moments leaves the impression that not much time has passed before Criseyde must leave Troy. But, as Troilus reminisces with Pandarus about how his love began, the lover situates this momentous event in the *preceding* April: 'Frend, in Aperil the laste – / As wel thow woost, if it remembre the – / How neigh the deth for wo thow fownde me' (III. 360–2: 'Friend, in last April – as you well know, if you remember it – how near to death from woe you found me').

The jumbling of time frames that occurs through attempting to capture lyric intensity in a form dependent on *seriatim* movement, to embed the lyric within the narrative, becomes clearer when setting Book V against Book III. Indeed, Book V's prologue displays the narrator's last attempt to embed lyric intensity within the narrative, to delay at least time's progress through a lyrical focus on the present, while at the same time telling how the narrative will progress:

> The gold-tressed Phebus heighe on-lofte
> Thries hadde alle with his bemes cleene
> The snowes molte, and Zepherus as ofte
> Ibrought ayeyn the tendre leves grene,
> Syn that the sone of Ecuba the queene
> Bigan to love hire first for whom his sorwe
> Was al, that she departe sholde a-morwe.

> (V. 8–14: The golden-haired Phoebus high above had melted clean all the snow three times with his beams, and Zephyrus just as often brought the tender green leaves back, since the son of Hecuba the Queen began to love her first for whom his sorrow was all, that she should depart the next day.)

Although the lines are lyrical, they lack the emotional intensity and closeness of Book III, and they increase the distance between the narrator-reader and his Criseyde. Indeed, circumlocutions such as 'the sone of Ecuba the queene' for 'Troilus' almost empty words of significance and encourage sliding past the fact these lines transfer: the lovers knew each other for three years. Rather than using poetry to convey love, these poetic lines convey emptiness and inform the reader in more ways than one of Criseyde's future absence.

The amount of time the lovers had together is thus marginalized not only by Book III's lyric focus on their first meetings, but also in an antithetical, rhetorical manner, by these lines' empty ornament. Further, these lines imply that without Criseyde, without all that inspires love and poetry, the narrator's dwelling in past texts becomes passionless, and his attempt to hold onto the lyric dissipates into focusing on its vehicle, poetic language, as time and the narrative's progress spread unevenly before him. The narrator's lyric poetry is thus emptied of significance, making Book V ripe for transferral, for creating new significance, and for the narrator's donning of the role of *critical reader*, a task which he is not altogether successful at doing.

Chaucer foreshadows Book V's dissonance in Book IV, in which Criseyde assures Troilus that she will return to him soon and assigns estimates to her absence. Although seeming precise because she quantifies, her estimates hover between alternating figures of 10 and 14 nights (IV. 1278, 1320, 1326, 1595, 1685), a point underscored in Book V, as Troilus attributes her prolonged absence to his miscalculation (V. 1186–90). These estimates help set up Book V's dissonance along temporal criteria that in effect stagger temporal progression. Thus, in Book V, events continually shift between the tenth day and about two months after Criseyde's departure, thereby structuring the book along a non-linear time scheme. Chaucer further underscores the disruption of chronological order by breaking up the unity of location: he has the narrator uncomfortably shift from the Greek camp to Troy's gates to Sarpedon's palace to different public and private places within Troy. These shifts differ markedly from the previous four books' settings in the lovers' private rooms, when movement is largely confined to Pandarus' huffing back and forth between the lovers.

In addition to disruptive time schemes and settings, Book V's structure is dissonantly constructed. For example, the tale of Criseyde's betrayal is interrupted by: the full texts of two of the lovers' letters, the narrator's insistent references to his literary sources, and his reintroduction of Criseyde with the poem's most complete and distancing description of the heroine (V. 806–26), sandwiched between descriptions of Diomede and Troilus (although descriptions tend to come in the early part of a narrative). In other words, the narrator is trying to do everything he can to avoid the moment in which Criseyde proves false to Troilus. In the readerly narrator's world, the story he finds is not the story he wants to read. He wants to see a faithful Criseyde, someone worthy of loving.

In presenting the story in this manner, Chaucer seems to break from the hermeneutic circling of lyric love, even though his tale is contextualized in the narrative of a lover's relationship with his beloved and lyric conventions are plentifully present. The narrator's positioning as a lover-poet/narrator-reader presents a new, that is different, set of perspectives along with a plethora of new, possible stories. One of those stories, however, doesn't emerge from the narrator's set of hermeneutic circles, but from his 'mirror image', Criseyde.

While in the Greek camp, Criseyde laments her faithlessness to Troilus as a past deed: 'Allas, of me, unto the worldes ende,/ Shal neyther ben ywriten nor ysonge/ No good word, for *thise bokes wol me shende*' (V. 1058–60, my italics: 'Alas, about me, to the end of the world, nothing will be written or sung that is good, for *these books will reproach me*'). As these lines imply, not only does she perceive *her* love *story* with Troilus at an end, Criseyde judges her own life according to literary models. She knows that if no harm can be said of her, then she can go down in history (fiction) as one of Love's saints, someone who might well be meditated upon in a cave. Thus, she decides 'To Diomede algate I wol be trewe' (V. 1071: 'At least I'll be true to Diomedes'). Attempting to star as one of love's saints in *somebody's* story, Criseyde leads a complex private life, making her at once simple and complex, an enigma always open to interpretation and hence always transferrable from one camp of readers to another.

And, indeed, Criseyde's transferrability stems from her potential to serve as the main figure in a number of narratives. Chaucer stresses her potential to be a universal heroine particularly in his initial introduction to her in Book I: she is at once helpless, in imminent danger of being killed or at least ousted from Troy (I. 85–91), and a cooly celestial beauty (I. 100–4). Further, she is an abandoned widow (I. 92–8) who acts and is treated as a young maiden heroine of romances

(I. 132 ff.). Even her stance is ambiguous: 'And yet she stood ful lowe and stille allone…With ful assured lokyng and manere' (I. 178–82: 'And yet she stood full humbly and quiet by herself … with a very assured appearance and manner'). Humble and proud, she is full of potential and ready to become a heroine.

Criseyde's ambiguous portrayal makes her ideally 'rewritable' text; that is, she is a source of constant wonder, even *in the world of the narrative*. On receiving her first letter, for example, Troilus puzzles almost endlessly over her meaning:

> But ofte gan the herte glade and quake
> Of Troilus, whil that he gan it rede,
> So as the wordes yave hym hope or drede.
>
> (II. 1321–3: But often, Troilus' heart did rejoice and quake, while he read it, according to how the words gave him hope or fear.)

And, on their first night together, Troilus seems to speak for the narrator as well as for himself when in attempting to read her expression, he tells her, 'Though ther be mercy writen in youre cheere,/ God woot, the text ful hard is, soth, to fynde' (III. 1356–7: 'Though there be mercy written in your face, God knows, the text is very difficult, truthfully, to find').

Metaliterarily, Criseyde's transferral to the Greek camp transforms her into a new heroine, a new generative metaphor, a *translatio* that inspires at least one Greek reader to lyric love (cf. IV. 829–30, 864–5). She refuses to close doors or forge links, and the question 'what if…?' constantly hovers over her. Like the Greeks who 'in diverse wise and oon entente' go to war with Troy (I. 62: 'in many ways and with one intent'), Criseyde finds many ways to make the best of Fortune's wheel, to transform failure into even minor victories. Indeed, it is precisely this trait that allows Criseyde to envision herself in a new romance; Troilus belongs to her *past* – that was a tragedy, and now it's time for another story.

Shakespeare's *A Midsummer Night's Dream*

Although Shakespeare's play stands just beyond our time frame, its use of Pyramus and Thisbe in the context of *translatio* as presented in a play-within-a-play makes *A Midsummer Night's Dream* (*c.* 1594–95) an ideal way to end this study.

In *A Midsummer Night's Dream*, the opening announcement and final-act celebration of Theseus' wedding to the captive Amazon Queen Hippolyta frames the frenetic tribulations of two pairs of young Athenian lovers. At first, both Demetrius and Lysander love Hermia, while she loves Lysander, and Helena, her friend, loves Demetrius. Two prominent sub-plots further complicate issues: first, Titania's discord with Oberon divides their fairy kingdom and disrupts the young lovers' allegiances and, second, a group of mechanicals, or craftsmen, prepare a play in honor of the royal wedding, an act that eventually entangles the humble Athenians into the play's other worlds (that of the nobles as well as of the fairy world). In the end, the fairy regents resolve their differences and realign the couples so that the young women are wed to their choices along with Theseus and Hippolyta. Finally, the noble Athenians *critically* view the mechanicals' play and receive the blessing of the fairies.

Although this seems like the conventional fare of lyric love, the play refashions some stereotypes. For example, when Helena chases Demetrius, she expresses her unconventional hunt in literary tradition's terms: 'Run when you will; the story shall be chang'd:/ Apollo flies, and Daphne holds the chase' (II. i. 230–1). Moreover, while Theseus uses the language of love to celebrate his union with Hippolyta, she has less to say about the event – after all, he defeated her in war, and she is his captive. Likewise, as they quarrel, Titania and Oberon accuse each other of having other lovers. This is not your traditional literary lovers' world.

In this context of multiply-stranded love with its potentially myriads of stories, spoken and not, the mechanicals refashion a classic Ovidian tale. Determined to be furthered – to be the players chosen to perform before the newly married King and Queen – the mechanicals work hard to present the tale of Pyramus and Thisbe. The problem is, the *tragedy* of the Ovidian lovers is not the most appropriate choice for a wedding ceremony, thereby creating dissonance at the very same time the choice suggests alternate readings, another *antithetical hypersign*. Indeed, at least some audience members may very well know that in addition to being an admirable ruler, Theseus wasn't the truest of lovers and that not too far in the future, Hippolyta will accidentally be killed by her best friend, Penthesilea, in a rescue attempt. The literary dissonance created in the play is placed in yet another perspective as well, since the mechanicals are as inept at their presentation as Chaucer's narrator is in forging through Criseyde's story.

To begin with, not only do the mechanicals choose a play with doubtful merit as an epithalamium, they choose a play that really doesn't have many acting parts. Although Peter Quince assigns actors to play the parents and the lion, in their *performance text*, the parents don't appear at all (in Ovid, they figure only as shadowy members of the tale's frame). Moreover, the players modify the distribution of parts during rehearsal (III. i. 45–67), and actors are recruited to play the moon and the wall. The lack of suitable roles is made more disso-nant still, since what is most notable about the mechanicals is their abuse of language, misuse which registers not in their world, but in 'our world', and, at the end of the play, in the world of the Athenian nobles. That is, in their own world, the mechanicals believe their language to fit in literary love's system.

Their malapropisms invite laughter, but also *critical interpretation* – audiences laugh because the language is deformed *when read against the literary system*. We witness the same kind of *critical interpretation* at the end of the play, when the nobles too critique the mechanicals' language. Sprinkling the players' performance with their comments, they are not only critical, they are inspired to 'write' as well, coming up with puns, similes, morals and applications. Thus, after Peter Quince has performed the prologue, mispunctuating as Merrygreek had done in *Ralph Roister Doister*, the nobles have this to say:

> *The.* This fellow doth not *stand upon points.*
> *Lys.* He hath rid his prologue *like a rough colt*; he knows not the stop.
> *A good moral*, my lord: it is not enough to speak, but to speak true.
> *Hip.* Indeed he hath play'd on his prologue *like a child on a recorder* –
> a sound, but not in government.
> *The.* His speech was *like a tangled chain*; nothing impair'd, but all
> disorder'd.   (V. i. 118–26, my italics)

In the players' world, this is one tough audience. On a *metaliterary* level, however, this scene shows how dissonant markers inspire, elicit, generate and almost necessitate, other texts. For not only do the nobles quip about the performance, after a while Bottom himself starts exchanging remarks *about the performance text* with the audi-ence. Thus, when Demetrius comments that the wall is among those left to bury the lovers, Bottom steps out of his role and responds, 'No, I assure you; the wall is down that parted their fathers.' (V. i. 351–2) – just as the wall between audience and players is removed in Athens.

Appropriately, it seems, the mechanicals had earlier wondered whether the nobles would understand their figured actions or be able to discern where reality ends and fiction begins. The mechanicals feared, for example, that the ladies might be frightened by the lion, or that the lovers' deaths might cause dismay. Upon the suggestion that they omit the killing, Bottom insists that Peter Quince need only write him a prologue, 'and let the prologue *seem to say* we will do no harm with our swords...' (III.i. 17–18, my italics). The italicized phrase may very well be a malapropism in the *world of the play*, but it is also, on the *metaliterary* level, an apt semiotic analysis. Obviously, swordfighting in a *performance text* is not real, but simply a representation, a sign, of a real sword fight – something that *seems* a sword fight. But just as valid, a prologue doesn't really 'say' – it can only 'seem to say', since words can't talk. In drama, however, the act of translating words into a *performance text* makes the words seem to say, so to speak. The players' semiotic acumen is foreshadowed, moreover, when they rehearse in the moonlight-flooded, magical woods.

When Peter Quince poses the problem of how to bring Moonshine into the performance, Bottom suggests they consult an almanac to see if the troupe can perform by natural moonlight (III. i. 53–4). Peter Quince, however, decides it's necessary to *represent* the moon on stage. In other words, he opts for the figuratively transforming conventions that allow an actor to represent an object in a *performance text*. In doing so, he also uses literary terminology: 'one must come in with a bush of thorns and a lantern, and say he comes to *disfigure*, or to present the person of Moonshine' (III. i. 59–61, my italics). Again, the malapropism is apt, since the figuring of Moonshine is actually a *disfiguring*, a refraction rather than a reflection – Peter Quince has opted to represent the *man in the moon*, not the moon, thereby adjusting more to the *signifier* (the actor playing the role) than to the *signified* (moonbeams).

Peter Quince transforms a literal action from a literary text and relies on audiences to transform it back to its literal 'reality' figuratively, in the meantime bringing other stories (like the man in the moon) to bear on the *hermeneutic drift*. But it is Bottom who most frequently causes dissonance. He is also the character most self-reflexively marked. As Peter Quince realizes, 'You have not a man in all Athens able to discharge Pyramus but he' (IV. ii. 7–8). At the same time, Bottom is also the most obviously associated with *translatio*, being the only character to undergo physical transformation in the play, a state underscored by the play's use of terms like 'translated' and 'transported' (III. ii. 32, IV. ii. 3–4), as reflected in Peter Quince's astonishment upon Bottom's return to his fellow players with his ass's head, 'Bless thee, Bottom, bless thee! Thou art translated' (III. i. 118–19).

When Bottom is transformed, then, he 'literally' becomes a *translatio*, a metaphor, a translation, a transformation. And since drama is figurative to begin with, Bottom thus functions something like a metaphor on metaphors. Thus, the figurative effect of the stage rejuvenates the dead metaphor that compares an idiotic mortal to an ass. And it is Bottom who inspires others to echo him, to move, transform and prolifically explode into other narrative forms as well. This is the essence of the metaphor and of the literary system itself: both create perspective-shifting transformations that generate continual movement.

At this juncture, returning to the mechanicals' rehearsal in the woods once again is revealing. There, in the beginning of Act III, Peter Quince matter-of-factly sets about his task:

> ... here's a marvail's convenient place for our rehearsal. This green plot shall be our stage, this hawthorn brake our tiring-house, and we will do it in action as we will do it before the Duke.   (III. i. 2–6)

What Peter Quince is doing, of course, is using language to transform a woodlands scene into a stage. But what would become apparent to an audience of Shakespeare's day viewing the *performance text* on a *bare* stage is that the actor playing Peter Quince figuratively intimates a stage in a woodlands scene for his own literal-minded 'audience', the mechanicals, while at the same time literally baring its *performative* reality to Shakespeare's audiences.

What is achieved here is a perfect balance, which holds various expressions of space and levels of meaning in one metaphorical, transforming moment (Marshall 1982). Critically, both the expressions of space and levels of meaning are defined by the audiences involved, and implied, in the scene. Thus, the mechanicals, the Athenian nobles and Shakespeare's own audiences define and interpret the interweaving of literal and figurative interpretation, while creating nodes at which to examine the interplay between *dramatic* and *performance texts*.

*   *   *

How audiences read, in the final analysis, determines how the literary system is re-envisioned, transformed and transferred. And the more perspectives they articulate as *literati*, the more strands will criss-cross along arcs structuring the literary system.

Note

1. The writer's positioning of the beloved – female or male – determines how she or he will be portrayed, an inherently rhetorical framing of the relationship (Bell 1998).

Conclusion

Regardless of what we read, whenever we read, we are reading a narrative created in a past moment. Even an e–mail message zapping your charges to your screen for your just completed purchases with amazon.com is conveyed as a narrative and one that was created at a past moment. The list of numbers and sparse text telling you of your purchases could not mean anything to you unless you understood it in the context of selling and buying in the twenty–first century, in the narrative of capitalist expansion, in the increasingly www–dependent exchange of information – a set of frameworks established in the narrative of bartering and refined and modified ever since.

Reading and narrating are activities we necessarily associate with book culture, but as we have hopefully seen, these activities entail more than the literal consumption of texts. How we order information, how we assess information, how we assimilate ideas, how we think, how we create – all these activities are informed by *and* inform our reading and narrating. What we read tells us something about who we are, but also about our literary system and, by extension, about the *literati* with whom we share and expand the literary system.

Because whatever we read is a reflection of a past moment; necessarily, we cannot understand all that went into the creation of a certain message – whether the person who generated it or the context in which it was generated. There will always be something we don't, cannot, know.

As discouraging as this may sound to those of us who enjoy digging around in the past, it is also *the* condition that allows and inspires *literati* to sustain and expand the literary system. If a past text or object were completely understood, or if the perfect poem were ever written, there would be no need to comment on it, there would be no inspiring energy to respond to it, there would be silence. If the literary system consisted of just such narratives, it would be a closed system.

We as readers would be just that – readers – without the writerly tendency to interpret, play, investigate.

Chronology

	Literary	Political	Cultural/Historical
1265–1321	Dante Alighieri		
1272–1307		Edward I, Plantagenet	
fl. 1288–1338	Robert Mannyng of Brunne		
1304–74	Francesco Petrarca		
1306–29		Robert I, King of Scots	
1307–27		Edward II, Plantagenet	
1309–77		Babylonian Captivity, papal court in Avignon	
1313–75	Giovanni Boccaccio		
~1320	*Ovide moralisé*		
1327–77		Edward III, Plantagenet	
1328		Treaty of Northampton, Scottish indepen-	

	Literary	Political	Cultural/Historical
		dence	
1329–71		David II, King of Scots	
~1330	Auchinleck MS. (*Sir Orfeo*)		
~1330–1408	John Gower		
1330–84		John Wycliff	
1337			William Merlee of Oxford made first scientific weather forecasts
~1337–~1410	Jean Froissart, author of *Les Chroniques*		
1337–1453		Hundred Years War between France and England	
~1340–1400	Geoffrey Chaucer		
~1342–~1416		Julian of Norwich	
~1344–51			Order of the Garter Established
1345			Bankruptcy of great Florentine banking houses of Bardi and Peruzzi

	Literary	Political	Cultural/Historical
1347–50			Black Death in England
~1350			First paper mill in England at Hertford
1351			Tennis becomes an open-air game in England
1352			Corpus Christi College, Oxford founded
1353	The Decameron		
1354			Mechanical clock developed at Strasbourg
~1359–1416		Owain ap Gruffydd (Owen Glendower) Welsh independence	
~1360			Clavichord and cembalo are being developed
~1370			Steel crossbow developed
~1370–1449	John Lydgate		
1371–90		Robert II, King of Scots	
~1373–~1439	Margery Kempe		

	Literary	Political	Cultural/Historical
1376	*Bruce*		
1377–99		Richard II, Plantagenet	
1378–1417		The Great Schism, papal courts in Avignon and Rome	
1381		The Peasants' Revolt	
~1381–85	*Troilus and Criseyde*		
~1386–90	*Confessio Amantis*		
~1387	Chaucer begins *Canterbury Tales Piers Plowman*, C-text		
1389		Turks defeat Serbs at Kosovo	
~1390	British Library, MS Cotton Nero A. x. 4,(*Sir Gawain and the Green Knight*) *Confessio Amantis*		
1390–1406		Robert III, King of Scots	
1394		Richard II wars against Ireland	

	Literary	Political	Cultural/Historical
1399–1413		Henry IV, Lancaster	
1403			Guild formed, eventually called the Stationers (book trade)
1411			St. Andrews University founded
~1412–20	*The Troy Book*		
1413		Joan of Arc burned at Rouen	
1413–22		Henry V, Lancaster	
1414–76			Medicis are bankers to the papacy
1420		Henry V acknowledged Duke of Normandy and heir to Crown of France	
1422	Earliest Record of Chester Plays		
1422–61		Henry VI, Lancaster	
~1422–92	William Caxton		
1443			English use quarantine and

	Literary	Political	Cultural/Historical
			cleansing to fight the Black Death
~1445	Legendys of Hooly Wummen		
1446–1515			Building of King's College Chapel, Cambridge
1453	Gutenberg prints Bible in Mainz, Germany		Vatican Library established
~1450–1500	Towneley Cycle		
1453		Fall of Constantinople to the Turks	
1455–85		Wars of the Roses	
1460			Winchester Cathedral completed
~1460–1529	John Skelton		
1461–70		Edward IV, York	
1464		Peace between England and Scotland	
1469–1527	Niccolò Machiavelli		
1470–71		Henry VI, Lancaster, restored	

	Literary	Political	Cultural/Historical
1471–83		Edward IV, York, restored	
1474	Caxton's *History of Troy*, first book printed in English (at Bruges)		
1474–1533	Ludovico Ariosto (author of *Orlando Furioso*)		
1475–1522		Gawin Douglas	
~1477–1535	Sir Thomas More		
1480			Leonardo da Vinci invents the parachute
1483		Edward V, York	
1483–85		Richard III, York	
1483–1546		Martin Luther	
1484			Botticelli's *Birth of Venus*
1485	Caxton prints Malory's *Morte D'Arthur*		
1485–1509		Henry VII, Tudor	
1489			Symbols + and – come into use
1492	Profession of book publisher	Columbus in the Americas	Leonardo da Vinci invents a

	Literary	Political	Cultural/Historical
	emerges (type founder, printer, and bookseller)	Jews expelled from Spain	flying machine
1495			Syphillis epidemic throughout Europe
1499–1500			Erasmus meets More at Oxford
~1499–1546	Sir Thomas Elyot		
1500		English annexes Ireland	First black lead pencils used in England
1502		Vespucci discovers Americas are not India	
1503			Leonardo da Vinci's *Mona Lisa* Canterbury Cathedral finished (begun ~1070)
~1503–42	Sir Thomas Wyatt		
~1503–56	Nicholas Udall		
1505			Christ's College, Cambridge
1507			Polydore Vergil named royal historiographer

	Literary	Political	Cultural/Historical
1509–47		Henry VIII, Tudor	
~1510	*Everyman*		
1513		Juan Ponce de Leon in Florida	
1514		James IV dies at Flodden Field	Pineapples first brought to Europe
~1514–18	*History of Richard III*		
1515–68	Roger Ascham		
1517			Martin Luther's 95 theses at Wittenberg Coffee first brought to Europe
1521			Beginning of the slave trade Diet of Worms condemns Luther for heresy
1521–22	*Speke Parrott*		
1524			First turkeys to Europe
1525			Hops introduced to England from Artois
1528			Severe outbreak of plague in

	Literary	Political	Cultural/Historical
			England
1529		Cardinal Wolsey replaced by More	
1529–37		Henry proclaims himself head of Anglican Church	Halley's comet
1531	*The Boke Named the Gouernour* First complete edition of Aristotle's works published by Erasmus		
1533		Henry marries Anne Boleyn and is excommunicated by pope Act of Restraint of Appeals (English ecclesiatical court severed from Rome)	
1534		Act of Supremacy Jesuit order founded by Ignatius Loyola Pope's authority abolished in England; Henry head of Church of England Decree forbidding English farmers to own more than 2000 sheep	

	Literary	Political	Cultural/Historical
1535		Thomas More executed Statute of Uses curbs power of English landowners	First diving bell Beginning of the London Exchange
1536		Anne Boleyn executed William Tyndale burned at the stake Union of England and Wales	
1536–39		Henry represses England's ca. 800 monasteries	
1539			First Christmas tree, Strasbourg
1540			Cathedral Michael Servetus discovers the pulmonary circulation of blood
1541			Hernando de Soto discovers Mississippi River
1542		Henry assumes title of King of Ireland Scottish invade England James V falls	

	Literary	*Political*	*Cultural/Historical*
1543		War with France	
1547–53		Edward VI, Tudor	
1549	Book of Common Prayer	Kett's rebellion	
~1550	*Ralph Roister Doister*		
1551			First licensing of alehouses and taverns in England and Wales
1552			St Andrew's Golf Club founded
1553	Thomas Wilson's *The Arte of Rhetorique*		
1553–58		Mary I, Tudor	
1554–1606	John Lyly		
1555	Worcester's Men become active		
1556	Stationers' Company of London granted monopoly of printing in England		
1557	Tottel's anthology of *Songes and Sonettes*		

	Literary	Political	Cultural/Historical
	containing Wyatt's poetry		
1558–1603		Elizabeth I, Tudor	
1559	Warwick's Men become active	Act of Settlement	
1561–1626	Francis Bacon		
1561			St Paul's Cathedral badly damaged by fire
1562	Norton and Sackville, Gorboduc		
1563			Another outbreak of the plague
1564			Horse-drawn coach introduced to England from Holland
1564–93	Christopher Marlowe		
1564–1616	William Shakespeare		
1564–1642			Galileo Galilei
1565	Arthur Golding's translation of first four books of Ovid's Metamorphoses		Pencils are manu-factered in England Sir Thomas Gresham founds

	Literary	Political	Cultural/Historical
			the Royal Exchange in London Royal College of Physicians, London, is to carry out human dissections
1567	Red Lion play-house built	O'Neill's rebellion in Ireland	
1568		Mary, Queen of Scots, flees to England	Geradus Mercator develops the cylindrical projection for maps
1569	Sussex's Men become active	Rebellion in England, sacking of Durham Cathedral	Mercator's map of the world Public lottery in London
1570		Papal bull excom-municating Elizabeth	
1572		Massacre of St Bartholomew's Day	
1573	Leicester's Men become active		
1574	Richard Burbage is licensed to open a theatre in London		
1576	The Theatre built		

	Literary	Political	Cultural/Historical
1577	Strange's Men become active; Blackfriars, Curtain, and playhouse at Newington Butts built; Raphael Holinshed's *Chronicles*		
1578	*Euphues*		
1579	Edmund Spenser's *Shepheardes Calender*		
1580	Oxford's Men become active Last performance of a miracle play in Coventry		Sir Francis Drake returns from circumnavigating the world Earthquake in London

Glossary

code: The system that allows individual units to be interpreted. Part of Jakobson's six-part communication model.

diachronic: A perspective on temporality which stretches out linearly over what is perceived to be a large stretch of time (see *synchronic*).

diegesis: A representation of events that is reported; the telling of a story which doesn't necessarily follow the chronological order (see *mimesis*).

figurative language: Language that conveys meanings in addition to denoted meaning.

icon: Peirce's term for a sign that resembles the thing being signified (see *index* and *symbol*).

index: Peirce's term for a sign that points to some connection between the sign and what it signifies (see *icon* and *symbol*).

interpretent: Peirce's term for the sign that a sign evokes in the mind of the interpreter.

intertext: A text shared or contained within another.

literary system: According to Corti, the communication system that includes not only those narratives considered canonical, but also any poem, image, or convention that allows us to read materials in a given period and given culture with understanding.

mimesis: A representation of events or images as they are enacted (see *diegesis*).

multiaccentuality: According to Vološinov, the reviving of the dialectic nature of a sign in times of social crises or revolutionary change (see *uniaccentuality*).

paradigm: The system of relationships that connects signs to other signs via difference and similarity. The fundamental principle underlying structuralist thought.

plot: The events of a narration in chronological ordering (see *story*).

signified: Saussure's term for the concept linked to a sound image (see *signifier*).

signifier: Saussure's term for the sound image conveying a concept (see *signified*).

story: The events as narrated (see *plot*).

symbol: Peirce's term for a sign that has the effect of law or convention (see *icon* and *index*).

synchronic: A perspective on temporality that opens up a slice of time and hence marginalizes the linear (see *diachronic*).

uniaccentuality: According to Vološinov, the attempt to suppress the dialectic nature of a sign (see *multiaccentuality*).

Annotated Bibliography

Primary texts

Anonymous. *Aucassin et Nicolette and Other Tales* (*c.* 1210–20). Trans. Pauline Matarasso. Harmondsworth: Penguin, 1971.

A delightful narrative poem that plays with society's conventions as well as with those of literature, even gender stereotypes – with a pregnant King and a Queen leading a war in which noone is to be killed, and ammunition consists of food.

Anonymous. *The Mabinogion* (*c.* 1300–1400). Trans. Charlotte E. Guest. Thrift Edition Series. New York: Dover, 1997.

The *Mabinogi* are 11 tales found originally in two medieval Welsh manuscripts: the White Book of Rhydderch (*c.* 1300) and the Red Book of Hergest (*c.* 1400), conveying ancient Celtic material that provides a different perspective on literature of this period, since tales, even those involving Arthur, are embedded in striking instances of magic and the supernatural.

Anonymous. *Medieval English Lyrics 1200–1400* (1200–1400). Ed. Thomas G. Duncan. Harmondsworth: Penguin, 1995.

Although I didn't treat medieval short lyric poems, they're worth a look. This edition gives marginal translations for words that may be difficult to the modern reader.

Ascham, Roger. *Letters of Roger Ascham* (1541–50). Ed. Alvin Vos, Trans. Maurice Hatch and Alvin Vos. New York: Peter Lang, 1989.

A collection of letters translated from the Latin providing an exceptionally effective way to gain one detailed view of the early modern era. Ascham's letters are rhetorically crafted and includes the tutor's reflections about Elizabeth I as well.

Baldwin, William. *Beware the Cat by William Baldwin: The First English Novel* (*c.* 1550). Eds. William A. Ringler, Jr., and Michael Flackmann. Los Angeles: Huntington Library Press, 1995.

This narrative is not only interesting historically as possibly the first English novel, but also for its use of Celtic motifs in a satirical framework.

Béroul. *The Romance of Tristran* (*c.* 1170–90) Ed. and trans. Norris J. Lacy. New York: Garland, 1989; along with Lacy's *Early French Tristan Poems* (*c.* 1150–90). 2 vols. Cambridge: D. S. Brewer, 1998.

Next to the Guenevere and Launcelot story, the story of Tristan and Isolde is the best-known love tale of the medieval period, much romanticized by Wagner.

Chrétien de Troyes. *Arthurian Romances* (*c.* 1170–90) Trans. William W. Kibler and Carleton W. Carroll. Harmondsworth: Penguin, 1991.

A translation from the Old French that provides the reader with all five Arthurian romances attributed to Chrétien de Troyes, purportedly the first poet to write at length of Arthur and his court.

Marie de France. *Lais* (*c.* 1160–80) Trans. Glyn Burgess and Keith Busby. Harmondsworth: Penguin, 1986.

A collection of short narrative poems that reveals a poet at work, whose sensitivity to characterization and ability to juxtapose images is very much worth reading.

Ovidius Naso, Publius. *Heroides and Amores* (*c.* 16–1 BCE). Ed. and trans. Grant Showerman; rev. G. P. Goold. Cambridge, Mass. and London: Harvard University Press and William Heinemann, 1986.

The first of Ovid's poetry presented in this facing-page translation is a collection of fictional letters written by heroines of classical literature, which was very popular in the period under study here.

Plato. *The Symposium and The Phaedrus: Plato's Erotic Dialogues* (*c.* 407–347 BCE). Trans. and Intro. William S. Cobb. Albany: SUNY Press, 1993.

Despite the title, these two texts don't earn an X-rating. They do explore love and provide a *locus classicus* (literally) for a number of love's conventions as have survived in the western literary system. The *Phaedrus* also plays with the relations between love and rhetoric.

Semiotics and rhetoric

Aristotle. *The Rhetoric of Aristotle: An Expanded Translation with Supplementary Examples for Students of Composition and Public Speaking* (*c.* 330 BCE). Ed. and Trans. Lane Cooper. Englewood Cliffs: Prentice-Hall, 1960.

A basic text for the student of rhetoric, made all the more useful through Lane Cooper's introduction and examples.

Barthes, Roland. *Elements of Semiology* (1964). Trans. Annette Lavers and Colin Smith. New York: Hill and Wang, 1967.

Probably a good place to start on a critical thinker, whose work is used in various disciplines and creates a rhetorical framework for Saussurian sign systems. For example, this study also treats his systems of clothing, food, cars and furniture.

—. *The Semiotic Challenge* (1985). Trans. Richard Howard. Berkeley: University of California Press, 1994.

An anthology of his essays, which may also be useful as a quick introduction to his work.

Booth, Wayne C. *The Rhetoric of Fiction*. Chicago: University of Chicago Press, 1983.

A seminal study, analyzing among other things the various poses of the narrator and how these elicit different kinds of responses from readers.

Deely, John. *Introducing Semiotic: Its History and Doctrine*. Bloomington: Indiana University Press, 1982.

As its title suggests, a historical survey of the semiotic discipline, which can prove very useful as an introduction to semiotic theory as well.

Derrida, Jacques. *Writing and Difference* (1967). Trans. Alan Bass. Chicago: University of Chicago Press, 1980.

It's hard to single out one of Derrida's deconstructionalist analyses, but this is perhaps the one closest to semiotic concerns. For an excellent overview of Derridean writing, see the relevant volume in the *Transitions* series (Wolfreys 1998).

Kennedy, George A. *A New History of Classical Rhetoric*. Princeton: Princeton University Press, 1994.

A clear and succinct overview of classical rhetoric and its tenets from ancient Greece to Boethius.

Kristeva, Julia. *Desire in Language: A Semiotic Approach to Literature and Art*. New York: Columbia University Press, 1980.

An anthology of essays of an important French feminist semiotician, whose work is based on some modification of Sigmund Freud and Jacques Lacan.

Noakes, Susan. *Timely Reading: Between Exegesis and Interpretation*. Ithaca: Cornell University Press, 1988.

A highly insightful study that explores the reading process as portrayed by writers, a process that moves between models of reading centered in the author (exegesis) and in the reader (interpretation).

Scholes, Robert. *Semiotics and Interpretation*. New Haven: Yale University Press, 1982.

The clearest introduction to semiotics I know of, with a glossary and working bibliography as well.

Sebeok, Thomas A. *An Introduction to Semiotics*. Toronto: University of Toronto Press, 1994.

A very useful entry to one important US school of semiotics that is grounded in a biological approach (zoösemiotics) and which treats six kinds of signs (signal, symptom, icon, index, symbol, name).

Overviews and anthologies

Blamires, Alcuin, ed., with Karen Pratt and C. W. Marx. *Woman Defamed and Woman Defended: An Anthology of Medieval Texts*. Oxford, Clarendon, 1992.

This collection provides texts that illustrate anti-feminist writings, along with those that presumably would defend women's honor.

Brooke, Tucker and Matthias A. Shaaber. *The Renaissance (1500–1660)*. A Literary History of England 2. New York: Appleton-Century-Crofts, 1967.

Although clearly dated, still a useful overview of the early modern literary scene for its inclusiveness and background references.

Lacy, Norris J., ed. *The New Arthurian Encyclopedia*. Assoc. eds. Geoffrey Ashe, Sandra Ness Ihle, Marianne E. Kalinke, and Raymond H. Thompson. New York: Garland and London: St James Press, 1991.

An excellent reference tool that provides alphabetically arranged articles of relevance to Arthur's story, along with a chronology and a table of contents arranged according to subjects.

Strayer, Joseph R., Editor-in-Chief. *Dictionary of the Middle Ages*. 13 vols. New York: Charles Scribner's Sons, 1982–89.

Another excellent reference tool for many aspects of the medieval literary system.

Wallace, David, ed. *The Cambridge History of Medieval English Literature*. Cambridge: Cambridge University Press, 1999.

A useful anthology for British literature from 1066–1550, with articles on various authors and themes, that provide important contextual materials as well as analyses.

Bibliography

Primary texts

Ælfric. *Ælfric's Lives of Saints, Being a Set of Sermons on Saints' Days Formerly Observed by the English Church* (c. 1000). Ed. Walter W. Skeat; Trans. Ms. Gunning and Ms. Wilkinson. London: Oxford University Press, 1966 rpt.

Andreas Capellanus. *De Amore, Libri Tres* (c. 1174). Ed. E. Trojel. Copenhagen: Gadiana, 1892.

Anonymous. *The Bachelor's Banquet* (1603). Ed. Faith Guildenhuys. Ottawa and Binghamton: Dovehouse Editions and MRTS, 1993.

Anonymous. *Biblia Sacra iuxta Vulgatem Versionem* (c. 390). Trans. St Jerome. Ed. Robert Weber. Stuttgart: Württembergische Bibelanstalt, 1969.

Anonymous. '*Everyman*' (c. 1500). In *Medieval Drama*. Ed. David Bevington. Boston: Houghton Mifflin, 1975, 939–63.

Anonoymous. '*Mary Magdalene from the Digby MS*' (c. 1500). In *Medieval Drama*. Ed. David Bevington. Boston: Houghton Mifflin, 1975, 687–753.

Anonymous. *The Mirror for Magistrates* (1559). Ed. Lily B. Campbell. New York: Barnes & Noble, 1960 rpt.

Anonymous. 'Pyramus and Thisbe'. In *Ovide Moralisé* (c. 1320). Ed. C. de Boer. Wiesbaden: Martin Sändig, 1966 rpt.: II. 18–39.

Anonymous. 'Robin Hood and the Knight' and 'Robin Hood and the Friar' (c. 1475). In *Specimens of the Pre-Shakespearean Drama*. Ed. John Matthews Manley. Boston: Ginn, 1903: I. 279–85.

Anonymous. *Sir Gawain and the Green Knight* (c. 1390). Eds. J.R.R. Tolkien and E. V. Gordon; rev. Norman Davis. Oxford: Clarendon, 1967.

Anonymous. *Sir Orfeo* (c. 1330). Ed. A. J. Bliss. London: Oxford University Press, 1954.

Anonymous. '*The Tryall of Chevalry*' (c. 1599–1603). In *A Collection of Old English Plays*. Ed. A. H. Bullen. New York: Benjamin Blom, 1964: III. 265–356.

Ascham, Roger. 'Report and Discourse of the Affairs and State of Germany' (1570). In *Roger Ascham English Works*. Ed. William Aldis Wright. Cambridge: Cambridge University Press, 1904: 125–69.

Augustinus Aurelius. *Sancti Augustini Opera: Confessionum Libri XIII* (c. 397–400). Eds. Martinus Skutella and Lucas Verheijen. Turnholt: Brepols Editores Pontificii, 1981.

—. P. Agaesse and A. Solignac, eds., *De Genesi ad litteram* (c. 400–426). 2 vols. (Paris: Desclee de Brouwer, 1972.

Barbour, John. *The Bruce* (1487). Ed. Walter W. Skeat. London: Oxford University Press, 1968 rpt.

Boccaccio, Giovanni. *Decameron* (1353). Ed. Vittore Branca. Torino: Giulio Einaudi, 1980.

Bokenham, Osbern. *Legendys of Hooly Wummen by Osbern Bokenham* (c. 1445). Ed. Mary S. Serjeantson. London: Oxford University Press, 1938.

Camden, William. *The History of the Most Renowned and Victorious Princess Elizabeth Late Queen of England* (1615). Ed. Wallace T. MacCaffrey. Chicago: University of Chicago Press, 1970.

Caxton, William. *The Book of the Ordre of Chyvalry* (1484). Ed. Alfred T. P. Byles. London: Oxford University Press, 1926.

Chaucer, Geoffrey. *The Riverside Chaucer* (c. 1360–1400). Gen. Ed. Larry D. Benson. Boston: Houghton Mifflin, 1987.

Chrétien de Troyes. *Chrétien de Troyes Erec et Enide* (c. 1170–90. Ed. and trans. Carleton W. Carroll. New York: Garland, 1987.

Dante Alighieri. *La Divina Commedia* (c. 1312–20). Ed. C. H. Grandgent; rev. Charles S. Singleton. Cambridge: Harvard University Press, 1972.

—. *De Vulgari Eloquentia* (c. 1303–04). In *Le Opere di Dante: Testo critico della società Dantesca Italiana.* Eds. M. Barbi *et al.* Firenza: Società Dantesca Italiana, 1960.

Elyot, Sir Thomas. *The Boke Named the Gouernour: Devised by Sir Thomas Elyot, Knight* (1531). Ed. Henry Herbert Stephen Croft. 2 vols. New York: Burt Franklin, 1967 rpt.

Froissart, Jean. *Chronicles* (c. 1369–1400). Ed. and trans. Geoffrey Brereton. Harmondsworth: Penguin, 1978 rpt.

Gascoigne, George. *George Gascoigne, The Posies* (1575 – 2nd edn). Ed. John W. Cunliffe. Cambridge: Cambridge University Press, 1907.

Geoffrey of La Tour-Landry. *The Book of the Knight of La Tour-Landry* (1484). Trans. William Caxton; Ed. Thomas Wright. London: Kegan Paul, Trench, Trübner, 1868.

Geoffrey of Vinsauf. *The Poetria Nova and its Sources in Early Rhetorical Doctrine* (c. 1200). Ed. and trans. Ernest Gallo. The Hague: Mouton, 1971.

Gibbon, Edward. *The History of the Decline and Fall of the Roman Empire* (1776). Ed. J. B. Bury. 7 vols. London: Methuen, 1909–14.

Gower, John. *The Complete Works of John Gower* (c. 1350–1408). Ed. G. C. Macaulay. Oxford: Oxford University Press, 1957 rpt.

Kempe, Margery. *The Book of Margery Kempe* (1430s). Ed. Lynn Staley. Kalamazoo: Medieval Institute Publications, 1996.

Langland, William. *Piers Plowman by William Langland* (1387 – C Edition). Ed. Derek Pearsall. London: Edward Arnold, 1978.

Lydgate, John. *Lydgate's Troy Book* (c.1412–20). Ed. Henry Bergen. London: Kegan Paul, Trench, Trübner, 1906.

Malory, Sir Thomas. *Le Morte D'Arthur* (1485 – Caxton edn). Ed. Janet Cowen; intro. John Lawlor. 2 vols. Harmondsworth: Penguin, 1977 rpt.

Mannyng, Robert. *Robert Mannyng of Brunne The Chronicle* (1338). Ed. Idelle Sullens. Binghamton: Binghamton University Press, 1996.

Marlowe, Christopher. *The Complete Works of Christopher Marlowe.* Vol. II: *Dr Faustus* (c. 1590). Ed. Roma Gill. Oxford: Clarendon Press, 1992 rpt.

More, Thomas. *St Thomas More: The History of King Richard III* (1557). Ed. Richard S. Sylvester. New Haven: Yale University Press, 1976.

Ovidius Naso, Publius. *The Art of Love and Other Poems with an English Translation* (1 BCE). Ed. and trans. J. H. Mozley; rev. G. P. Goold. Cambridge: Harvard University Press, 1985.

—. *Metamorphoses with an English Translation* (c. 8 CE). Ed. and trans. Frank Justus Miller; rev. G. P. Goold. 2 vols. Cambridge: Harvard University Press, 1994.

The Paston Family. *The Paston Letters* (c. 1450s). Ed. Norman Davis. Oxford: Oxford University Press, 1983.

Shakespeare, William. *The Riverside Shakespeare* (1588–1613). Ed. G. Blakemore Evans, with the assistance of J. J. M. Tobin. Boston: Houghton Mifflin, 1997.

Skelton, John. '*Speke Parott*' (1521). In *John Skelton: The Complete English Poems*. Ed. John Scattergood. New Haven: Yale University Press, 1983, 230–46.

Udall, Nicholas. '*Ralph Roister Doister*' (c. 1553). Ed. W. Carew Hazlitt. In *A Select Collection of Old English Plays*. New York: Benjamin Blom, 1964 rpt, 53–161.

Vergilius Maro, Publius. *Virgil Aeneid with an English Translation* (c. 19 BCE). Ed. and trans. H. Rushton Fairclough. 2 vols. Cambridge: Harvard University Press, 1956.

Wyatt, Sir Thomas. *Sir Thomas Wyatt, The Complete Poems* (1557 – Tottel's edn). Ed. R. A. Rebholz. New Haven: Yale University Press, 1978.

Semiotics, rhetoric and theory

Alcuin. *The Rhetoric of Alcuin and Charlemagne: A Translation, with an Introduction, the Latin Text, and Notes* (c. 790–800). Ed. and trans. Wilbur Samuel Howell. Princeton: Princeton University Press, 1941.

Allen, Judson Boyce. *The Ethical Poetic of the Later Middle Ages: A Decorum of Convenient Distinction.* Toronto: University of Toronto Press, 1982.

Anonymous. *[Cicero] ad C. Herennium: De Ratione Dicendi (Rhetorica ad Herennium)* (c. 86–82 BCE). Ed. and trans. Harry Caplan. Cambridge: Harvard University Press, 1977.

Augustinus, Aurelius. *De Doctrina Christiana* (c. 397–426). Ed. and trans. R. P. H. Green. Oxford: Clarendon, 1995.

Bahti, Timothy. *Allegories of History: Literary Historiography after Hegel.* Baltimore: Johns Hopkins University Press, 1992.

Baldwin, Charles Sears. *Medieval Rhetoric and Poetic to 1400: Interpreted from Representative Works.* St Clair Shores, MI: Scholarly Press, 1972 rpt.

Black, Max. *Models and Metaphors: Studies in Language and Philosophy.* Ithaca: Cornell University Press, 1962.

Brannigan, John. *New Historicism and Cultural Materialism.* Houndmills: Macmillan, 1998.

Breisach, Ernst, ed. *Classical Rhetoric and Medieval Historiography.* Kalamazoo: Medieval Institute Publications, 1985.

Caplan, Harry. *Of Eloquence: Studies in Ancient and Medieval Rhetoric.* Eds. Anne King and Helen North. Ithaca: Cornell University Press, 1970.

Corti, Maria. *An Introduction to Literary Semiotics* (1976). Trans. Margherita Bogat and Allen Mandelbaum. Bloomington: Indiana University Press, 1978.

Derrida, Jacques. 'White Mythology: Metaphor in the Text of Philosophy'. Trans. F. C. T. Moore. *New Literary History*, vol. 6 (1974), 5–74.

Eco, Umberto. *The Limits of Interpretation*. Bloomington: Indiana University Press, 1994.

—. *Semiotics and the Philosophy of Language*. London: Macmillan, 1984.

Elam, Keir. *The Semiotics of Theatre and Drama*. London: Routledge, 1994 rpt.

Greenblatt, Stephen J. *Renaissance Self-Fashioning: From More to Shakespeare*. Chicago: University of Chicago Press, 1980.

Greimas, A. J. *Sémantique structurale*. Paris: Larousse. 1966.

Haslett, Moyra. *Marxist Literary and Cultural Studies*. Houndmills: Macmillan, 1998.

Innis, Robert E., ed. *Semiotics: An Introductory Anthology*. Bloomington: Indiana University Press, 1985.

Irvine, Martin. *The Making of Textual Culture: 'Grammatica' and Literary Theory, 350–1100*. Cambridge: Cambridge University Press, 1994.

Jakobson, Roman. 'Closing Statement: Linguistics and Poetics' (1960). In Innis 1985, 147–75.

Lakoff, George and Mark Johnson. *Metaphors We Live By*. Chicago: University of Chicago Press, 1980.

Lanham, Richard A. *The Motives of Eloquence: Literary Rhetoric in the Renaissance*. New Haven: Yale University Press, 1976.

Lausberg, Heinrich. *Handbuch der literarischen Rhetorik: Eine Grundlegung der Literaturwissenschaft*. 2 vols. München: Max Hueber, 1960.

Mink, Louis O. *Historical Understanding*. Eds. Brian Fay, Eugene O. Golob and Richard T. Vann. Ithaca: Cornell University Press, 1987.

Nöth, Winfried. 'Semiotic Aspects of Metaphor'. In Paprotté and Dirven, 1–16.

Paprotté, Wolf and Dirven, René. *The Ubiquity of Metaphor: Metaphor in Language and Thought*. Amsterdam: John Benjamins, 1985.

Peirce, Charles Sanders. *Collected Papers of Charles Sanders Peirce*. Eds. Charles Hartshorne and Paul Weiss. Cambridge, Mass.: Belknap Press of Harvard University Press, 1960.

Ricoeur, Paul. *The Rule of Metaphor: Multi-disciplinary Studies of the Creation of Meaning in Language* (1975). Trans. Robert Czerny with Kathleen McLaughlin and John Costello. Toronto: University of Toronto Press, 1977.

de Saussure, Ferdinand. 'The Linguistic Sign' (1916). Trans. Wade Baskin. In Innis, 28–46.

Sidney, Sir Philip. *An Apology for Poetry* (c. 1582). Ed. Geoffrey Shepherd. Manchester: Manchester University Press, 1980 rpt.

Traugott, Elizabeth Closs. '"Conventional" and "Dead" Metaphors Revisited'. In Paprotté and Dirven, 25–29

Vance, Eugene. *Mervelous Signals: Poetics and Sign Theory in the Middle Ages*. Lincoln: University of Nebraska Press, 1986.

Vološinov, V. N. *Marxism and the Philosophy of Language* (1929). Trans. Ladislav Matejka and I. R. Titunik. New York: Seminar Press, 1973.

White, Hayden. *Metahistory: The Historical Imagination in Nineteenth-Century Europe*. Baltimore: Johns Hopkins University Press, 1973.

Wolfreys, Julian. *Deconstruction • Derrida*. Houndmills: Macmillan, 1998.

Overviews and anthologies

Braunmuller, A. R. and Michael Hattaway, eds. *The Cambridge Companion to English Renaissance Drama*. Cambridge: Cambridge University Press, 1990.
S. P. Cerasano and Marion Wynne-Davis, eds. *Renaissance Drama by Women*. London: Routledge, 1996.
F. L. Cross and E. A. Livingstone, eds. *The Oxford Dictionary of the Christian Church*. London: Oxford University Press, 1974.
Herbert G. Wright, ed. *Early English Versions of the Tales of Guiscardo and Ghismonda and Titus and Gisippus from the Decameron*. London: Oxford University Press, 1937.

Secondary sources

Aers, David. *Community, Gender, and Individual Identity: English Writing 1360–1430*. London: Routledge, 1988.
Auerbach, Erich. *Literary Language and Its Public in Late Latin Antiquity and in the Middle Ages* (1958). Trans. Ralph Manheim. New York: Pantheon Books, 1965.
Barber, Richard and Juliet Barker. *Tournaments: Jousts, Chivalry and Pageants in the Middle Ages*. Woodbridge: Boydell Press, 1989.
Beer, Jeanette ed. *Medieval Translators and Their Craft*. Kalamazoo: Medieval Institute Publications, 1989.
Bell, Ilona. *Elizabethan Women and the Poetry of Courtship*. Cambridge: Cambridge University Press, 1998.
Beltz, George Frederick. *Memorials of the Most Noble Order of the Garter, From its Foundation to the Present Time*. London: William Pickering, 1841.
Benson, C. David. *The History of Troy in Middle English Literature: Guido delle Colonne's Historia Destructionis Troiae in Medieval England*. Woodbridge: D. S. Brewer, 1980.
Bevington, David M. *From Mankind to Marlowe: Growth of Structure in the Popular Drama of Tudor England*. Cambridge: Harvard University Press, 1962.
Bloomfield, Morton W. *The Seven Deadly Sins: An Introduction to the History of a Religious Concept and with Specific Reference to Medieval English Literature*. East Lansing: Michigan State College Press, 1952.
Borsi, Franco and Stefano. *Paolo Uccello: Florenz zwischen Gotik und Renaissance*. Trans. Marianne Albrecht-Bolt. Stuttgart: Belser, 1993.
Briscoe, Marianne G. and John C. Coldewey, eds. *Contexts for Early English Drama*. Bloomington: Indiana University Press, 1989.
Charity, A. C. *Events and their Afterlife: The Dialectics of Christian Typology in the Bible and Dante*. Cambridge: Cambridge University Press, 1966.
Chartier, Roger and Guglielmo Cavallo, eds., *Die Welt des Lesens*. Trans. H. Jochen Bußmann, Ulrich Enderwitz, Klaus Jöken, Bernd Schwibs, and Martina Kempter. Frankfurt and Paris: Campus and Editions della Maison des Sciences de l'Homme,1999.

Colish, Marcia L. *The Mirror of Language: A Study in the Medieval Theory of Knowledge.* New Haven: Yale University Press, 1968.

Curtis, S. J. *History of Education in Great Britain.* London: University Tutorial Press, 1965.

Curtius, Ernst Robert. *European Literature and the Latin Middle Ages* (1948). Trans. Willard R. Trask. Princeton: Princeton University Press, 1973.

Donaldson, E. Talbot. *Speaking of Chaucer.* New York: W. W. Norton, 1970.

Duclow, Donald F. '*Everyman* and the *Ars Moriendi*,' *Fifteenth Century Studies,* vol. 6 (1983), 93–113.

Freeman, Michelle A. *The Poetics of Translatio Studii and Conjointure: Chrétien de Troyes's Cligés.* Lexington: French Forum, 1979.

Gellrich, Jesse M. *The Idea of the Book in the Middle Ages: Language Theory, Mythology, and Fiction.* Ithaca: Cornell University Press, 1985.

Ginsberg, Warren. 'Ovid's *Metamorphoses* and the Politics of Interpretation.' *Classical Journal,* vol. 84 (1988-89), 222–31.

Goez, Werner. *Translatio Imperii: Ein Beitrag zur Geschichte des Geschichtsdenkens und der politischen Theorien im Mittelalter und in der frühen Neuzeit.* Tübingen: J. C. B. Mohr, 1958.

Haug, Walter. *Literaturtheorie im deutschen Mittelalter: Von den Anfängen bis zum Ende des 13. Jahrhunderts, Eine Einführung.* Darmstadt: Wissenschaftliche Buchgesellschaft, 1985.

Holmes, Grace. *The Order of the Garter: Its Knights and Stall Plates, 1348 to 1984.* Windsor: Oxley & Sons, 1984.

Hughes, Felicity A. 'Gascoigne's Poses'. *Studies in English Literature,* vol. 37 (1997), 1–19.

Jongkees, A. G. '*Translatio studii*: Les Avatars d'un Thème Médiéval.' In *Miscellanea Mediaevalia in memoriam Jan Frederik Niermeyer.* Groningen: J. B. Wolters, 1967, 41–51.

Katz, David S. *The Jews in the History of England 1485–1850* (Oxford: Clarendon Press, 1994.

Keiser, George R. 'The Mystics and the Early English Printers'. In *The Medieval Mystical Tradition in England.* Ed. Marion Glasscoe. Cambridge: D. S. Brewer, 1987, 9–26.

Kelly, Douglas. '*Translatio studii*: Translation, Adaptation, and Allegory in Medieval French Literature'. *Philological Quarterly,* vol. 57 (1978), 287–310.

Knight, Stephen. *Robin Hood.* Oxford: Basil Blackwell, 1994.

Knowles, David. *The English Mystical Tradition.* London: Burns & Oates, 1961.

Lancashire, Anne. 'Medieval to Renaissance: Plays and the London Drapers' Company to 1558'. In *The Centre and its Compass.* Robert A. Taylor, *et al.*, eds. Kalamazoo: Medieval Institute, 1993, 297–313.

Luck, Georg. *The Latin Love Elegy.* London: Methuen, 1969.

Lyne, R.O.A.M. *The Latin Love Poets: From Catullus to Horace.* Oxford: Clarendon, 1980.

Lytle, Guy Fitch and Stephen Orgel, eds. *Patronage in the Renaissance.* Folger Institute Essays. Princeton: Princeton University Press, 1981.

Marshall, David. 'Exchanging Visions: Reading *A Midsummer Night's Dream*'. *ELH,* vol. 49 (1982), 543–75.

Matzke, John E. 'Contributions to the History of the Legend of Saint George, with Special Reference to the Sources of the French, German and Anglo-Saxon Metrical Versions', *PMLA*, vol. 10 n.s. (1902), 464–535, and 11 n.s. (1903), 99–171.

Monson, Don A. 'Andreas Capellanus and the Problem of Irony'. *Speculum*, vol. 63 (1988), 539–72.

Moore, Dennis. 'Making Sense of an Ending: Morgan Le Fay in *Sir Gawain and the Green Knight*'. *Mediaevalia*, vol. 10 (1984), 213–33.

Olson, Glending. *Literature as Recreation in the Later Middle Ages*. Ithaca: Cornell University Press, 1982.

Partner, Nancy F. *Serious Entertainments: The Writing of History in Twelfth-Century England*. Chicago: University of Chicago Press, 1977.

Patterson, Lee W. *Negotiating the Past: The Historical Understanding of Medieval Literature*. Madison: University of Wisconsin Press, 1987.

Reiss, Timothy J. *Knowledge, Discovery and Imagination in Early Modern Europe: the Rise of Aesthetic Rationalism*. Cambridge: Cambridge University Press, 1997.

Rowe, George E. 'Interpretation, Sixteenth-Century Readers, and George Gascoigne's "The Adventures of Master F.J."' *ELH*, vol. 48 (1981), 271–89.

Scattergood, V. J. and J.W. Sherborne. *English Court Culture in the Later Middle Ages*. London: Gerald Duckworth, 1983.

Spiegel, Gabrielle M. *Romancing the Past: The Rise of Vernacular Prose Historiography in Thirteenth-Century France*. Berkeley: University of California Press, 1993.

Staley, Lynn. *Margery Kempe's Dissenting Fictions*. University Park: Pennsylvania State University Press, 1994.

Tristram, Hildegard L. C. 'Aggregating Versus Integrating Narrative'. In Willi Erzgräber and Sabine Volk, eds., *Mündlichkeit und Schriftlichkeit im englischen Mittelalter*. Tübingen: Gunter Narr, 1988.

Weiss, Adrian. 'Shared Printing, Printer's Copy, and the Text(s) of Gascoigne's *A Hundreth Sundrie Flowres*', *Studies in Bibliography*, vol. 45 (1992), 71–104.

Wetherbee, Winthrop. *Chaucer and the Poets: An Essay on Troilus and Criseyde*. Ithaca: Cornell University Press, 1984.

—. *Platonism and Poetry in the Twelfth Century: The Literary Influence of the School of Chartres*. Princeton: Princeton University Press, 1972.

Zink, Michel. *Froissart et le temps*. Paris: Presses Universitaires de France, 1998.

Index